Instability in the terms of trade of primary commodities, 1900-1982

FAO ECONOMIC AND SOCIAL DEVELOPMENT PAPER

64

Pasquale L. Scandizzo
and
Dimitris Diakosawas

FOOD AND AGRICULTURE ORGANIZATION OF THE UNITED NATIONS
Rome, 1987

The designations employed and the presentation
of material in this publication do not imply the
expression of any opinion whatsoever on the
part of the Food and Agriculture Organization
of the United Nations concerning the legal
status of any country, territory, city or area or
of its authorities, or concerning the delimitation
of its frontiers or boundaries.

M-70

ISBN 92-5-102531-2

All rights reserved. No part of this publication may be reproduced, stored in a retrieval system, or transmitted in any form or by any means, electronic, mechanical, photocopying or otherwise, without the prior permission of the copyright owner. Applications for such permission, with a statement of the purpose and extent of the reproduction, should be addressed to the Director, Publications Division, Food and Agriculture Organization of the United Nations, Via delle Terme di Caracalla, 00100 Rome, Italy.

© **FAO 1987**

CONTENTS

	Page
PREFACE	iv
ACKNOWLEDGEMENTS	v
LIST OF TABLES	vi
LIST OF FIGURES	x
ABBREVIATIONS	xi

CHAPTER I — TERMS OF TRADE OF PRIMARY COMMODITIES: THE CONTROVERSY AND ITS ORIGINS (1–20)

	Page
Introduction	1
Terms of Trade: A Critical Survey	3
Some Conclusions	18
Notes	20

CHAPTER II — THE EMPIRICAL EVIDENCE ON TRENDS IN THE TERMS OF TRADE (21–58)

	Page
Introduction	21
Measuring the Secular Movements of the Terms of Trade	22
A Disaggregated Analysis of Terms of Trade Movements	31
Upswings and Downswings	42
The Question of Productivity Increases	47
Some Conclusions	54
Notes	58

CHAPTER III	**TERMS OF TRADE INSTABILITY: THE TRADITIONAL APPROACH**	59-86
	Definitions and Methodological Problems	59
	Review of the Literature	63
	Alternative Measures of Instability	67
	Increased Instability in the Terms of Trade	72
	Some Conclusions	85
	Notes	86
CHAPTER IV	**TERMS OF TRADE INSTABILITY: THE SPECTRAL ANALYSIS VIEW**	87-103
	Detection of Trends and Instability	87
	Method of Analysis	90
	Empirical Results	96
	Some Conclusions	102
CHAPTER V	**BENEFITS AND COSTS FROM TRADE: THE CASE OF AGRICULTURAL EXPORTS COMMODITIES**	104-158
	Introduction	104
	Terms of Trade and Cost-Benefit Analysis	105
	Measuring the Welfare Consequences of Terms of Trade Changes	110
	The International Market for Tropical Commodities	116
	Overall Considerations	153
	Notes	158
CHAPTER VI	**CONCLUSIONS AND POLICY IMPLICATIONS**	159-167
	Some General Remarks	159
	Have Terms of Trade of Primary Commodities Been Falling?	161
	The Benefits from Trade	163
	The Question of Instability	164
	Policy Implications	165

		Page
APPENDIX I	Graphs	168-182
APPENDIX II	Notes on Time Series of Productivity	183-188
	Regression Results for Terms of Trade during Downswing and Upswing Periods	189-192
	Regression Results on the Question of Productivity Increases	193-194
APPENDIX III	Tests of Increased Instability	195-197
APPENDIX IV	Regression Results Used in Spectral Analysis	198-203
APPENDIX V	Estimates of Degree of Currency Overvaluation and of Trends and Instability in the Benefits from Trade and its Components	204-214
BIBLIOGRAPHY		215-227

PREFACE

Controversies on issues of terms of trade of primary commodities - and, by extension, on trade-based development prospects of developing countries - have a long, complicated and inconclusive history. The subject, or rather the subjects, are elusive on account of the multiplicity of theoretical measures, and data sets on which these can be applied, as well as the different welfare interpretation each of these measures possesses. No wonder public policy debates continue to be replete with contrasting claims about economic effects related to terms-of-trade vagaries.

The authors of this study have attempted to clarify the logical connections of alternative terms-of-trade measures and their significance as welfare indicators and also to answer the questions: Have the primary commodities of terms of trade been declining over as long a period as consistent data permit us to measure? Have they exhibited unusually large and increasing instability? What can be inferred regarding net gains from primary commodity trade? In answering these questions, the authors have been careful to implement and compare alternative measurement and estimation approaches and also to place their work in the context of the earlier and more recent literature. The help of the World Bank in making available for the purposes of this study perhaps the longest and most consistent set of annual international market prices of individual primary commodities is gratefully acknowledged.

Some conclusions drawn by the authors will appear to some readers controversial as seen from the perspective of the new "consensus" regarding macroeconomic and sectoral policies of developing countries. Other readers will be struck by the absence of strong results, i.e., confirmation or rejection of sharply formulated hypotheses expressing notions perhaps more vaguely held by many policy analysts and policy makers. Controversial conclusions should be welcome. As long as their methodological basis is not specious, they enliven the intellectual debate on important analytical and policy matters and help to instil caution that consensus is likely to weaken. The absence of strong results is in itself worthy of attention. Besides incidentally explaining the persistence of terms-of-trade-related claims and counterclaims in the service of special interests, it may point to a chronically misplaced emphasis on long-term issues and associated resource allocation implications at the expense of more palpable and less risky issues of cyclical foreign exchange management. This is one of the possible conclusions the reader may draw, but it may also be that other models we have not been able to think of could detect more definite patterns in the data and establish firmer conclusions.

H.W. Hjort
Director
Policy Analysis Division
Food and Agriculture Organization of the United Nations

ACKNOWLEDGEMENTS

We are gratefully indebted to Enzo Grilli and Ron Duncan, Assistant Director and Chief of the Commodity Studies and Projections Division of the World Bank, for kindly making the data on commodity prices available to us.

A special intellectual tribute is due to Apostolos Condos, Senior Economist in the Policy Analysis Division of FAO. This study was originated under his supervision. His stimulating discussions, comments and criticisms on the subject matter, at each stage of the project, played a vital role in bringing the study to fruition.

We should also like to place on record our indebtedness to Mr. J.M. Caballero, an economist with the Policy Analysis Division of FAO, whose most helpful comments facilitated improvement of earlier versions of this study. We have also benefited from comments by and discussions with other FAO staff members. Unfortunately, individual acknowledgements are impossible.

Throughout the project it was the authors' fortune and pleasure to have research assistance provided by Ms. Gabriella Coletti. Equally fervent thanks are due to Ms. Caroline Costello, who bore the main burden of typing successive versions of the text and tables with remarkable speed, accuracy and diligence. Finally, thanks go to Ms. Sanna Fellows, who did the painstaking editorial work.

Needless to say, any remaining errors, random or otherwise, are the responsibility of the authors.

LIST OF TABLES

		Page
2.1	Classification of Studies According to Different Theses on Secular Trends of the Terms of Trade, 1817-1986	28
2.2	Analysis of Changes in the Terms of Trade Between DCs and LDCs, 1817-1986	30
2.3	Commodity Description and Data Sources	32
2.4	Trends in the Terms of Trade for Individual Commodities, 1900-82	37
2.5	Time Breakdown: Trends in the Terms of Trade	40
2.6	Chow Test for Structural Breaks in the Trends of Terms of Trade	43
2.7	Test of the Prebisch Asymmetry Hypothesis	45
2.8	Barter Terms of Trade as a Function of Trends and Productivity	51
2.9	Trends in the Single Factorial Terms of Trade, 1900-82	52
2.10	Comparison of BTT and SFTT Trend Estimates for Agricultural Commodities	53
2.11	Time Breakdown: Trends in the Single Factorial Terms of Trade	55
2.12	Chow Test for Structural Breaks in the Trends of Single Factorial Terms of Trade	56
3.1	Main Empirical Studies on Commodity Terms of Trade Instability	64
3.2	Estimates of Instability Levels	66
3.3	Alternative Traditional Measures of Barter Terms of Trade Instability, 1900-82	71
3.4	Spearman Rank Correlation Coefficient between Traditional Instability Indices of Barter Terms of Trade, 1900-82	73
3.5	Test of Increased Instability for Barter Terms of Trade, 1900-82	75
3.6	Time Breakdown: Instability in the Terms of Trade	77

		Page
3.7	Chow Test for Structural Breaks in the Instability of Terms of Trade	78
3.8	Increased Instability for the Single Factorial Terms of Trade, 1900-82	81
3.9	Comparison of Results of Instability Analysis	82
3.10	Time Breakdown: Instability in the Single Factorial Terms of Trade	83
3.11	Chow Test for Structural Breaks in the Trends of Single Factorial Terms of Trade	84
4.1	Stationarity Tests on the Terms of Trade Series, 1900-82	93
4.2	Stationarity Tests Under Different Detrending Procedures, 1900-82	97
4.3	Spearman Rank Correlation between Different Detrending Procedures	98
4.4	Spearman Rank Correlation between Different Frequency Bands	99
4.5	Variability over Frequency Interval of 2-6 Years	99
4.6	Variability over Frequency Interval of 6-12 Years	100
4.7	Variability over Frequency Interval of More than 12 Years	100
4.8	Variability Over the Whole Spectrum	101
5.1	Product Composition of World Exports	117
5.2	Product Composition of Developing Countries' Exports	118
5.3	Developing Countries' Export Earnings from Raw Materials	119
5.4	Percentage of Cocoa, Coffee, Tea and Sugar Exports Over Total Exports (f.o.b. Prices)	120
5.5	Cocoa Production, by Main Countries	122
5.6	Trends in Real Cocoa Producer Prices in Major Producing Countries	123

		Page
5.7	Cocoa Exports, by Main Countries	126
5.8	Cocoa Export Price Elasticities	127
5.9	Cocoa: Net Nominal Protection Coefficients (NNPC) with and without the Adjustment for Market Share, and Nominal Protection Coefficients (NPC), 1961-82	128
5.10	Cocoa: Decomposition of Benefits from Trade	130
5.11	Coffee Production, by Economic Regions and Main Countries	132
5.12	Coffee Exports, by Economic Regions and Main Countries	133
5.13	Coffee Export Price Elasticities	135
5.14	Coffee: Net Nominal Protection Coefficients (NNPC) with and without the Adjustment for Market Share, and Nominal Protection Coefficients (NPC), 1961-82	136
5.15	Coffee: Decomposition of Benefits from Trade	137
5.16	Sugar Production, by Economic Regions and Main Countries	139
5.17	Sugar Exports by Economic Regions and Main Countries	140
5.18	Sugar Export Price Elasticities	143
5.19	Sugar: Net Nominal Protection Coefficients (NNPC) with and without the Adjustment for Market Share, and Nominal Protection Coefficients (NPC), 1961-82	144
5.20	Sugar: Decomposition of Benefits from Trade	145
5.21	Tea Production, by Economic Regions and Main Countries	147
5.22	Tea Exports, by Economic Regions and Main Countries	148
5.23	Tea Export Price Elasticities	150
5.24	Tea: Net Nominal Protection Coefficients (NNPC) with and without the Adjustment for Market Share, and Nominal Protection Coefficients (NPC), 1961-82	151

		Page
5.25	Tea: Decomposition of Benefits from Trade	152
5.26	Net Nominal Protection Coefficients (NNPC) with and without the Adjustment for Market Share, and Nominal Protection Coefficients (NPC), 1961-82	153
5.27	Decomposition of Benefits from Trade	155
5.28	Trends in the Benefits from Trade and its Components	156
5.29	Instability Levels of Benefits from Trade and its Components	156
5.30	Trends in Instability of Benefits from Trade and its Components	157
A.2.1	Terms of Trade During Downswing Periods	189
A.2.2	Terms of Trade During Upswing Periods	191
A.2.3	Regression Results for Productivity	193
A.2.4	Regression Results for the Single Factorial Terms of Trade	194
A.3.1	Kendall's Tau Test of Increased Instability for Barter Terms of Trade, 1900-82	196
A.3.2	Heteroscedasticity Test of Increased Instability: Kendall's Tau Test	197
A.4.1	ARIMA Model Specifications for Terms of Trade, 1900-82	199
A.4.2	Estimation Results of the Harmonic Version	201
A.4.3	Spearman Correlation Coefficient between Traditional Instability Indices and Indices Based on the Spectrum for BTT, 1900-82	203
A.5.1	Base Years Used in Estimating Parity Exchange Rates	204
A.5.2	Degree of Currency Overvaluation (NNPC/NPC), 1961-82	205
A.5.3	Trends in the Benefits from Trade and its Components: Country Results	205
A.5.4	Trends in Instability in the Benefits from Trade and its Components: Country Results	209
A.5.5	Instability of Benefits from Trade and its Components: Country Results	213

LIST OF FIGURES

		Page
2.1	Barter Terms of Trade as a Function of Trend and Productivity	53
5.1	Excess Supply Curve	110
5.2	Non-Linear Excess Supply Function	112
5.3	World Cocoa Production and Prices	124
5.4	World Coffee Production and Prices	134
5.5	World Sugar Production and Prices	141
5.6	World Tea Production and prices	149

ABBREVIATIONS

ARIMA	= integrated autoregressive - moving average process
BKS	= Bartlett's Kolmogorov-Smirnov statistic
BTT	= barter terms of trade
c.i.f.	= cost, insurance, freight
C.V.	= coefficient of variation
DBT	= domestic barter terms of trade
DC	= developed countries
DFTT	= double factorial terms of trade
DY	= dummy year
DYC	= dummy country
FK	= Fisher's Kappa statistic
f.o.b.	= free on board
GBTT	= gross barter terms of trade
GLS	= generalized least square
ha	= hectare
IBT	= international barter terms of trade
ITT	= income terms of trade
LDC	= less developed countries
MA	= moving average
m.t.	= metric tons
NBTT	= net barter terms of trade
NPC	= nominal protection coefficient
NNPC	= net nominal protection coefficient
$NNPC^*$	= optimum NNPC
NSP	= net social payoff
OLS	= ordinary least square
SFTT	= single factorial terms of trade

CHAPTER I

TERMS OF TRADE OF PRIMARY COMMODITIES:

THE CONTROVERSY AND ITS ORIGINS

Introduction

Primary commodity markets have offered an opportunity for much economic debate on a number of key issues. First, secularly declining terms of trade of primary commodities are used to explain the widening gap between developing (LDCs) and developed countries (DCs). Second, they are regarded as a contributing factor to the creation of a structural condition of unequal exchange between a "dominating" industrial centre and a "dominated" agrarian periphery. And third, they are thought to be a source of instability, often causing financial vulnerability to foreign exchange equilibria and fragility to international market institutions.

More recently, the domestic determinants of primary commodity markets have been of interest to economists. The reason being that since the mid-1970s, a renewed awareness has emerged as regards welfare costs of government policies on import substitution and currency overvaluation. It is alleged that these policies have tended to penalize agricultural commodities of LDCs for two reasons: (i) they have directly discriminated against export crops within the country through taxation and overvalued exchange rates; and (ii) they have prevented any effective agreement among producers to restrict and regulate their supply in foreign exchange markets.

Despite the strength of claims of both strands of thought on commodity markets, an examination of the literature does not reveal conclusive theoretical arguments or consistent empirical evidence for either the issue concerning declining terms of trade and increasing instability, or the causes of the weak performance of primary producers.

This is not surprising perhaps, since market performance is an inherently empirical complex phenomenon. Thus, theoretical arguments, based as they are on simplifying assumptions, are unlikely to be compelling. Empirical evidence, on the other hand, may also fail to convince because of the many facets of market performance, the numerous time periods and the different interpretation that can be placed upon concepts such as "trends" and "instability".

While recognizing the complexities and difficulties involved, this study's objective confronts the terms of trade issue by examining simultaneously over the past 90 years, three main questions: (i) Have the terms of trade of primary commodities been declining in any meaningful sense? (ii) Have they shown unusually large instability and has such instability been increasing? (iii) And what has been the relationship between terms of trade, domestic policies and country-welfare?

There are two clear advantages in pursuing these issues: (i) the tremendous amount of theoretical and empirical work available in the general area of terms of trade, instability and welfare; and (ii) the availability to draw on previous findings and, hence, the opportunity of using the longest data series and widest literature survey.

With assistance from World Bank and FAO staff, perhaps the longest and most concise set of annual data on individual commodity prices at the international market level were assembled for this study. Also, an extensive and previously unavailable data series on land productivity by commodity were compiled from various sources, even though perhaps with less success in terms of consistency and accuracy. Country-level data on domestic prices, border prices, income and exchange rates were assembled from FAO and other UN sources.

The study is structured as follows. The remainder of Chapter I surveys the main <u>theoretical arguments</u> on the issue of the secular trends of the terms of trade of primary commodities. Chapter II examines the main <u>empirical studies</u> that helped to originate the controversy on declining trends, and analyzes the evidence with a fresh set of data. Chapter III extends the study to the question of the price instability of primary commodities, examines past studies and analyzes data using traditional measures of trend and variability. Chapter IV confronts again the issue of distinguishing the basic tendency of prices and their variability from the phenomenon of instability, by using spectral analysis. Chapter V examines the issue of measuring the benefits and costs from policies affecting terms of trade and domestic prices for the agricultural export commodities. Finally, Chapter VI summarizes conclusions reached and offers suggestions on policy issues.

Terms of Trade: A Critical Survey

Classical economists for more than a century claimed that the terms of trade of primary commodities would be improving over time. Only in the early 1950s was this argument radically challenged by Prebisch (1950) and Singer (1950), who claimed that the terms of trade of primary commodities were subject to declining long-term trends.

Since the development of this controversy in the 1950s, the concept of "terms of trade" has been subject to careful scrutiny, and several specifications and complementary definitions have been added to its original meaning. Thus, it is useful to look in some detail at the various concepts assigned to terms of trade, because different definitions correspond to alternative concepts, and hence reflect different phases, twists and arguments of the controversy.

Terms of trade can be said to denote the ratio between the value of one commodity bundle in terms of another. Unfortunately, however, values can be defined, measured and aggregated in many ways, and in the case of the terms of trade, there are a number of alternative concepts that subsequently emerge. These concepts fall into two groups:

- Those that relate to the exchange ratio between commodities; and
- Those that relate to the exchange ratio between productive resources.

In the first group, three types of terms of trade can be distinguished:

a) <u>Gross Barter Terms of Trade</u>: GBTT = $\frac{Qm}{Qx}$

This is the ratio between the volume of imports and the volume of exports. An increase in GBTT is regarded as favourable since more imports can be obtained with given exports.

b) <u>Net Barter Terms of Trade</u>: NBTT = $\frac{Px}{Pm}$

This is the ratio between the prices of exports and the prices of imports. It is the most widely used concept of terms of trade. If its export prices have declined relative to the prices the country has to pay for its imports, its terms of trade are said to have deteriorated. When trade is balanced, then GBTT is equal to NBTT:

$$\frac{GBTT}{NBTT} = \frac{Qm}{Qx} \cdot \frac{Pm}{Px} = \frac{Vm}{Vx} = 1$$

c) <u>Income Terms of Trade</u>: ITT = $\frac{Px}{Pm} \cdot Qx$

It measures the capacity to import based on exports and gives the purchasing power of exports. A rise in ITT indicates that the country can obtain a larger volume of imports from the sale of its exports.

The aforementioned concepts of terms of trade are no unambiguous indicators of a country's trade performance because:

1) <u>Deterioration of a country's terms of trade does not necessarily result in it being worse off</u>. Terms of trade trends provide information only about changes in prices and/or values of tradables and give no indication of either the real value of exports or the intra-country distribution of export earnings. It is possible to have opposite movements

in the NBTT and the ITT. The NBTT might be deteriorating while the ITT might be improving. If, for example, the prices of exports in terms of imports fall by a smaller percentage than the percentage increase in productivity, the country is clearly better off (i.e., it obtains a greater quantity of imports per unit of factors embodied in its exports). In other words, the deterioration of the NBTT may partly be offset by increasing productivity.

2) Even if there is growth in the economy, NBTT may deteriorate. In theory, the possibility exists that the type and the rate of development may cause so severe a deterioration in the NBTT that the gain from growth in output is more than offset by the loss from the adverse terms of trade, so that the country ends up with lower real income after growth. If for example, the "factor saving" due to an increase in factor supply or to technical progress is so export-biased that the terms of trade worsen, the negative income effect of the actual deterioration in the terms of trade may be greater than the positive effect of the expansion in output (Bhaghwati's (1958) immiserizing growth concept).

3) Terms of trade measures do not allow for the re-exportation of factor returns. In the same vein, if imports are financed by borrowing, it is not certain that the economy will be better off. A similar argument applies to exports when there is foreign control. Furthermore, NBTT fail to take explicitly into account changes in export-productivity and changes in the volume of exports. Even if NBTT are improving, this may lead to a loss of export receipts and thus to a deterioration in the balance of payments. The effect of a higher export price on the balance of payments of a single country may also be different from the effect on a group of countries exporting the same commodity.

4) Terms of trade do not take into account commodity composition. The commodity composition is also not considered in the terms of trade measures. For example, terms of trade can improve for basic goods and deteriorate for non-basic goods, resulting in higher welfare for the country.

In the second group of terms of trade measures, one may distinguish between:

Single-Factorial Terms of Trade: $\text{SFTT} = \frac{Px}{Pm} \cdot Zx$ and

Double-Factorial Terms of Trade: $\text{DFTT} = \frac{Px}{Pm} \cdot \frac{Zx}{Zm}$

where Zx = export productivity index, or according to Emmanuel (1972) the productivity of labour in the production of exports

Zm = import productivity index

As can be seen from above, even if NBTT deteriorate, SFTT may improve or a deterioration in NBTT may be offset by improvement in SFTT. [1]/ SFTT represent a correction to NBTT to account for the growth in productivity in the exporting country. They measure the purchasing power of one unit of a domestic resource: for example, labour in international markets. DFTT, on the other hand, represent the exchange value of domestic resources of the exporting country in terms of domestic resources of its trading partners.

Whereas SFTT is useful in examining the question of whether a country's absolute development stage has changed, DFTT give the relative situation in each trading partner accounting for gaps in productivity, if any, between the two countries. Neoclassical economists are concerned with SFTT since it emphasizes the absolute gains from trade, with each country seen in isolation, while structuralists and unequal exchange theorists emphasise DFTT since they are concerned with the distribution of gains from trade. The following attempts to briefly outline the views that different economic schools tend to hold on the role and evolution of the terms of trade in developing countries.

Classical School

As mentioned before, classical economists since the time of Adam Smith have believed that terms of trade would shift in favour of primary commodities. Their prediction was based on the assumption of diminishing returns in the production of primary products from a limited stock of land and other natural resources (e.g., mineral deposits), occurring as population expanded and/or per capita consumption increased. This decline would then inevitably result in rising relative prices for primary goods. This movement in the terms of trade was viewed in the context of a static technology.

In his Wicksell Lectures, Lewis (1969) presents a simple framework to explain the evolution of terms of trade of LDCs. He divides commodities between those produced in both trading partners--DCs and LDCs-- and those produced only in one of the trading country groups. The commodities produced in both country groups can be identified as "basic", while those produced in either country group may be called "specific" commodities. The basic commodities are identified as food and the specific ones as coffee and steel. DCs produce steel and food and LDCs, coffee and food. Labour is the only input in production in both country groups and there is a fixed technological coefficient for the production of each commodity. This implies that there is a linear transformation curve between steel and food for DCs and between coffee and food for LDCs. The terms of trade depend not on the type of commodities, that is, manufacture versus primary commodities, but on the conditions in the trading countries that determine wages. Food is used as a numeraire where the price of each specific good is expressed. Terms of trade are identified by the relative price of steel and coffee. The model is mainly derived from the classical tradition and is a special case of a Ricardian system with three goods and two country groups.

In the Lewis's growth model of unlimited supply of labour from the subsistence sector, wages are determined by the average productivity of labour in food production. Prices of all commodities are determined by the amount of labour required per unit of output multiplied by the wage rate.

Thus, technological progress in food production will raise the wage rate, which in turn will increase the price of specific commodities. The ultimate impact will improve the terms of trade. On the other hand, technological progress in specific commodities will reduce the labour required per unit of output without affecting the wage rate. This will induce the price of these commodities to fall and worsen the terms of trade.

Because of the linearity assumption and the fact that food is produced in both trading regions a uniform improvement in productivity in either region will not have spillover effects to the other region. For example, a uniform increase in the productivity in both sectors in DCs will not affect the welfare of LDCs, and vice versa. A uniform increase in productivity leaves relative prices unchanged.

Lewis argues that over the last eighty years, productivity has increased faster in agriculture than in manufactures in DCs, while LDCs have achieved some technical progress in their export crops--cocoa, coffee, rubber--("specific"), but not in their subsistence crops ("food"). In his framework, this is tantamount to declining terms of trade for LDCs, since the cost of a unit of food in terms of steel is falling. Had technical progress occurred in their basic commodity, food, their terms of trade would have improved.

Neoclassical School

For the Neoclassical economists, movements in the terms of trade depend on the rate of increase in each country's import demand. This, in turn, is determined by shifts in offer curves, which may be attributed to different types of development.

The type and the degree of bias (i.e., neutral, export or import bias, ultra-import or ultra-export) and the rate of development in each country, determine the movements in the terms of trade. For neoclassical economists, therefore, the key determinants of terms of trade movement is growth in consumption and production. If the foreign offer curve is elastic, the volume of exports may increase enough to improve the ITT, despite deterioration in the NBTT.

NBTT of LDCs will deteriorate if consumption of importables increases more than domestic production. Given that demand for their export goods is income inelastic, LDCs will witness a continuous decline in their terms of trade, if they attempt to expand their exports at the same rate as that of DC exports.

While neoclassical views are very general, they consciously ignore institutional, cyclical and technical changes of terms of trade. For example, Södersten (1980) argues that "there is no need to fall back upon highly dubious theories about the influences of market forms, of labour-unions, etc. Simpler reasons can be given for why the terms of trade might go against the LDCs and why growth through trade might prove a fruitless venture for these countries".

Within the neoclassical paradigm, a number of theoretical models of behaviour of terms of trade have been formulated, each of which has stressed particular aspects of supply and demand factors involved. Edgeworth (1894) in a very simple model shows that a country that is completely specialized in the production of a single export good will be made worse off by an increase in the quantity produced, if the good itself is not domestically consumed. When two countries are completely specialized in the production of two different commodities, Johnson (1955) shows that the terms of trade will move against the country whose rate of growth, weighted by its income elasticity of demand, is higher. Hicks (1953) considers the case of incomplete specialization, that is the case where two countries produce both an exportable and an importable commodity, and shows that technical progress improves a country's terms of trade if it occurs in the importable commodity and worsens them if it occurs in the exportable commodity. This result is extended by Findlay and Grubert (1959) who show that:

- Neutral technical progress in a commodity will improve a country's terms of trade for the importable commodity and worsen them for the exportable one.

- Technical progress biased towards the factor in which the commodity is less intensive, will improve the terms of trade for the importable commodity and worsen them for the exportable commodity.

- Technical progress biased towards the factor in which the commodity is more intensive, may improve or worsen the terms of trade, depending on the extent of the technical progress and its factor bias. [2]

Bhagwati (1958) applies a more general model in which the country is not specialized in either production or consumption showing that growth could be "immiserizing". Johnson (1959) provides a taxonomic synthesis of the effects on the terms of trade of capital accumulation, population growth and various types of technical progress corresponding to different patterns of income elasticity.

In the standard neoclassical models of a comparative-static type, the fundamental determinants of terms of trade are tastes, technology and factor endowments of the trading partners. In a dynamic two-country framework, however, Findlay (1981) shows that the growth of effective labour in the more developed region, the North, together with the technology of primary production, the real wage and the propensity to save out of profits in the less developed region, the South, are the main determinants of the terms of trade. In Findlay's model, the North is assumed to have full employment and a variable real wage that clears the labour market. The North follows the orthodox neoclassical growth models of the Solow-type with constant returns to scale and with capital and labour as the inputs. Capital consists of a stock of manufactures. The labour force grows over time at a constant rate and labour-augmenting technical progress is also assumed to take place. The South develops along the Lewis-type with unlimited supply of labour. It is assumed to have a dual economy structure with a fixed real wage and a variable employment level. The South produces only primary goods, and there is again a neoclassical production function with labour and capital as the inputs. Capital, as before, consists of a stock of manufactures. The growth rate of the South depends on the rate of profits and the savings ratio. Profits themselves are a function of the terms of trade.

In a steady equilibrium, the growth rates of the two outputs, manufactures and primary products should be equal. An interesting feature of the model is that it shows how productivity increases may influence national incomes and per capita incomes asymmetrically in the two countries. Findlay demonstrates that an increase of productivity in the North will benefit both the North and the South. Growth that occurs due to technical progress in the North will improve its terms of trade which, in turn, through dynamic linkages will trigger off the growth process in the South. In contrast, however, an increase in the productivity of capital in the South will cause a deterioration of its terms of trade and will lead to a fall in per capita income. Therefore, the North is the active partner and the South the passive one as the former can keep its productivity gains where the latter will have to give them away by decreasing terms of trade. It should be pointed out that Findlay's conclusion is consistent with that of Prebisch-Singer on the secular deterioration of terms of trade for the South. The structural difference in the determination of the growth rates of the two country-groups produce asymmetrical consequences on the terms of trade of changes in technology and the propensity to save. It should be pointed out, however, that in the long run equilibrium level, the rate of deterioration approaches zero.

Structuralist School

For the structuralists, the terms of trade of developing countries are bound to deteriorate progressively and inexorably, as long as the present international economic order prevails. The causes of this deterioration are said to be differences in the distribution of the gains from increased productivity, diverse cyclical movements of primary products and industrial prices, and disparities in the rates of increase in the demand for imports between the DCs and LDCs.

The most profound proponents of this school are considered to be Prebisch and Singer. Their main challenge is directed at the validity of the trade theory assumption of classically competitive factor and product markets in both the centre and the periphery. Three major strands in the argument can be identified:

- The income elasticity of demand for imports from the South is low in the North, while it is high in the South for imports from the North.

- Technological progress in the North tends to reduce the demand for imports from the South, while technological progress in the South tends to occur in the export sector.

- The structure of product and factor markets tends to be much more monopolistic in the North than in the South.

Neoclassical economic theory suggests that, where competition exists, technological changes resulting in increased productivity will lead to reduced prices. Prebisch argues that this process operates at the periphery, bringing down export prices to the benefit of consumers at the centre.

However, at the centre more monopolistic forces are believed to operate, particularly in the labour market where union power is seen as extracting the gains from increased productivity in the form of higher wages and in the product market where firms are seen as having sufficient market power to pass on higher wage-costs in the form of higher prices to consumers both at the periphery and at the centre.

Thus, as a result of differences in competitive structure, the prices of primary exports from the periphery are depressed relative to those of imported manufactured items, and trade will act as an "exploitative" force on behalf of the centre. The centre has the best of both worlds as consumer of primary commodities and as producer of manufactures, while LDCs have the worst of both worlds as consumers of manufactures and as producers of primary products. The increase in productivity in the periphery's export-sector will increase output, which with the centre's low-income elasticity of demand would tend to decrease the periphery's export prices.

On the other hand, the periphery's own high-income elasticity of demand for imports will tend to preserve the price level of industrial products. Productivity gains in the centre are absorbed by factors, but in the periphery they are given away in the form of lower export prices. Consequently, a deterioration in the terms of trade would result in depriving developing countries of the fruits of their own technological progress.

The Prebisch and Singer thesis has been disputed both on grounds of theory and fact. At the theory level the following points may be stressed:

1) <u>The entire argument of the "secular deterioration hypothesis" has been restricted to the NBTT only</u>. But as pointed out before, deterioration of NBTT cannot be identified with being worse off. Also important are changes in the ITT. In fact, the LDCs have increased their volume of exports in such a way that their ITT (buying power) have increased. The crucial point, however, is that this growth of import purchasing power has lagged behind that of the industrialized nations, not only because the growth of world trade in agricultural and mining products has lagged behind that in manufactures, but also because the LDCs' share of trade in agricultural primary commodities has steadily fallen: from 40.5 percent in 1955 to 29.8 percent in 1983.

2) <u>Why is it that prices in the periphery decrease relatively more on the downswing than they improve on the upswing, so that the end result is a deterioration in the NBTT for these countries?</u> For Prebisch-Singer, the explanation lies in the market forms: while monopolistic firms are common in DCs, the export-industries in most LDCs are competitive. But the question is why monopolistic market conditions, tend in the long run, to better the terms of trade for a country, while free competition would tend to worsen them? To make such a statement one needs to look at the effect of different market forms on productivity. $\underline{3/}$ What is of interest is not the market forms per se, but their influence on the growth of supply. By applying a comparative-static price theory, one may conclude that the monopolist can restrict his output to maintain a higher price level.

On the other hand, by focusing on the effects of different market forms on production, one can argue that the rate of technical progress tends to be higher under monopolistic conditions than under competition. Ceteris paribus, the faster output grows, the more adverse will be the development of relative commodity prices. If one accepts this view, one may draw the conclusion that the more monopolistic the country export-sector, the worse the prospects for the terms of trade. A conclusion which is opposite to Prebisch's assertion.

3) <u>Aggregation of primary products cannot be representative of the wide variety of primary products exported by poor countries</u>. Some primary producing countries are also importers of primary products. For example, although Haberler (1964) appears to accept the notion that for a typical LDC, exports will be predominantly primary products and imports mostly industrial goods, he doubts that NBTT would move uniformly up or down for such a wide range of products. He argues that it would be "a very strange coincidence" if these terms moved parallel in the long-run for all countries, since some export coffee, others mineral products, wheat, etc. Even if no general case of declining terms of trade can be established, it may be true, that a case for a particular country (or group of countries), or a particular raw material or group of them can be found. But such a finding will not imply that NBTT of LDCs are secularly declining.

Furthermore, some primary products imported by LDCs are commodities predominantly produced in DCs. Therefore, the terms of trade between primary products and manufactured ones are not the same as the terms of trade between poor and rich countries. Spraos (1980), although accepting this argument as theoretically correct, doubts its practical relevance because "the evidence does not suggest a lesser deterioration of the NBTT for the primary products which originate predominantly in LDCs". However, a recent study by Thirlwall and Bergevin (1985) claims that "the terms of trade of LDCs have fared marginally worse than for DCs, in the period prior to 1973, if the influence of petroleum is excluded".

4) <u>Monopolistic trade unions</u>: It is argued that even if trade unions and firms actually possessed sufficient monopoly powers, the existence of such monopoly elements would explain movements in the absolute domestic prices and not changes in relative world prices of manufactures and primary goods. World prices depend on world conditions of supply and demand, and a country with a relatively high domestic price level may simply find itself out of international markets unless it makes some adjustment in its domestic prices or exchange rate.

Unequal Exchange

Unequal exchange gives a clear answer to the question of the effect of trade on LDCs: exploitation resulting from wage differential and equalization of the rate of profit.

The unequal exchange thesis stems from Emmanuel's work (1972). In his model he distinguishes two groups of countries: the periphery and the centre. His concept of unequal exchange is based on the labour theory of value and provides a theoretical foundation for the unfair division of welfare between the two groups of countries, due to the labour of the periphery being rewarded much less than the comparable labour of the centre in international trade. The exchange is unequal because the periphery exchanges goods in which more labour-time is embodied for goods in which less labour-time is embodied. Specialization on the basis of comparative advantage is bound to yield detrimental effects.

It is important to stress the difference between the Emmanuel and the Prebisch thesis since the secular deterioration hypothesis is concerned with the terms of trade and the distribution of gains from trade <u>over time</u> and not <u>at any point in time</u>, as in the Emmanuel case. According to this thesis, the continuously increasing power of trade unions in DCs to secure high real wages generates, via higher prices of manufactures, continuously deteriorating terms of trade for LDCs. Thus whereas in Prebisch the emphasis is on peripheral countries as primary producers, for Emmanuel the source of their exploitation is low wages regardless of whether they are producing manufactures or primary products.

Relative prices are assumed to play no role in the determination of the composition of the bundle of commodities consumed. Wages are determined independently by historical and moral factors. Differences in wages are attributed to different degrees of exploitation of labour rather than to differences in labour productivity. While the assumption of labour immobility across countries is retained, capital is treated as an internationally mobile factor. As in the Marxist paradigm, the value of goods is proportional to the amount of social labour-time embodied in their production: current labour (variable capital) and past labour (constant capital). The surplus value of any good is the excess of its value over the wages required to be paid to the workers.

Two core assumptions of Emmanuel's thesis are that (i) real wages are exogenously determined in each country; and (ii) the rate of profit on capital is equalized across countries. The terms of trade result as a consequence of these two fundamental assumptions. The price of production for a good produced in a high-wage country will be higher than for the same good produced in a low-wage country with the same technique.

The most striking outcome of Emmanuel's thesis is that a country might be the victim of unequal exchange and at the same time enjoy substantial improvement in its terms of trade and absolute real income. For example, if workers in the centre are able to secure for themselves part of the increase in productivity, the DFTT will move against the periphery. The commodity terms of trade for the periphery, however, although are not as favourable as they would be if there were no increase in the real wage in the center, might still be better than they were initially before the productivity increase in the center.

A point of paramount importance is that even if real wages and interest rates are equalized in both trading groups, the DFTT are not equal to unity, since the labour content of the capital-abundant country's exports is less than that of its imports. The unequal exchange theory, therefore, implies that if production prices are actually used in international exchange, value will pass on balance from poor to rich countries through exchange, if either rich ones have a higher "organic composition of capital" or higher wages. Emmanuel, however, dismissed the former and is mainly concerned with the latter.

What are the main limitations of this theory? *First*, it does not explain the differences in wages between the centre and periphery, since these are not dependent on productivity. The assertion that wages determine development and income levels is difficult to uphold from the point of view of logic and from a historical perspective. According to Bettelheim (1970), Emmanuel's treatment of wages as independent of productivity gives rise to the impression that to correct the inequality of exchanges it would be sufficient to change wages. He advocates that Emmanuel wrongly neglects the possibility that a low-wage country may be able to develop manufacturing export-industries with modern technology and thus earn high profits that will provide a basis for rapid industrialization (such as Japan's development). Amin (1976) also argues that it is the imperialistic domination of peripheral social formation by the centre that fosters unequal exchange rather than wage-differentials.

Second, the distinction between centre and periphery seems naive. It neglects intra-country differentiation and competition between capital and labour. It replaces exploitation by classes with exploitation by countries.

Third, the assumption that all exports to DCs are specific, that is, non-competing products, is very unrealistic. Although this might be true for some products and countries, it is certainly not the case for others.

Fourth, its policy implications are flawed. If LDC exports consist of non-competing products, LDCs have no freedom of manoeuvre in relation to their DC trading partners. It is not sufficient to show that the gains from trade are unequal and from that to conclude that LDCs are exploited. Although one may agree that the international market is unjust, the incremental effects are most important. The fundamental issue is whether international trade reduces absolute levels of incomes for the periphery.

Some conclusions

Theories about terms of trade formation present a great variety of hypotheses, schools of thought, forms, empirical arguments and policy implications. In reviewing them, one cannot avoid the impression that ideological predilection and inventiveness were at the root of all the arguments about (i) the tendency for LDCs' terms of trade to deteriorate; (ii) the unfairness of the distributions of the gains from trade; and (iii) the unequal exchange of values. On the other hand, in the case of neoclassical economics, it is clear that the theoretical machinery is unable, despite its power, to formulate unambiguous forecasts on patterns, size and growth of relative prices.

The terms of trade controversy, therefore, is unlikely to be settled on the basis of theoretical arguments. As in most cases of important conjectures and predictions about the course of economic variables, economists are often caught between structuralist and neoclassical theories.

Nevertheless, theories of terms of trade formation do provide a wide range of variants to the basic model of international trade and comparative advantage. With these variants, they achieve the result of showing the limitations of the classical paradigm and of unravelling the chain of circumstances which may cause the world of trade not to be the best possible one.

However, more than an antidote to Panglossian illusions on the "fairness" of the real world, the theoretical models examined are useful to set the stage against which one may evaluate the claim of deteriorating the terms of trade. Within the framework of these competing theories, confronting such an empirical claim with the best empirical data available will have the result not only of verifying the claim as such, but also of testing the theories by counterfactual evidence.

The study of the alternative theoretical models within which the terms of trade can be seen to evolve is of further importance, because it shows the complexity of the issues involved and the limitations of any empirical test confined to individual aspects of these issues. As this chapter has tried to show, terms of trade come in many forms and are not generally the ultimate object of the theory or the empirical analysis, since their improvement or deterioration does not necessarily imply that the country is better or worse off. Furthermore, some terms of trade may improve and some may deteriorate. Deterioration and improvement may be defined in different ways and may be unevenly, and perhaps unfairly, distributed between DCs and LDCs, and within these country groups.

As a concluding remark to this first chapter, therefore, any attempt to provide either a "comprehensive" test of the competitive claims on the terms of trade, or of a satisfactory "piecemeal" test is futile. The comprehensive test would be inevitably paired to a controversial, highly simplified theoretical model of irreplicable empirical complexity. The piecemeal test, on the other hand, will always be vulnerable to the objection that it does not embody the structure of any definite theory and is thus unable to reject it.

Even though this difficulty is well known, it is nevertheless, believed that the piecemeal test--the only possibility under the circumstances--is sufficiently interesting to justify the major research commitment required by this study.

Notes

1/ Spraos (1983) argues that if there is chronic unemployment and the expansion of production of exportables draws on such labour, then the employment dimension in that sector should be considered along with productivity. In fact, he has defined the following employment-corrected double factorial terms of trade (ECDFTT):

$$ECDFTT = \frac{Px}{Pm} \cdot \frac{Zx}{Zm} \cdot Nx = \frac{Px}{Pm} \cdot \frac{Qx}{Zm} = \frac{Vx}{Pm} \cdot \frac{1}{Zm}$$

Where N_x = employment in the sector producing exportables

Q_x = production in the sector producing exportables

V_x = value of exportables

2/ For a formula showing the quantitative relationship, see Takayama (1972), p.394.

3/ As shown in Chapter II, this study's analysis provides little support to this argument. Similar results are also reported by Thirlwall and Bergevin (1985).

CHAPTER II

THE EMPIRICAL EVIDENCE ON TRENDS IN THE TERMS OF TRADE

Introduction

Terms of trade changes and variability have attracted the attention of development economists in several ways. First, the economic significance of the various terms of trade definitions and measurements has been debated and at times questioned. Second, the notion of their long-term trends and secular movements has been closely examined. Third, the variability around these trends and various measures of instability has been the object of further investigation. Fourth, the determinants of both trends and variability have been analyzed.

This chapter has the objective of making a contribution to this field by examining, in some detail, the issue of secular trends of terms of trade of fourteen individual primary commodities and three commodity aggregates between 1900 and 1982. The data used are perhaps the largest and most accurate collection of a time series of prices for primary products assembled to date. They have been put together from a variety of different sources and through painstaking effort in the course of a major World Bank research project. [1]

The plan of this chapter is as follows: the next section is devoted to theoretical and methodological problems involved in measuring secular movements in the terms of trade. A survey of past research on the trends in the terms of trade is also presented. This is followed by a description of data used in this study and presents the results of the analysis of secular movements in the terms of trade between 1900 and 1982 and during selective sub-periods. Next, the Prebisch's hypothesis on the asymmetry between upswings and downswings in commodity prices is examined. The question of the contribution of productivity changes to movements of the various terms of trade is also briefly explored. Lastly, there is a summary of the main findings and some conclusions are drawn.

Measuring the Secular Movements of the Terms of Trade

a) Earlier attempts

As discussed in the previous chapter, the debate on the terms of trade started with a seminal article by Prebisch (1950), which is still very relevant because it embodies most of the main elements of the many controversies that have followed. The "seeds of controversy" in Prebisch's article concerned:

- The theoretical foundations of the notion of "terms of trade";
- The methodology used to measure these "terms" and their presumed decline against developing countries; and
- The choice of data.

While at the time Prebisch would probably not have ascribed great significance to the issue, his use of the net barter terms of trade (NBTT) between primary products and manufactures, implied that this gross measure could be considered a proxy for an actual gain from trade of the developed countries at the expenses of the developing ones. Most of the critics of this type of presumption denied that the price ratios, however corrected, would ever be able to reflect real income changes. The reasons invoked were basically two:

- Deterioration in the price ratios may be the result of an expansion of trade from developing countries in response, for example, to a cost reduction; and

- Because utility can only be measured ordinally, a comparison of two different levels of money values has no welfare significance.

Both of these points are made by Baldwin (1955), who illustrates the first objection with the example of Great Britain, which "during the first half of the nineteenth century, has been carried into international prominence on the wave of a secular decline in its commodity terms of trade". On the second objection, Baldwin observes that modern welfare economics have shown that the only way to measure changes in real income is to make strong value judgements involving assumptions on interpersonal comparisons of utility. However, different welfare conclusions will generally follow from different sets of such value judgements. Therefore, the real income implications of welfare comparisons are more often a matter of choice for the reader than empirically falsifiable propositions.

That some significance could be attached to even crude comparisons of terms of trade over time was proved, however, by the theorists of what can be called the "free trade" group. Several theorems on the desirability of a ceteris paribus improvement in the terms of trade were thus due to Kemp (1962), Samuelson (1962), and Krueger and Sönneschein (1967). These latter authors, in particular, showed that the relationship between the improvements of the welfare position and the terms of trade of a "small" country could be broken down into two parts:

- The relationship between the improved terms of trade and a new potential welfare position; and

- The relationship between the degree of improvement of the terms of trade and the degree of improvement of the welfare position.

Perhaps not surprisingly, the authors proved that while terms of trade improvements can be taken as an indication that potential improvements in welfare have become possible, one cannot use terms of trade changes to measure welfare changes. In other words, it is not always the case that the more the terms of trade improve, the greater the welfare gains will be.

The criticism of the methodology used to analyze the terms of trade changes and the subsequent efforts at refining it can also be illustrated with reference to Prebisch's pioneering article. The objections raised at the time and recurring thereafter are basically four:

- The arbitrariness of the time span;
- The omission of major explanatory variables;
- The statistical procedure; and
- The data inadequacy.

These objections are somewhat standard in the sense that they apply to most attempts of economic measurement. Their relevance to the terms of trade issue, therefore, has to be judged in terms of the special circumstances surrounding the specific measurements attempted. Concerning the arbitrariness of the time span, the dependence of the conclusions on the beginning and the end period can be tested with sensitivity analysis, or with more complex statistical methods (e.g., spectral analysis). As Spraos (1980) shows, the qualitative part of Prebisch's conclusions seem to stand the quite extensive tests of sensitivity, while the quantitative part is obviously much weaker. Other analyses based on shorter time series, also reported by Spraos (1980), show even less robust results.

A more relevant objection relating to time trend analysis is that any test on the decline of the terms of trade should be performed in ceteris paribus conditions, i.e., the intervening exogenous factors should be accounted for. The major factors whose effect should be "extracted" from the usual terms of trade measure to obtain a "net" measure free of exogenous bias are: (i) freight and insurance costs; (ii) trade composition; (iii) quality; and (iv) productivity.

Freight and insurance costs are important for all components of the terms of trade measure based on c.i.f. prices. In the original Prebisch study, the developing country price component was, in fact, measured by the c.i.f. prices of primary product imports, while manufactured exports (the developed country price component) were measured at f.o.b. prices. Because freight and insurance costs fell precipitously in the period immediately preceding World War I, the failure to account for this omitted variable could be largely responsible for the negative trend measured (e.g., see Ellsworth (1956) and Bairoch (1975)).

A second major source of bias may be traced to the failure to account for changes in trade composition and, in a similar way, to the changing quality of the products imported and exported. The basket of goods traded between developing and developed countries has indeed changed drastically since the beginning of the century, and it is even doubtful if exports of primary products can still be considered the core of developing country exports. Furthermore, a large part of the trade expansion of the last 50 years has occurred within developing countries and there are signs that this will continue at an accelerated pace.

Trade composition has also changed through a twofold quality effect: the product mix has evolved in favour of higher quality goods, and the quality of the individual goods has improved.

This phenomenon has mainly concerned manufactures, but primary exports have also evolved in the same direction. Spraos (1980), for example, reports that in Kenya the proportion of coffee beans of highest quality (AA) rose from 0.2 percent harvested in 1957/58 to 16.3 percent in 1964/65, and that the percentage of cotton output with a staple length of 28 mm or more rose in Greece from 11.3 percent in 1954 to 97.3 percent in 1970. The proportion of primary products processed before shipment (e.g., cocoa butter instead of cocoa beans) has also drastically increased.

Productivity changes are also related to quality changes as a source of bias. The literature on the terms of trade is unclear as to the consequences of differential changes in productivity between developing and developed countries. On one hand, productivity is considered a major force in determining decreases in unit costs. As stated in the previous chapter, the so called SFTT and DFTT have been devised to account for input-saving technological progress. The SFTT, for example, are defined as the product of the barter terms of trade (i.e., the ratio of export and import prices) by an index of the productivity of the factors of production in export industries. The DFTT, on the other hand, are obtained by multiplying the barter terms of trade by a ratio of indices of factor productivity in the export and import industries, respectively. (For a discussion of the two measures see, for example Robertson, 1915).

Both these measures, however, are attempts to convert relative price changes into relative income changes. They do not separate the changes in prices due to productivity increases from the autonomous changes that may be the subject of a trend. In other words, adoption of the SFTT or the DFTT does not eliminate the problem of separating the changes in the terms of trade due to productivity increases from changes due to exogenous factors.

The statistical procedure used to analyze the measure selected is also subject to controversy. Because the time span is arbitrary and major explanatory variables may have been omitted, the statistical test devised can easily be faulted on grounds of bias and incompleteness. Regression tests produce further elements of uncertainty, linked to the arbitrariness of the functional form. Even in the simple case of a test of a linear trend coefficient, the choice of a quadratic equation or of a higher order polynomial may completely change the statistical results. 2/

Finally, the question of data reliability should be examined with some care. Prebisch originally used two partially overlapping series (those of Schlote and the Board of Trade, as given in the United Nations, 1949) to give a run of index numbers from 1876-80 to 1946-47 for the NBTT of merchandise trade in the United Kingdom. Apart from the single source provided by one United Nations publication, however, it is very hard to trace the origin and the components of the series used. Commodity coverage and techniques of measurement prior to or around 1900 are sufficiently uncertain for one to be tempted to disregard the corresponding numbers as possibly misleading on accounting and statistical grounds.

A second series by the League of Nations referred to by Prebisch and later used in modified form by Lewis (1952), utilised the ratio between unit value of British primary imports to the unit value of British exports and imports of manufactures. This series was modified by the League itself with data from a larger trade pool for the years after 1929. Later on, Lewis (1952) tried to improve it by adding data from the imports and exports of manufactures of the United States and by using other subsidiary information and by applying a more balanced procedure to splice the partially overlapping indices available from Schlote and the League.

More precisely, for the years 1871-1929, the League used the Sauerbeck wholesale price index as a proxy for the price of traded primary products, and a weighted average of British export and import prices of manufactures (derived from Schlote's series) for the prices of traded manufactures. 3/ Since 1930, the League series has used a wider set of data compiled from 67 country statistics (see Review of World Trade, 1938).

On the other hand, the Lewis series, for the years 1871-1920 was based on a weighted average of the Schlote index for U.K. imports and exports of raw materials, while an unweighted average of the Schlote index of U.K. exports and imports was used for manufactures. After 1920, Lewis put together the U.K. and U.S. index of food and raw materials and of manufactures, giving equal weights to each of the two countries. Since 1930, he has used the same data used by the League.

A third index, compiled by the United Nations from national indices (weighted according to national trade shares) starts from 1900, but up to 1913, only 60-65 percent of world exports and 50-55 percent of exports of primary products were used in the index computation.

All these indices suffer from common shortcomings: uneven commodity coverages, questionable weighting procedures, switching definitions, abuse of averaging methods, and difficulty of tracing the manipulations from the many different data sources.

In conclusion, even though the question of <u>statistical reliability</u> has not figured prominently in the debate on the terms of trade, it should be dealt with as a major object of concern. Since the original controversy erupted, however, the statistical tools of time series analysis have evolved sufficiently to allow a much more rigorous testing of the basic hypotheses.

b) <u>Empirical evidence from earlier to more recent studies</u>

As may be seen from Table 2.1, which is an updated version of Nguyen (1981), a review of the most important studies on the trends of terms of trade of LDCs (and primary commodities) shows that no conclusive comfort to either side of the controversy is warranted. Empirical studies have come up with estimates of positive, negative and no secular trends, depending on the time period explored, the definitions used and the estimation techniques employed. As mentioned in the previous sections, disputes have arisen about what measure of the particular terms of trade variable is relevant, how to treat quality changes, what sample period is desirable, and so on. Out of the most important studies selected, about a third confirm the Prebisch hypothesis, and about a fourth disprove it.

Table 2.1: **Classification of Studies According to Different Theses on Secular Trends of the Terms of Trade, 1817-1986**

Rising terms of trade of LDCs and/or primary products	Declining terms of trade of LDCs and/or primary products	Trends that are not empirically convincing or analytically justifiable
Ricardo, D. (1817)	Kindleberger, C.P. (1943;1950;1956) a/	Schlote, W. (1938)
Malthus, T.R. (1820)		Rostow, W.W. (1951)
Torrens, R. (1815;1821)	Martin, K. and Thackeray, F.G. (1948)	Young, J. (1951)
Mill, J.S. (1848)		Viner, J. (1952)
Jevons, W.S. (1865)	UN (1949; 1950)	Meier, G.M. (1952;1968)
Marshall, A. (1903;1926)	Singer, H. (1950)	Haberler, G. (1954;1959; 1961a;1961b;1964)
Keynes, J.M. (1912)	Triantis, S.G. (1952)	
Robertson, D.H. (1915)	Myint, H. (1954-55)	Baldwin, R.E. (1955)
Graham, F.D. (1932)	Lewis, W.A. (1955)	Ellsworth, P.T. (1956)
Clark, C. (1938;1942)	Myrdal, G. (1956a;1956b; 1957a; 1957b)	Morgan, T. (1959;1963)
Kahn, A.E. (1946)		Bhagwati, J. (1960)
Viner, J. (1946)	Atallah, M.K (1958)	Cairncross, A.K. (1961)
Haberler, G. (1947;1958)	Prebisch, R. (1959;1964)	Baer, W. (1962)
Lewis, W.A. (1949;1952)	Lerdau, E. (1959;1965)	Lipsey, R.E. (1963)
Robinson, A. (1954)	Nurkse, R. (1953;1959)	Flanders, M.J. (1964)
Mikesell, R. (1954)	Bernstein, E.M. (1960)	Kindleberger, C.P. (1964;1968)
Aubrey, H. (1955)	Schultz, T.W. (1961) b/	
Moret, M. (1957)	Hall, R. (1962)	Johnson, H.G. (1967)
Montgomery, S. (1960)	Kaldor, N. (1963)	Kemp, M.C. (1968)
Bairoch, P. (1970)	Wilson, T. et al (1969)	Clement, M. et al. (1968)
Law, A. (1975)	Porter, R. (1970)	Bhatia, B.M. (1969)
	Emmanuel, A. (1972)	Streeten, P. (1974)
	Brecher, R.A. (1974)	UNCTAD (1975)
	Commonwealth (1975)	d'Hérouville, H. (1975)
	Behrman, J. (1977)	Yotopoulos, P.A. and Nugent, J.B. (1976)
	Ray, G. (1977) c/	
	Adams, F. and Behrman, J. (1982)	Henner, H.F. (1976)
	Singer, H. (1982)	Schloss, H.H: (1977)
	UNCTAD (1982)	Singer, H. (1982)
	Sundrum, R. (1983) d/	Södersten, B. (1980)
	Josling, T. (1984)	Jabara, C. (1980)
	Labys, W. and Polak, P. (1984)	Hallwood, P. (1982) e/
	Chu, K. and Morrison, T.K. (1984,1986)	
	Sapsford, D. (1985)	
	Thirlwall, A. and Bergevin, J. (1985)	

a/ Deterioration for LDCs but not for primary products.
b/ T.W. Schultz has found a rather stable evolution for the period 1904-50.
c/ Between 1845-1975, there were only 33 years with rising "real" prices of primary commodities.
d/ Over the 1960s period. For the 1970s, he reports rising terms of trade of LDCs.
e/ For the two sub-periods examined, (1957-69 and 1970-80), he found statistically significant trends.

Table 2.2, which reports the results classified in terms of causes of change, suggests that in the 1970s "real" commodity prices responded more quickly and sharply than before to changes in economic activity in industrial countries (Enoch and Panic, 1980; Labini, 1982; Hallwood, 1982; etc.). Furthermore, the pronounced commodity "real" price instability in the decade commencing in 1972 is explained mainly by the sharp increase in the fluctuations of the dollar exchange rates vis-á-vis other major currencies (Chu and Morrison, 1984 and 1986).

Overall, empirical evidence of a general decline in the LDC's NBTT over a long historical period up to the Korean War is lacking. Only in the post-Korean War period is there some evidence of a decline in the NBTT for most LDCs.

The relationship between prices of primary and manufactured goods appears to be characterised by short periods in which the terms of trade rose more sharply in favour of the former (i.e., 1950-54, 1973-74 and less markedly in 1962-64, 1969-73). Typically these short periods seem to be interspersed by longer ones in which prices for manufactures rise relative to those of primary commodities. The available data for the period 1950-75 show that the NBTT for LDCs as a whole (excluding fuel exports) have declined at a statistically significant trend rate of 1.1 percent a year.

The NBTT for LDC primary commodities (excluding fuel) against imported manufactured goods show a statistically significant trend decline at 1.6 percent a year for the same period.

A study on the NBTT and ITT of DCs and LDCs during 1950-65 (Wilson, T., et al., 1969), taking a 1950-53 average as the base year and thus including the mid-1950s boom years, showed that LDCs' NBTT fell to 98.3 in 1954-57, to 92.3 in 1958-61 and to 90.7 in 1962-65. Their ITT consistently improved, reaching 156.8 in 1962-65. Moreover, for certain countries both the NBTT and ITT improved.

Table 2.2: **Analysis of Changes in the Terms of Trade Between DCs and LDCs, 1817-1986**

Causes of changes	Selected Studies
A. Rising trends	
(1) Diminishing returns in agriculture and extractive industries	Ricardo, Malthus, Torrens, J.S. Mill, Jevons, Marshall, Keynes, A. Robinson
(2) Predictions based on econometric models: demand and supply conditions will turn against manufactures and DCs	Lewis (1952), Aubrey
B. Declining trends	
(a) Supply side:	
(1) Wage rises of unionized workers in DCs and monopoly pricing	UNCTAD, Prebisch A, Singer H, Myrdal, Emmanuel, Kaldor
(2) Chronic surplus of primary products due to secular fall in raw material content of industrial output	Bernstein, Singer, Kaldor (1963)
(3) Wages in LDCs export sector fixed by peasant-earnings level because of unlimited supply of labour	Lewis
(4) Lack of flexibility in economic adjustments in LDCs and structural rigidity in primary production	Kindleberger (1956), Myrdal
(5) Production stocks and past real prices of commodities	Bosworth and Lawrence (1982), Hwa (1979), Sapsford
(b) Demand side:	
(1) Falling demand by DCs due to technological progress which reduces primary inputs in manufactured output and to synthetic substitutes	UNCTAD, Bernstein, Prebisch, Singer, Kaldor, Sundrum
(2) Protectionism in DCs which reduces imports from LDCs	UNCTAD, Prebisch
(3) Engel's law	Kindleberger (1943;1950), UNCTAD, Prebisch, Schultz, Nurkse, Porter
(4) Differences in cyclical movements of product prices: in prosperity, prices of primary products rise faster than those of manufactures, but this "gain" is more than compensated, in depression, by drastic falls in relative prices of primary products	Prebisch, Triantis, Martin and Thackeray
(5) Economic activity of DCs	Chu and Morrison (1984;1986), Sapsford

A noteworthy point is, that while many LDCs enjoyed a considerable improvement in their terms of trade in 1973 and the first half of 1974 as a result of the general upswing of primary commodity prices, some countries with relatively large imports of food and petroleum suffered further deterioration in their terms of trade.

The question then arises whether the apparent improvement of the terms of trade of many primary products vis-á-vis manufactured goods in 1973 and early 1974 invalidate the Prebisch thesis for future deterioration, or whether these improvements have been an atypical episode.

Furthermore, the price trends of the main categories of primary commodities are different, and divergencies can be expected to be found not only among the main groups but also within them. For example, the study by Adams and Behrman (1982) demonstrates that the secular patterns for coffee and cocoa and for wheat and maize are quite similar, but those for copper and tin differ markedly. The explanation given by the authors is that market structures differ substantially in some cases, even within commodity groups.

In terms of summary, one may agree with Spraos (1980), that although it is an open question whether there was much or little deterioration, the statistical evidence is consistent with the view that there was some. The statistical series chosen by Prebisch did, however, exaggerate the rate of deterioration. From World War II to the 1970s the evidence points to a deteriorating trend in the relative price of primary goods.

A Disaggregated Analysis of Terms of Trade Movements

Table 2.3 reports the data sources used for the empirical analysis that follows. As shown, data on international prices have been assembled commodity by commodity, in an attempt to maintain stability, as far as possible, among the characteristics of grade, quality and packaging of the product. Subsequently, price indices have been computed for seven different commodity aggregates. Each price index is a weighted arithmetic average of world export values of each commodity for 1975.

Table 2.3: **Commodity Description and Data Sources**

Commodity	Description	Weight (%)	Source of data
Coffee	Santos 4, spot N.Y., 1900-72; Guatemalan prime washed, spot N.Y., 1973-82	7.4	Pan America Coffee Bureau, Annual Coffee Statistics, various issues; U.S. Bureau of Labour Statistics
Cocoa	Guayaquil cocoa in London, 1900-06; Bahia in N.Y., 1907-12; Accra spot N.Y., 1913-82	2.8	Commodity Research Bureau, Commodity Year Book, 1939; Gill and Duffus, Cocoa Statistics, December 1978, IBRD Commodities Division
Tea	Formosa, fine, spot N.Y., 1900-17; all tea in London Auction, 1918-82	1.9	Commodity Research Bureau, Commodity Year Book, 1939; International Tea Committee, Annual Bulletin Statistics, various issues
Sugar	World raws, spot price, 1900-47; f.a.a. Cuba basis, 1948-60; f.o.b. and stowed Greater Caribbean ports (including Brazil), bagged, 1961-70; f.o.b. and stowed Caribbean ports (including Brazil), in bulk, 1971-82	19.7	International Sugar Council, The World Sugar Economy, Vol. II, 1963; Journal of Commerce, USDA, Sugar Report
Wheat	Canadian No. 1, northern basis in score, Port William-Port Arthur, 1900-47; Canadian No. 1, Western red spring in store, Thunder Bay, 1948-82	19.7	FAO, Monthly Bulletin of Agricultural Economics and Statistics; Canadian Grain Commission, Grain Statistics Weekly; IBRD, Commodities Division
Maize	Cash contract prices at Chicago, 1900-11; U.S. No. 3, Yellow, c.i.f. Rotterdam, 1912-47; U.S. No. 2 yellow f.o.b. Gulf ports 1948-82	12.0	Commodity Research Bureau, Commodity Year Book, 1939; U.S. Bureau of Labor Statistics, USDA, Grain Market News
Rice	Thai 5 percent brokes, f.o.b. Bankok	5.0	USDA, Rice Market News; IBRD, Commodities Div.
Cotton	Average price of middling 7/8 cotton at designated spot markers	7.7	USDA, Statistics on Cotton and Related Data; IBRD, Commodities Division
Wool	Raw, territory fine combining wool-scored basis, Grades 64's, 70's, 80's, in Boston	3.5	Commodity Research Bureau, Commodity Year Book, various issues; IBRD, Commodities Division
Rubber	RSS No. 1, spot New York	2.8	Rubber Statistical Bulletin, various issues
Copper	Elecholytic, domestic refinery, f.o.b. refinery	9.4	Engineering and Mining Journal
Tin	New York Market	2.3	Engineering and Mining Journal
Lead	Common, New York market	1.4	Engineering and Mining Journal
Zinc	Prime Weater, spot St. Louis	4.6	Engineering and Mining Journal

All individual commodities and aggregate price indices have been deflated by the U.S. index of unit value of exports of manufactured goods. For each commodity and for each aggregate, therefore, the ratio of international prices and manufactures export unit value is proposed as a measure of the commodity's BTT.

Although the U.S. index of unit value of exports of manufactured goods may not appear a satisfactory indicator of the prices faced by developing countries, its choice is justified for two reasons: (i) it is the only reliable deflator available for a period as long as the one that this study considers (1900-82); (ii) it is highly correlated to the alternatives that would be available for shorter periods (in particular, the U.S. wholesale price index for which the correlation coefficient is 0.999 during the period).

It is interesting to first examine the general evolution of these terms of trade measures on a commodity basis by visual impression on the basis of simple time charts (See Appendix I, Graphs 1 - 19). Commodities can be classified into three groups: (i) clearly increasing secular trends; (ii) clearly decreasing; and (iii) stationary or uncertain. The first group comprises only coffee and tin. The second group, the seemingly most numerous one, comprises tea, wool, wheat, food, rice, coffee, all agricultural goods and rubber. The third group includes cotton, cocoa, sugar, maize, lead and zinc.

On a visual basis, therefore, and considering the whole sequence, there seems to be no doubt that the terms of trade of all primary commodities exported by developing countries, with only two exceptions, show a tendency to decrease or to remain stationary. Indeed, the visual impression that conveys this conclusion is so strong that it is hard to imagine any statistical test capable of reversing it.

On the other hand, it is also clear that the visual impression may be misleading for some of the very reasons discussed in the introductory section: (i) the arbitrariness of the base year; (ii) the omitted exogenous factors; and (iii) the lack of rigour of the visual test. If a statistically justifiable testing procedure is to be used, however, the nature of the null hypothesis must be specified more carefully with reference to the following two points:

- First, the objective of the test is stated as the falsification of the hypothesis that the terms of trade for each particular commodity and/or for any of their aggregate indices have been decreasing over time. Obviously, this does not mean "decreasing all the time", but just decreasing in some acceptable a priori sense.

- Second, in this chapter single regressions by ordinary least squares are used as a means to obtain statistics on the evolution of terms of trade over time. The assumption is that the underlying evolution of the terms of trade can be measured by linear and quadratic yearly trend variables, once the rest of the variance of the dependent variable is accounted for through appropriate explanators.

These two points, however, are not sufficient to clarify the form of the test, since a "decline in the terms of trade" in terms of a trend can be measured in several different ways. Consider a quadratic trend equation of the form:

$$Y_i = a + bt + ct^2$$

A measure of underlying evolution is offered by the following statistics:

I) First derivative: $\frac{\partial Y_i}{\partial t} = b + 2ct$

II) Linear trend coefficient: $(\partial Y/\partial t) - 2ct = b$

III) Quadratic trend coefficient: $-\frac{\partial^2 Y/\partial t^2}{2} = c$

IV) Value of **t** for which the first derivative changes sign: $\bar{t} = -\frac{b}{2c}$

Each of these statistics can be interpreted as revealing different characteristics of an underlying trend. The first derivative is the statistic more intuitively associated with the concept of a fall or a rise in the dependent variable, since it measures the variation of terms of trade for a unit increase in time. In a quadratic equation, however, its value is not independent of time and even its sign can be reversed with the passage of time if the signs of the two coefficients **b** and **c** are not identical.

The linear trend coefficient **b** and the quadratic trend coefficient **c** have the virtue of being invariant with respect to the value of the trend variable. Their interpretation, however, is indistinct and rests on the assumption that the linear component of the trend reflects a basic tendency to decline or to increase, while the quadratic component portrays the trend to "turn around" or "reverse" this basic tendency.

Finally the value of **t** for which the first derivative changes sign gives us some information on a possible dichotomous behaviour of the data in the period considered. In other words, the answer to the question: "Have the terms of trade been declining in the period 1900-82?" can be in the affirmative for sub-period A (i.e., 1900-60) and in the negative for sub-period B (i.e., 1960-82).

In order to estimate a trend equation, the series were transformed into logs, and both a linear and a quadratic specification were attempted applying a Generalized Least Squares (GLS) estimation procedure accounting for autocorrelation. More specifically, the procedure used can be summarized in the following steps:

a) Estimates of the model using the Ordinary Least Square (OLS) method were obtained;
b) Autocorrelations up to 5 lags of the residuals were computed;
c) The Yule-Walker equations were solved to obtain the autoregressive parameters, and a preliminary estimate for the variance;

d) The autoregressive parameters, which were not significant at least at the five percent level were removed in order of significance; and

e) All the variables from the original data were transformed and the parameters were re-estimated using the OLS regression.

This procedure is thought to be more powerful than those which use iterative methods to correct for the presence of autocorrelations, because with the latter, convergence may not be achieved at a global minimum or maximum. Furthermore, a number of observations equal to the number of lags are lost, with a consequent loss of degrees of freedom.

Results derived from the regression analysis

Having established that a diagrammatic portrayal of the data can only be a very first step in the analysis, specific tests on the basis of the measures I and IV were performed. Table 2.4 shows the estimates of these four measures obtained by fitting quadratic or linear (depending on which one gives better fit) trend equations for the whole period 1900-82. The equations fitted are mostly significant both in the linear and quadratic terms. The $\bar{R}^2$s are seldom very high, but this is to be expected in an equation having only the linear and the quadratic trend as explanatory variables over 82 years of observations. On the other hand, given the simplicity of the equation, it is perhaps surprising that in a number of cases a sizeable portion (30 to 65 percent) of the variance of the terms of trade is explained by the regression.

Overall, the following conclusions are suggested by the estimates of the table. First, the basic tendency, as expressed by the linear trend, is negative for all commodities and all aggregates except beverages, cocoa, coffee, lead and tin. The time paths, however, for beverages and lead can be regarded as trendless since the fit of the equations is very poor. Second, there is a tendency to reverse the linear trend, (i.e., the linear coefficient and the quadratic coefficient have opposite signs) given a sufficient time, also for virtually all products.

Table 2.4: **Trends in the Terms of Trade for Individual Commodities, 1900-82**

Commodity	Intercept	Trend	Trend squared	$\bar{R}^2$	First derivative (elasticity)	Time of trend reversal (no. of yrs.)
Beverages	4.465 (26.864)***	0.005 (1.584)		0.006	0.005	
Cereals	4.833 (78.274)***	-0.006 (5.860)***		0.277	-0.006	
Food	4.596 (56.965)***	-0.003 (2.038)**		0.026	-0.003	
Non-food	5.992 (45.793)***	-0.017 (6.267)***		0.313	-0.017	
Maize	4.694 (41.067)***	0.008 (1.280)	-0.0002 (2.252)**	0.153	-0.008	20.00
Rice	4.805 (53.916)***	-0.006 (3.344)***		0.091	-0.006	
Cotton	4.902 (32.572)***	0.013 (1.530)	-0.0002 (2.248)**	0.071	-0.006	32.50
Wool	5.306 (72.617)***	0.022 (5.399)***	-0.0004 (8.028)**	0.659	-0.011	27.50
Rubber	7.323 (21.943)***	-0.060 (3.205)***	0.0004 (1.709)*	0.306	-0.027	75.00
Coffee	4.266 (22.912)***	0.010 (2.531)**		0.051	0.010	

Table 2.4: (cont.)

Commodity	Intercept	Trend	Trend squared	$\bar{R}^2$	First derivative (elasticity)	Time of trend reversal (no. of yrs.)
Cocoa	4.881 (16.453)***	-0.046 (2.796)***	0.0006 (2.981)***	0.046	0.003	39.33
Tea	4.913 (24.437)***	0.012 (1.074)	-0.0002 (1.331)	-0.007	-0.004	30.00
Sugar	4.466 (20.427)***	-0.032 (2.574)**	0.0003 (2.038)**	0.077	-0.007	53.33
Wheat	4.787 (67.151)***	-0.007 (4.599)***		0.280	-0.007	
Copper	4.991 (28.706)***	-0.027 (2.719)***	0.0003 (2.548)**	0.058	-0.002	45.00
Tin	4.059 (41.252)***	-0.013 (2.244)***	0.0003 (4.326)***	0.484	0.012	21.67
Lead	4.729 (48.191)***	0.001 (0.326)		-0.024	0.001	
Zinc	4.345 (32.018)***	-0.009 (1.232)	0.0001 (1.312)	-0.016	-0.001	45.00
Total agriculture	4.999 (52.636)***	-0.008 (4.045)		0.149	-0.008	

*** = Indicates significance at the 1 percent level.
** = Indicates significance at the 5 percent level.
* = Indicates significance at the 10 percent level.

Sub-periods

As pointed out by Sapsford (1985), the unconvincing evidence for deteriorating terms of trade in primary commodities in the 1900-82 period might be because the underlying parameters of the NBTT's growth path did not remain constant.

In order to consider this problem, intercept and slope dummy variables were introduced in the trend equations estimated above. In doing so, however, the problem remained of how to select the years for which the structural shift may have happened. The following different procedures were applied:

1) Divide the sample period 1900-82 into <u>sub-periods</u> of 10, 15 and 20 years;
2) Use 1900-50 and 1950-82 as <u>break periods</u>; [4]
3) Identify periods which have been marked by <u>historical events</u>. These include:

Pre-World War I:	1900-13
World War I and Inter-War Period:	1914-39
World War II-Korean War:	1940-53
Post-Korean War period until the first "oil shock":	1954-73
Post first "oil shock" period:	1974-82 [5]

For each period identified, a search procedure was applied in the range of $\pm$ 3 years and the one with the highest $\bar{R}^2$ was eventually used in the regressions.

While the regressions estimated are available from the authors on request, Table 2.5 synthesizes the main features of the results for the five alternative groupings of the data tested. For each grouping experiment, Table 2.5 reports four series of results:

Table 2.5: Time Breakdown: Trends in the Terms of Trade

	N_1			N_2			N_2^1			N_3			N_4			N_5		
	No. of time specific		Signific. trend	No. of time specific		Signific. trend	No. of time specific		Signific. trend	No. of time specific		Signific. trend	No. of time specific		Signific. trend	No. of time specific		Signific. trend
	A	B	C D	A	B	C D	A	B	C D	A	B	C D	A	B	C D	A	B	C D
Beverages	1	0		1	1	+*	0	1	+**	0	0		2	3	+**	1	2	+***
Cereals	1	0	-**	1	2		1	2	-*	0	0		1	2		4	3	-**
Food	0	0	-**	2	3		2	3		1	1		2	2		5	4	
Non-food	1	0	-***	0	1	-***	0	1	-***	0	0	-**	2	2		2	2	-***
Coffee	0	0		3	3	+***	1	1		1	1		3	3		4	2	+***
Cocoa	1	1	-*** +***	3	4		3	2	+**	2	2		2	4	+***	4	3	
Tea	1	1		3	3		3	2	+** -*	3	3		1	1	+***	2	4	+**
Sugar	0	0	-*	2	2		2	2		1	1		3	3		6	6	
Wheat	0	0	-***	2	2	-***	2	3	-*** +***	0	0	-*	1	1		4	4	-***
Maize	0	0		2	3	-***	2	3		2	1	+*** +***	1	1		4	4	-**
Rice	0	0	-**	1	1	-*	1	1	+** -**	3	2		4	4		6	5	-***
Cotton	1	1		1	2		1	2		1	1		1	1		4	5	+*
Wool	1	1	-*** +**	0	0		0	0		0	0		3	2	+***	4	5	
Rubber	1	1	-**	1	0		1	0		0	0		2	2	+***	2	2	
Copper	0	0		2	1	+*	0	1	+***	2	2		3	2		4	4	
Tin	0	0		2	0		2	2	+**	1	1		0	0	+*	1	0	+**
Lead	1	0		2	1	+**	2	1	+**	4	4	+**	2	1	+***	1	2	
Zinc	1	1	-***	2	3	+*** -***	2	2	+**	0	0		4	4	+*** -***	3	4	
Total agriculture	0	0	-***	1	3	-**	1	2		0	1	-***	3	4	-***	2	1	-***

N_1 = Two break periods: 1900-50, 1950-82.
N_2 = Historical period breaks: 1900-13, 1914-39, 1940-53, 1954-73, 1974-82.
N_2^1 = Historical period breaks: 1900-13, 1914-39, 1940-53, 1954-70, 1971-82.
N_3 = Every 20-year breaks.
N_4 = Every 15-year breaks.
N_5 = Every 10-year breaks.
A = Constant dummies.
B = Coefficient dummies.
C = Linear trend.
D = Quadratic trend.
*** = Indicates significance at the 1 percent level.
** = Indicates significance at the 5 percent level.
* = Indicates significance at the 10 percent level.

- The number of time specific intercept dummies whose coefficient is significantly different from zero, at least at the 90 percent confidence level under the "t" bilateral test;
- The number of time specific slope dummies with the same characteristics;
- The sign; and
- The level of significance of the linear and quadratic trend coefficients.

Consider first the results column by column. For the <u>first grouping</u> (N_1 : 1900-50, 1950-82), significant differences in the intercepts of the trend equations were found for 10 out of 19 cases, while significant differences in the slopes were found for 11 cases. When significant, linear trend slopes were always negative, while in the only two cases in which a quadratic term was significant, it was also positive.

For the <u>second grouping</u> (N_2 : 1900-13, 1914-39, 1940-53, 1954-73, 1974-82), the results were more mixed, with many more sub-period coefficients showing significance and with only a few cases with a significant trend coefficient common to all the sub-periods.

The <u>third grouping</u> (N_2^1), which differs from the second only for the last two sub-periods (1954-70 and 1971-82 instead of 1954-73 and 1974-82, respectively), shows a higher number of significant common trend coefficients, but negative trends throughout are limited to only two cases (cereals and non-food), while the positive common trend coefficients are much more numerous (cocoa, tea, copper, tin, zinc).

The <u>fourth grouping</u> (N_3 : every 20-year breaks) shows a smaller number of significant time specific coefficients and a higher number of significant and negative ones (cereals, non-food, total agriculture and wheat) for the whole period.

The <u>fifth grouping</u> (N_4 : every 15-year breaks) has a higher density of positive signs for the non-time specific trend coefficient and, as could be expected due to the higher number of parameters, also shows a higher number of significant time-specific coefficients.

The <u>final grouping</u> (N_5 : every 10-year breaks), however, does not confirm several of the positive trend coefficients put in evidence with the previous grouping (i.e., the 15-year breaks), while a number of negative ones emerge from insignificance.

Reading the table by row, on the other hand, suggests that some results are much more robust than others. A significant secular declining linear trend for non-food, for example, is present in all the estimated equations. For total agriculture, similar results are obtained for five groupings, while for cereals it is observed for four out of six of the groupings considered.

Table 2.6 shows the results of the standard Chow (1960) test on the simultaneous significance of the differences in the parameters of the regressions of the sub-groups within each grouping. Clearly the groupings with shorter sub-series are consistently more successful in identifying significantly different sub-period parameters. The results for the groupings with fewer sub-periods, however, are more interesting, as they suggest that long-term trends of different size and sign may coexist within the same 80 year-long time series. In the case of N_1, it appears that significantly different trend equations for the two break periods 1900-50 and 1950-82 can be estimated for only 7 out of the 19 commodities or aggregates considered, while for N_3 (the 20-year breaks), it is only 6 out of the same 19 cases.

Upswings and Downswings

The main argument given by Prebisch to explain the alleged deterioration of the terms of trade was that changes in the primary commodity prices are asymmetrical. More specifically, he claimed that primary commodity prices are more sticky upwards and flexible downwards. In the downswing, primary commodities fall by more than they rise on the upswing, relative to prices of manufactured goods. The rationale underlying this theory is that manufacture prices are cost-determined under monopolistic conditions, while commodity prices are determined in highly competitive markets. [6]

Table 2.6: **Chow Test for Structural Breaks in the Trends of Terms of Trade**

Commodity	N_1	N_2	N_2^1	N_3	N_4	N_5
Beverages	***				***	***
Cereals		***	***		***	***
Food		***	***	***	***	***
Non-food	***	***	***		***	***
Total agriculture	**	***	***	**	***	***
Coffee	***	**			***	***
Cocoa	**	**			***	***
Tea		**			***	***
Sugar		***	***		***	***
Wheat		***	***		***	***
Maize		***	***	***	***	***
Rice						
Cotton						
Wool	***	**	**		***	***
Rubber	***	***	***	**	***	***
Copper		***	***		***	***
Tin			***		**	
Lead		***	***	**	**	**
Zinc		***	***	***	***	

N_1 = Two break periods: 1900-50, 1950-82;

N_2 = Historical period breaks: 1900-13, 1914-39, 1940-53, 1954-73, 1974-82;

N_2^1 = Historical period breaks: 1900-13, 1914-39, 1940-53, 1954-70, 1971-82;

N_3 = Every 20-year breaks;

N_4 = Every 15-year breaks;

N_5 = Every 10-year breaks.

*** = Indicates significance at the 1 percent level.
** = Indicates significance at the 5 percent level.

If the hypothesis of asymmetric response is valid, one would expect the elasticity of primary commodities with respect to prices of manufactured goods to be larger for downfalls than for upturns. 7/ Such a claim was tested by constructing a simple one-equation model for each commodity. The model can be described as follows:

$$\log(P^c_{it}) = a + bD_t + c\log(P^m_t) + d(D_t \log P^m_t) + eT + U_t$$

where P^c_{it} = the price index of primary commodity i, at time t

P^m_t = the price index of manufactures at time t

T = time trend variable

D_t = dummy variable such that

$$D_t = \begin{cases} 1 & \text{if } P_{it} < P_{it-1} \quad \text{(downswings)} \\ 0 & \text{otherwise} \quad \text{(upswings)} \end{cases}$$

U_t = error term

The coefficient **c** of the equation is the price elasticity of primary commodity i with respect to manufactures in times of prosperity (when manufacture prices are rising). The corresponding elasticity for the years in which manufacture prices are declining is equal to the sum of the coefficients **c** and **d**.

For the Prebisch hypothesis to be true the following relation should be satisfied:

$$c+d > c = d > 0$$

Thus, if the coefficient **d** is positive and statistically significant, the Prebisch hypothesis is valid. 8/

The equation was estimated by a Generalized Least Square (GLS) technique and adjustment of autocorrelation was made. The regression results are reported in Table 2.7. As can be seen, the Prebisch hypothesis

Table 2.7: Test of the Prebisch Asymmetry Hypothesis

Commodity	Intercept	Time	Manuf. price	Interc. dummy	Slope dummy a/	$\bar{R}^2$	Chow test
Beverages	0.409 (0.777)	0.010 (1.842)*	0.790 (4.200)***	−0.003 (0.017)	0.001 (0.010)	0.510	3.185 (2,75)**
Cereals	0.179 (0.699)	−0.007 (3.095)***	1.020 (11.058)***	−0.152 (0.844)	0.048 (0.974)	0.810	0.626 (2,76)
Food	−0.436 (−1.492)	−0.007 (2.501)**	1.160 (10.996)***	0.007 (0.042)	−0.001 (0.017)	0.793	0.015 (2,77)
Non-food	1.940 (4.802)***	−0.013 (3.338)***	0.818 (5.625)***	0.453 (2.459)**	0.110 (2.176)***	0.398	3.662 (2,77)**
Total agriculture	0.237 (0.753)	0.010 (3.165)***	1.069 (9.418)***	−0.158 (0.993)	0.038 (0.871)	0.691	0.418 (2,77)
Coffee	0.190 (0.308)	0.014 (2.291)**	0.800 (3.602)***	−0.027 (−0.099)	0.003 (0.36)	0.538	0.001 (2,77)
Cocoa	−0.174 (0.213)	0.0002 (0.022)	0.975 (3.438)***	−0.108 (0.363)	0.029 (0.362)	0.206	4.391 (2,77)***
Tea	1.792 (4.442)***	0.010 (2.557)**	0.488 (3.365)***	0.124 (0.686)	−0.033 (0.658)	0.529	0.198 (2,77)
Sugar	−2.140 (3.739)***	−0.021 (4.057)***	1.634 (7.942)***	0.135 (0.312)	−0.048 (0.399)	0.547	0.002 (2,77)
Wheat	−0.162 (0.602)	−0.010 (4.168)***	1.131 (11.691)***	−0.105 (0.544)	0.034 (0.647)	0.805	0.029 (2,76)
Maize	0.551 (1.522)	−0.004 (1.231)	−0.908 (6.966)***	−0.232 (0.888)	0.063 (0.866)	0.655	0.283 (2,77)

Table 2.7: (cont.)

Commodity	Intercept	Time	Manuf. price	Interc. dummy	Slope dummy a/	$\bar{R}^2$	Chow test
Rice	0.803 (1.999)**	-0.001 (0.324)	-0.768 (5.270)***	-0.213 (1.324)	0.079 (1.779)**	0.520	6.499 (2,75)*
Cotton	1.077 (2.913)***	-0.001 (0.336)	0.803 (5.989)***	-0.243 (1.638)	0.069 (1.676)**	0.600	0.002 (2,76)
Wool	1.947 (4.387)***	-0.004 (0.932)	0.707 (4.418)***	-0.291 (1.343)	0.073 (1.218)	0.367	0.914 (2,75)
Rubber	2.392 (3.000)***	-0.031 (3.824)***	1.025 (3.592)***	-0.642 (1.935)*	0.143 (1.566)*	0.226	3.249 (2,77)**
Copper	0.815 (1.610)	0.002 (0.296)	0.753 (4.212)***	-0.341 (1.794)*	0.085 (1.633)*	0.405	1.719 (2,77)
Tin	-0.868 (1.918)*	0.010 (2.316)**	1.009 (6.179)***	-0.045 (0.203)	0.004 (0.058)	0.738	(0.276) (2,77)
Lead	0.467 (1.238)	0.003 (0.900)	0.877 (6.451)**	-0.026 (0.140)	-0.004 (0.080)	0.688	0.717 (2,77)
Zinc	0.275 (0.734)	0.005 (1.338)	0.770 (5.685)***	-0.349 (1.486)	0.082 (1.266)	0.715	0.915 (2,77)

a/ One tail test.

*** = Indicates significance at the 1 percent level.
** = Indicates significance at the 5 percent level.
* = Indicates significance at the 10 percent level.

is supported for only five cases (i.e., non-food, rice, cotton, rubber, copper). In all other instances, the slope dummy coefficient is statistically insignificant with either a negative or a positive sign. 9/

From the above five commodities, only for non-food and rubber, is the elasticity in the turnfall years substantially higher than the corresponding elasticity in the upswing years. For the remaining three commodities, the difference is rather marginal. 10/

Since the above results, on the whole, reject the asymmetry hypothesis, a decision was taken to examine the trends in the terms of trade themselves, when prices of manufactured goods were falling and when they were rising. The results are shown in Table A.2.1 and Table A.2.2. At first sight, these tables indicate that the terms of trade deteriorated in nine cases when manufacture prices were falling, and in eleven cases when manufacture prices were rising. A noteworthy point is that there were three cases in the period of upswings (beverages, coffee, tin) and two in the period of downswings (coffee, tin) where terms of trade improved.

The conclusion to be drawn from the above analysis is that the hypothesis of asymmetrical changes in primary commodity prices is inadequate in explaining the deterioration, if any, in the terms of trade which occurred during periods of upswings and downswings.

The Question of Productivity Increases

The conclusions obtained so far, hold for the tests performed for the BTT. Would they hold also for factor terms of trade, that is, for any price measure that took into account productivity increases? As mentioned earlier, the question of accounting for movements in productivity is really twofold:

- Real income measures of the terms of trade can be obtained by combining measures of productivity increase with measures of relative price movements; and

- Productivity increases or decreases may be one of the main causes of movements in the terms of trade.

These two characteristics can be combined through the following simple model that considers the evolution of both the BTT and of land productivity.

(1) $\dot{P}_t = b\dot{T} + c\dot{Q}_t + g\dot{S}_t$

(2) $\dot{Q}_t = a\dot{T} + d\dot{Z}_t$

where:

$\dot{P}_t$ = rate of change of BTT

$\dot{T}$ = " " " of trend

$\dot{S}_t$ = " " " of BTT shifters

$\dot{Q}_t$ = " " " of land productivity

$\dot{Z}_t$ = " " " of land productivity shifters

Summing $\dot{P}_t$ and $\dot{Q}_t$ according to (1) and (2) yields:

(3) $\dot{V}_t = \dot{P}_t + \dot{Q}_t = (b + a)\dot{T} + c\dot{Q}_t + g\dot{S}_t + d\dot{Z}_t$

where $\dot{V}_t$ = rate of change of real revenue per acre of the agricultural commodity considered (i.e., SFTT)

Expression (3) can also be written in the form:

(4) $\dot{P}_t = (b + a)\dot{T} + (c - 1)\dot{Q}_t + g\dot{S}_t + d\dot{Z}_t$

where the coefficient of the productivity variable can be interpreted as the joint effect of the correction due to the dependent variable (i.e., the definition of the SFTT) and the impact of productivity shifts on the barter terms of trade.

Even though equation (4) is observationally equivalent to equation (1), its parameters have a different interpretation. In particular, equation (4) trend parameter is the combination of the trend effect upon both BTT and productivity. The productivity parameter, on the other hand, allows separation of the impact of productivity upon the BTT from the impact upon the SFTT.

Given this framework, estimates are obtained of the effect of productivity changes in exporting countries, with reference to equations (1), (2), (3) and (4), using a product-by-product approach. In doing so, land productivity as the variable embodying technical progress is used, because this is really the only productivity variable that can be estimated for a sufficiently large number of years on a product-by-product basis. As a consequence, this part of the analysis is limited to agricultural commodities.

The length of the time series available poses very serious problems to the construction of equally long time series of output per hectare for the major export commodities. Appendix II contains a detailed account of the sources and country data used to compile the yield series selected for use in this analysis. Graphs 20-26 in Appendix I show that, with few exceptions, average land productivity has undergone a rapid increase in the latter part (roughly the last 35 years) of this century. This increase is particularly steep for cereals, where the so-called "green revolution" clearly claims more conspicuous recent successes. It is more moderate for other traditional commodities, especially tree-crops like cocoa and tea, where technical progress tends to be counterbalanced by the aging of the plantations.

Given these estimates of yield evolution, Table 2.8 presents a set of equation results yielding the impact of productivity on the terms of trade. The results refer to the BTT of each commodity, defined as the international price of the commodity deflated by the U.S. unit value of manufactured exports, and can be interpreted according to equation (1) or equation (4). For each crop, two explanatory variables and two dummies are considered: trend; the corresponding yield; a dummy variable for the years in which data for all producing countries were available (generally 1955-82); and a dummy variable for the years that exclude one or more major producers for lack of data.

As Table 2.8 shows, the trend variable is highly significant in four cases (cocoa, wheat, maize and coffee), while it is not significant, at least at the 10 percent significance level, in two (rice and tea). While the coefficient of the trend variable is negative for the two cereals, it is positive for coffee and cocoa. [11]/

For the yield variable, on the other hand, the results are even more mixed. Statistical significance is found only for maize and tea. The sign of the productivity effect on the BTT is estimated to be negative for maize, sugar, wheat and cocoa, and positive for tea, rice and coffee. These results suggest that only for wheat—a crop now exported mainly by developed countries—the BTT has shown a twofold tendency to deteriorate under the impact of both a secular decline and a negative influence of the increase in productivity. For coffee, on the other hand, the evidence shows an opposite tendency for the BTT to improve under the joint impact of the two factors, while the secular trend in the terms of trade (as reflected in the coefficient of the trend variable) seems also to be positive, once the negative effect of the increase in productivity is taken into account. Finally, maize and tea summarize the two opposite cases of crops affected only by a secular decline in BTT (maize) or by positive BTT effects of productivity increases (tea).

Consider now the estimation of equation (3) under the assumption $c=g=d=0$. This equation is interesting because it allows comparison of the time profile of the SFTT and the BTT. Using the same procedure used and illustrated for BTT, the estimates of trend equations for SFTT presented in Table 2.9 were obtained. Table 2.10, which shows how these estimates compare with those presented earlier (Table 2.4) for BTT, suggests that adjustment for productivity makes a substantial difference in judging the tendency to decline of the terms of trade for the case of tea, sugar, rice and wheat. For the remaining four commodities (coffee, cocoa, maize), the sign of the first derivative (elasticity) is the same for both the BTT and SFTT equations. Consideration of the productivity, however, seems to have the effect of reducing the absolute value of the elasticity with respect to the trend in the case where this parameter is negative and of increasing it when it is positive (Table 2.10 and Figure 2.1).

Table 2.8: **Barter Terms of Trade as a Function of Trends and Productivity**

	Intercept	Trend	Trend squared	Productivity	DY	DYC	$\bar{R}^2$
Tea	0.795 (0.323)	1.363 (1.113)	-0.212 (1.120)	0.507 (1.551)*	-0.007 (0.039)		-0.116
Maize	5.378 (6.021)***	0.306 (1.946)**	-0.075 (2.677)**	-0.123 (1.958)*	-0.049 (0.662)		0.159
Rice	3.412 (1.441)	0.045 (0.256)	-0.041 (1.209)	0.156 (0.624)	-0.033 (0.324)		0.081
Wheat	6.508 (4.441)***	0.191 (1.420)	-0.055 (2.172)**	-0.216 (1.294)	-0.017 (0.273)		0.250
Coffee	2.862 (2.224)**	-0.320 (1.214)	0.107 (1.898)*	0.186 (1.291)	-0.110 (0.542)		0.043
Cocoa	13.793 (5.036)***	-5.785 (3.239)***	0.902 (3.389)***	-0.089 (0.331)	-0.206 (0.824)	-0.233 (1.506)*	0.279
Sugar	5.653 (3.675)***	-0.159 (1.606)		-0.206 (0.741)	0.226 (1.083)	-0.216 (1.250)	0.060

*** = Indicates significance at the 1 percent level.
 ** = Indicates significance at the 5 percent level.
  * = Indicates significance at the 10 percent level.
 DY = Dummy year.
DYC = Dummy country.

Table 2.9: Trends in the Single Factorial Terms of Trade, 1900-82

Commodity	Intercept	Trend	Trend squared	$\bar{R}^2$	First derivative (elasticity)	Time of trend reversal (No. of yrs.)
Coffee	3.473 (15.199)***	0.010 (2.070)**		0.027	0.0100	
Cocoa	2.780 (12.894)***	0.010 (2.370)**		0.021	0.0100	
Tea	3.427 (10.289)***	0.054 (3.258)***	-0.0005 (2.967)***	0.103	0.0130	54.00
Sugar	5.389 (25.341)***	-0.020 (1.709)*	0.0003 (1.981)*	0.019	0.0050	33.33
Wheat	4.499 (37.988)***	-0.011 (1.664)	0.0002 (2.064)**	0.036	0.0050	27.50
Maize	5.200 (58.468)***	-0.017 (3.382)***	0.0002 (2.850)***	0.125	-0.0004	42.50
Rice	5.392 (38.837)***	-0.024 (3.084)***	0.0003 (3.269)***	0.088	0.0009	40.00

*** = Indicates significance at the 1 percent level.
** = Indicates significance at the 5 percent level.
* = Indicates significance at the 10 percent level.

Table 2.10: **Comparison of BTT and SFTT Trend Estimates for Agricultural Commodities**

Commodity	BTT		SFTT	
	First derivative (elasticity)	Time of trend reversal (No. of yrs)	First derivative (elasticity)	Time of trend reversal (No. of yrs)
Coffee	0.010	–	0.0100	–
Cocoa	0.003	39	0.0100	–
Tea	–0.004	30	0.0130	54
Sugar	–0.007	53	0.0050	33
Wheat	–0.007	–	0.0050	28
Maize	–0.008	20	–0.0004	43
Rice	–0.006	–	0.0009	40

Sources: Table 2.4 and Table 2.9.

Figure 2.1: **Barter Terms of Trade as a Function of Trend and Productivity**

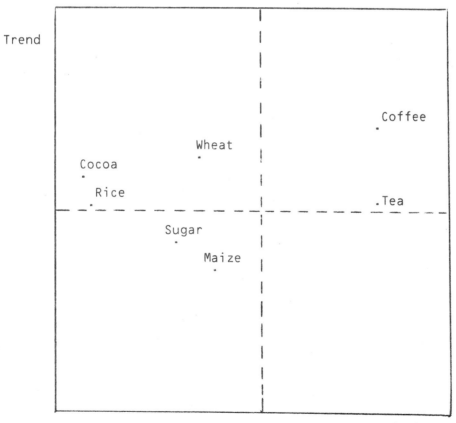

Sub-periods

The procedures and the sub-periods used for the BTT were also applied for the SFTT. Table 2.11 synthesizes the main features of the results and Table 2.12 displays the results of the standard Chow test on the stability on the parameters in each sub-grouping. Comparing Table 2.11 with Table 2.5 we see that the results for SFTT, in general, are in agreement with those obtained for the BTT. However, there are some individual cases where the results for the SFTTs tend to be more sound as the trend variables are significant at the 1 percent level. These cases occur for cocoa in the 20-year sub-period and cotton for the 20-year and 10-year sub-periods.

Some Conclusions

Tests of deteriorating terms of trade of primary commodities are difficult to design and perform both for reasons of methodology and lack of data. This chapter has made an effort to look at the problem on the basis of the most reliable evidence that can be put together on the subject, attempting, at the same time, to use a simple and coherent methodology.

There is evidence of a long-term decline in the barter terms of trade for most commodities. At the same time, however, the series analysed show a tendency to reverse this trend over periods ranging from 20 to 50 years. Rather than a trend, therefore, these results suggest a very long cycle whose full detection is made impossible by the insufficient length of the time series available.

If sub-periods are examined, the above conclusions are strengthened by the fact that in the case where the sub-periods were kept reasonably long, the signs of the trend slopes remained stable, even though they were significantly different from one sub-period to the other in terms of absolute value.

Table 2.11: Time Breakdown: Trends in the Single Factorial Terms of Trade

	N_1				N_2				N_2^1				N_3				N_4				N_5			
	No. of time specific		Signific. trend		No. of time specific		Signific. trend		No. of time specific		Signific. trend		No. of time specific		Signific. trend		No. of time specific		Signific. trend		No. of time specific		Signific. trend	
	A	B	C	D	A	B	C	D	A	B	C	D	A	B	C	D	A	B	C	D	A	B	C	D
Coffee	0	0			3	3	+***		1	1			1	1			3	3			2	3		
Cocoa	1	1	-***	+***	3	4			3	2	+**		2	3	+***	-***	2	4	+***	-**	3	1		
Tea	1	1			3	3			3	2	+**	-*	1	1			1	1	+***	-***	1	1	+**	
Sugar	0	0	-*		2	2			2	2			1	1	-*		3	3			3	3	-**	
Wheat	0	0	-***		2	2			2	3			1	2			1	1			5	5	-***	+**
Maize	0	0			2	3	-***	+**	2	3	-***	+***	2	2		-**	1	1			4	4		
Rice	0	0	-**		1	1	-*		1	1			2	2			4	4			2	2	-***	

N_1 = Two break periods: 1900-50, 1950-82.
N_2 = Historical period breaks: 1900-13, 1914-39, 1940-53, 1954-73, 1974-82.
N_2^1 = Historical period breaks: 1900-13, 1914-39, 1940-53, 1954-70, 1971-82.
N_3 = Every 20-year breaks.
N_4 = Every 15-year breaks.
N_5 = Every 10-year breaks.

A = Constant dummies.
B = Coefficient dummies.
C = Linear trend.
D = Quadratic trend.

*** = Indicates significance at the 1 percent level.
** = Indicates significance at the 5 percent level.
* = Indicates significance at the 10 percent level.

Table 2.12: **Chow Test for Structural Breaks in the Trends of Single Factorial Terms of Trade**

Commodity	N_1	N_2	N_2^1	N_3	N_4	N_5
Coffee	**	**				
Cocoa		**				***
Tea		**			***	
Sugar		***	***	**		***
Wheat		***	***		***	
Maize		***	***			
Rice						

N_1 = Two break periods: 1900–50, 1950–82.

N_2 = Historical period breaks: 1900–13, 1914–39, 1940–53, 1954–73, 1974–82.

N_2^1 = Historical period breaks: 1900–13, 1914–39, 1940–53, 1954–70, 1971–82.

N_3 = Every 20-year breaks.

N_4 = Every 15-year breaks.

N_5 = Every 10-year breaks.

*** = Indicates significance at the 1 percent level.
 ** = Indicates significance at the 5 percent level.

When productivity adjustments were considered, however, the results were more mixed. Within the group of agricultural commodities for which it was possible to perform the tests, the introduction of land productivity as a separate explanatory variable in the equation, confirmed a negative trend for BTT of wheat and maize, and a positive one for cocoa and coffee.

Similar results were also obtained for the trends of the SFTT of the same agricultural commodities, even though in this case significant negative trends were obtained also for rice, and reversals of the sign of the trends were estimated to occur within 28 and 54 years for all commodities, except coffee and cocoa.

In conclusion, the statistical analysis performed shows that the evidence on <u>the negativity of trends in the terms of trade is weak</u>, limited to a sub-set of primary commodities, subject to sign reversal within a period, at most, equal to half a century, and within the group of agricultural goods, significantly affected by the time pattern of productivity.

Notes

1/ We owe thanks to Enzo Grilli and Ron Duncan, the two authors of the World Bank study, for the opportunity to use such valuable data.

2/ In his 1980 article, Spraos does not seem to be aware of this problem, since he claims that his regressions are "... intended very simply to test whether a trend is present in the data and thus supplement the impressions gained by visual inspection of the time series. Their object is not to explain the observed movement of the terms of trade, nor to obtain efficient predictors, nor even to seek 'the best fit on time'..."

3/ The Sauerbeck index was the unweighted average of prices of 37 commodities (more important commodities, however, were represented more than once through different grades). The Economist index, recently used by Ray (1977), was the unweighted average of 22 commodities until 1911, of 44 commodities between 1911 and 1927, and of 58 commodities thereafter.

4/ This is the breakdown used by Sapsford (1985).

5/ For the fourth historical period break (post-Korean War until the first oil crisis) we also tested 1970 as a break year instead of 1973, as a possible contender to capture the effects of the collapsing of the Bretton Woods international monetary system at the end of the 1960s. However, only for two cases (sugar and tin) were the dummies for this sub-period significant under the latter approach. On the contrary, using the "oil shock" as a break year (1973) there were seven cases (coffee, cocoa, tea, sugar, cotton, rubber and zinc) with significant dummy coefficients in the period under consideration.

6/ See Kaldor (1983) for a detailed exposition of the argument.

7/ During the 83 years covered in the analysis, there were 31 years with manufactured prices falling and 52 years with manufactured prices rising. The largest decline in the index was observed in 1921 (11.23 percent) and the highest increase in 1978 (21.08 percent).

8/ Our results are in conformity with those of Thirlwall and Bergevin (1985) who found very little evidence for the Prebisch hypothesis of asymmetric changes in commodity prices. It should, however, be pointed out that Thirlwall and Bergevin allowed for changes only in the slope, and assumed that the intercept remained constant during downswings.

9/ These results are confirmed by the standard Chow (1960) test. As shown in Table 2.7, only for beverages, non-food, cocoa, rice and rubber, and thus the hypothesis that the data cannot be pooled is rejected.

10/ The Besley et al. (1980) test for multicollinearity detected that only for sugar was multicollinearity a serious problem between the quadratic trend variable and the yield variable. For this reason the quadratic trend variable from the regression was dropped.

11/ The regression results for equations (2) and (3) are reported in Appendix II, Table A.2.3 and Table A.2.4 respectively.

CHAPTER III

TERMS OF TRADE INSTABILITY: THE TRADITIONAL APPROACH

Definitions and Methodological Problems

Instability is an elusive concept in applied economics for at least three reasons. First, instability depends on the definition of the underlying economic model and on the identification and measurement of its explanatory variables, even if only a trend is considered as the appropriate mode. In other words, instability refers to the residual stochastic variable generated after the effect of the exogenous variables has been measured and the original variable has been purged of it.

Second, instability can be defined with reference to several different concepts of "average" variability. Thus, for example, instability can be defined as "unexpected" variability, or as "excess" variability, or as the variability of a time series once the trend and given cyclical components have been taken into account.

Third, once the concept has been defined, a wide range of statistics can be used to measure its variability. These measures are generated by the fact that the distance between a set of realized and a set of predicted points can be defined in a variety of ways, depending on the weights given to the different couples of points and the functions used to combine these weighted individual measurements.

Fourth, errors in sampling, prediction and data measurements make it difficult to identify sources of instability in economic analysis. As a consequence, it is often difficult to understand whether measures of instability refer to (i) instability of the original variable (say, production or prices); (ii) instability of the parameters of the underlying economic model; (iii) instability of the omitted explanatory variables; or (iv) the inappropriateness of the model or the functional form utilized.

These difficulties in defining and measuring instability are compounded when attempts are made to compare instability measures over time or across countries. In this case, a further problem is due to the possible instability of the underlying economic model. If instability is measured after accounting for a deterministic trend, for example, one could find that the predicted area values on the basis of a linear trend are closer on average to realized values, and hence residual instability is lower, for period A rather than for period B. If two equations are estimated for the two periods, however, the increase in instability could simply be the result that a linear trend as a specification performs better for period A than for period B. If only one equation is estimated, the increase in instability could be the result that a linear trend is not appropriate, or is appropriate for only one of the two periods or that its coefficient is unstable over time.

A reasonable approach to the definition of the concept of instability was proposed by Coppock (1977). According to this author:

> Instability should not be understood to mean any deviation from a fixed level. It means _excessive_ departure from some _normal_ level. However, there is no way of determining _a priori_ the meaning of _excessive_ and _normal_.

Hence, a presumption has to be made as to what constitutes "normal" versus "excessive" variability.

A simple way of interpreting Coppock's approach, encompassing the implicit assumptions of most instability studies is as follows: for many economic phenomena there exists a time trend. Over a lengthy period of time there may be a tendency for economic variables to rise or fall by a given average percentage amount. This long-term trend is affected by secular movements in certain exogenous variables. At any point of time, however, there may be short-term factors at work causing the series to deviate from the value that might have been expected on the basis of the trend. According to this interpretation, in most of the instability studies the influence of trend is removed from the data before instability is measured, on the ground that such a trend is predictable and can be readily adapted to by economic agents. This clearly reflects some judgement on acceptable variability, which is due to trend and an unacceptable variability, which is due to deviation from the trend.

Because it is considered explicitly or implicitly as a measure of the "unexpected" or "unpredictable" changes, in general, instability does not coincide with variability. In the same way, stability might not necessarily imply stagnation either. In a study by Lam (1980), for instance, instability was identified with the fast growth of export earnings. This led him to adopt an index that was non-detrended and positively depended on export growth rates. Consequently, his empirical findings of positive correlation between export earnings instability and economic growth were inevitably a mixture of trend, instability and residual variability.

A number of alternative indices of instability can be constructed depending on: (i) the selected form of the "target" level; and (ii) the specific way the deviations are measured.

Most commonly, targets or normal levels have been identified by Ordinary Least Square (OLS) and Moving Average (MA) methods. Deviations of the actual values from the target line, on the other hand, can be measured as the sum of absolute deviations or the sum of square deviations. The obvious way to obtain a single index of instability is to express the deviations as a relative or percentage figure: for instance, to weigh deviations by the trend values or to express them as a percentage of the average of the original series (Coppock 1977, p.5).

The OLS method involves a linear function of time either in the log of the time series, yielding the exponential index, or directly yielding the linear index. The main problem of this method is that the process of squaring weighs large deviations proportionately more than small ones. Thus, unless the dependent variable is random and normally distributed and the values of the independent variable (time) are fixed, countries with the larger but less frequent deviations in the economic variable under consideration (i.e., terms of trade, export earnings, etc.) are assigned a higher instability than countries with smaller, but more frequent fluctuations. A further issue of some importance is the assumption of normality, which is required in order to perform conventional significance tests. A priori, the normality assumption might seem perfectly appropriate for a disturbance that is specifically attributed, for example, to the influence of weather. In other cases, however, the situation is much less clear. Disturbances, for example, might be equated with the impact of unspecified policy changes and it is not immediately obvious that these would be normally distributed nor, indeed, serially independent.

For the MA method, the index is defined as the sum of the absolute deviations of each year's economic variable--real commodity prices P_t in this case--from an n-year MA, with the value of n specified by the assumption:

$$I = \Sigma \left| \frac{P_t - MA}{MA} \right|$$

This method has been criticized insofar as the choice of MA and weights are arbitrary. The interval **n** determines the degree of smoothing, and hence, the degree of instability measured by the index. Thus, theoretical considerations should determine the period used in choosing **n**. Another criticism is related to the point that the MA uses only a subset of data to estimate trend value and generates oscillatory movement in the residual, that is, a Yule-Slutsky oscillatory series (Malinvaud, 1966, p.376).

If the cycle is greater than the MA, then instability will be understated. Furthermore, if the curve of a series is convex to the time axis in a certain range, the MA gives lower values for all terms of the series than does the original, and if concave, it gives higher values than the original. This implies that it may be inappropriate to use it to eliminate short-term random fluctuations in phenomena subject to strong seasonal fluctuations, as both cyclical maxima are decreased and cyclical minima are increased. In general, if the period/amplitude is not constant, the MA method will not eliminate the cyclical component. In such a case, it is better to begin with an analysis of the pattern of raw data.

Chapter III is structured as follows. A brief review is given of the literature concerning studies related to the measurement of instability and the issue of terms of trade instability. Then some empirical evidence of the sensitivity of instability in the terms of trade on the index chosen is presented. Lastly, investigation is made into the issue of whether instability has increased over time. This is done concerning both BTT and SFTT.

Review of the Literature

Most of the empirical studies of instability deal with export earnings. The available empirical evidence concerning fluctuations in commodity terms of trade suggest that commodity prices have been sharply fluctuating, particularly in short periods. Table 3.1 reports the main empirical studies that explicitly considered either the question of instability in commodity terms of trade or instability in export earnings of primary commodities.

On average, current indices of terms of trade instability of primary commodities have sharply increased over time. Hallwood (1982), for example, reports that for the 1970-80 period instability in the BTT more than trebled in comparison with instability experienced during 1957-69.

The studies reviewed show that fluctuations in commodity prices have been relatively larger than those for manufactured goods. For the 1950-79 period, the primary commodity price instability index was almost twice as large as that for manufactures, and for the 1962-79 period, the index of the former was over three times the magnitude of that for the latter (Adams and Behrman, 1982). Generally, in the 1960s commodity prices experienced higher instability than in the 1950s. Instability in the primary producers' terms of trade increased in the 1970s compared with earlier years. A statistical significant relationship between instability in the terms of trade and industrial production has existed since 1921, but it was only in the 1970s that the elasticity became greater than one.

Table 3.1: **Main Empirical Studies on Commodity Terms of Trade Instability**

Author	Date	Period covered	Instability index used
Coppock, J.	(1962)	1946-58	Log-variance index
MacBean, A.	(1966)	1946-59	Moving average index
IMF-IBRD	(1969)	1953-65	Detrended coefficient of variation
Sciavo-Campo G.	(1969)	1954-66	Log-variance index
Leith, J.	(1970)	1948-58 1957-67	Log-variance index and absolute percentage Deviations from linear trend
Massell, B.	(1970)	1950-66	Standard deviations from log-linear trend
Naya, S.	(1973)	1950-60	Detrended coefficient of variation
Lawson, C.	(1974)	1950-69	Standard deviations from log-linear trend
Commonwealth Secretariat	(1975)	1954-72	Detrended coefficient of variation
Knudsen, O. and A. Parnes	(1975)	1958-68	Index based on the permanent income hypothesis
Labys, W. and Perrin, Y.	(1976)	1954-73	Detrendend coefficient of variation
Behrman, J.	(1977)	1950-75	Standard error
World Bank	(1978)	1955-76	Deviations from five-year moving averages
Hwa, E.	(1979)	1955-75 a/	Non-detrended coefficient of variation
Hallwood, P.	(1979)	1871-13 1957-80	Average annual absolute percentage deviations of the terms of trade from a log-linear trend
Lancieri, E.	(1979)	1961-72	Absolute deviations from log-linear trend
Hallwood, P.	(1982)	1957-80	The same as above
Adams, G. and Behrman, J.	(1982)	1950-79	Standard errors of the regressions
Glezakos, C.	(1983)	1961-74	Square root deviations from Linear and Log-Linear trends; absolute percentage deviations from adaptive expectations trend
Sarkar, G.	(1983)	1951-70 1963-75	Square root of the percentage deviations from a five-year geometric moving average; absolute percentage deviations from a five-year geometric average; and the square root of the square of the deviations from a log-linear trend
Josling, T.	(1984)	1970-79	Average percentage deviations around trend fitted to the agricultural income terms of trade
Chu, K. and Morrison, T.	(1984)	1957-82	Percentage standard error of estimates of a semi-log regression and the average annual absolute percentage deviations from a trend
Labys, W. and Polak, P.	(1984)	1955-81	Deviations from five- and three-year averages; annual average percentage change

a/ For coffee, cocoa and rubber; 1963-73 for cotton; 1956-75 for sugar and copper; and 1960-75 for tin.

As regards instability experienced by individual commodities, the study by Berhman (1977) shows that over the 1953-72 period, high instability was experienced by sugar, cocoa, sisal, copper, linseed oil and zinc; moderate instability by coffee, cotton, rubber, jute, wool, rice; and low instability by tin, tea, iron ore, wheat, bauxite, bananas, tobacco, and groundnut oil (Table 3.2). [1]

A review of literature on the degree of correlation between various instability indices makes it clear that the sensitivity of instability is a matter of debate among economists. The first attempt to examine the correlation between instability indices was made by Coppock (1977) who found that the correlation coefficients for the log-variance index and the index using the average of percentage deviations around the log-linear trend for export earnings over 1959-71 was 0.897. [2] MacBean (1966) concluded that "as long ... as each index is calculated for the same period of time, the results are invariably highly correlated". Later comparisons of instability indices of export earnings made by Knudsen and Parnes (1975) confirmed Coppock's results of high correlation. In particular, they found that the correlation coefficient between the log-variance index and the deviations from the exponential trend index was 0.94; and between the deviations from an exponential trend index and a five-year moving average, 0.86.

Other studies, however, were less conclusive. Glezakos (1970), for instance, found that the correlation between the five-year moving average index used by MacBean and the log-variance index of Coppock was only 0.44. Leith (1970) also pointed out that, depending on the period chosen and on whether the sample includes only DCs or LDCs, the correlation coefficient between the log-variance index and the deviations from a linear trend index varies from a high of 0.75 to a low of 0.50. Furthermore, the study by Offut and Blandford (1981) confirms the findings of Glezakos and Leith of a low correlation coefficient between instability indices. The 1981 study compares the rank correlation among the coefficient of variation, three- and five-year moving averages, the log-variance index, and average percentage indices for average yield, output, price and revenue, for ten U.S. field crops over the 1950-70 period. The authors found very little

Table 3.2: **Estimates of Instability Levels**

Commodity	World Bank (1978) 1955-76	Behrman (1977) 1950-75	Adams & Behrman (1982) (nominal prices) 1950-79	Lancieri (1979) (nominal prices) 1961-72	Sarkar (1983) 1954-72	Labys & Polak (1985) Deviation from moving averages 3-Year, 5-Year 1955-81	Labys & Polak (1985) Annual average change 1955-81	Hwa (1979) [a] 1955-75
				%				
Beverages			25					
Cereals			28					
Food								
Non-food								
Total agric.				6.4				
Coffee	6.5	19	43	7.0		7.1	12.1	22
Cocoa	2.6	31	52	13.7		10.2	16.8	42
Tea	1.3	13		3.0		4.8	6.2	
Sugar	13.9	39	42	13.6		18.8	30.3	111
Wheat	0.6	20	26	2.3		4.5	7.9	
Rice	1.6	23		8.3		7.0	14.1	
Maize	2.3	18		3.6		4.6	6.9	
Cotton	4.0	24	31	4.1		4.7	6.8	36
Wool	0.6	27		7.0				
Rubber	3.5	21				7.9	12.1	36
Copper	5.0	2	21			9.1	15.3	46
Tin	1.7	17	29			5.3	8.1	40
Lead	0.4	28				9.2	14.7	
Zinc	0.7	33				8.4	14.4	
Manufactured goods			18					
Terms of trade (All primary comm.)			18		18			
Terms of trade (overall)								
Developing countries						54		
Developed countries						59		

[a] Cotton: 1963-75; Sugar: 1956-75; Copper: 1956-75; Tin: 1960-75.

concurrence among rankings and made the conclusion that "the results of this application should eliminate any remaining scepticism as to the dependence of the characterization of instability on the choice of empirical technique" (p.6).

From this brief review, no clear picture emerges from the empirical evidence: indeed, much of the evidence is conflicting. A number of reasons to explain the inconclusiveness of the studies are readily found. First, the results depend not only on the period chosen and the group of countries included in the sample, as Leith argued, but also on the nature of the variable with respect to which instability is measured. Some economic variables such as export-earnings may display a pronounced trend; others, such as price series, might include high outliers. Second, every index has its own specific characteristics and weaknesses. It is well known, for example, that the log-variance index is sensitive to the period of the data series, since a major part of the index depends only on the first and last observation (Knudsen and Parnes, 1975, p.12). The moving average indices, on the other hand, which use only subsets of the data in determining trend values, are more strongly influenced by outliers. Therefore, one may find a high correlation among the log-variance index, moving average index and non-detrended measures, which are influenced by outliers, simply if these outliers happen to be the last observation of the sample. Third, when, as in the Knudsen and Parnes' (1975) study, the deviations are squared, the squaring increases the possibility of a high correlation between this index and the exponential one. Fourth, all the studies, except the (1981) one by Offut and Blandford, attempt broad generalizations by comparing two or three indices.

Alternative Measures of Instability

This section begins by listing seven different indices of instability, all of which have been used in one form or another in previous empirical studies. The indices are classified into two groups: (i) those that measure deviations from the mean of the series, i.e., non-detrended indices; and (ii) those that measure deviations from a trend, i.e., detrended indices. The latter contains indices that are based on the OLS method (mentioned earlier) to estimate the trend.

a) **Non-detrended indices**

1. The coefficient of variation index: $\text{C.V.} = 100 \times \dfrac{\sqrt{\dfrac{\Sigma(P_t - \bar{P})^2}{N}}}{\bar{P}}$

where P_t = price index in year t;
 $\bar{P}$ = mean value of price index;
 N = number of observations.

This is the simplest index, most commonly used and easily interpretable, but if the data exhibit any form of time trend, this index overstates instability relative to non-trending series.

2. The corrected coefficient of variation index:

$$\text{Corr. C.V.} = 100 \times \sqrt{\dfrac{\Sigma(P_t - \bar{P})^2}{N-1}} \times \dfrac{\sqrt{(1-\bar{R}^2)}}{\bar{P}}$$

where $\bar{R}^2$ = adjust. correlation coefficient.

This is an improvement on the previous index since it explicitly takes into account the explanatory power of the equation.

b) **Detrended indices**

3. The arithmetic mean of the absolute values of the deviations from a trend line fitted by OLS expressed as a percentage of the mean of the series:

$$H = 100 \times \dfrac{\Sigma |P_t - \hat{P}_t|}{(N-1)\bar{P}}$$

4. The square root arithmetic mean of the absolute values of the deviations from a trend line fitted by OLS as a percentage of the mean of the series:

$$\text{EPSILON} = 100 \times \frac{\sqrt{\Sigma |P_t - \hat{P}_t| / N - 1}}{\bar{P}}$$

5. The sum of the square of deviations from a linear trend, normalized by the trend itself:

$$\text{FI} = 100 \times \Sigma \left(\frac{P_t - \hat{P}_t}{\hat{P}_t} \right)^2$$

6. The linear trend index, the standard error of the estimate as a percentage of the mean of the observations:

$$\text{GI} = 100 \times \frac{\sqrt{\Sigma (P_t - \hat{P}_t)^2 / N - 1}}{\bar{P}}$$

7. The exponential index, the average of percentage absolute deviations around the log-linear trend (i.e., $(P_t = (1 + r)^t \cdot u_t)$

$$\text{EXPON} = 100 \times \frac{\Sigma \left| \frac{P_t - \hat{P}_t}{\hat{P}_t} \right|}{N - 1}$$

where P_t = the logarithmic least square estimate of the trend value for time period t (in natural numbers).

$\hat{P}_t$ = is the antilog of $\ln P_t$: $P_t = e^{\ln \hat{P}_t}$

The above instability measures were computed for each commodity and aggregate index of NBTT specified, with reference to the period 1900-82.

The results reported in Table 3.3 support the hypothesis that the magnitude of instability is very sensitive to the particular index employed. The coefficient of variation indices, for example, display high differences between one another, and the non-detrended coefficients produce systematically higher instability than the detrended ones. For rubber, the uncorrected index gives instability at 103.65 percent, whereas the corrected one gives instability at 51.89 percent. The only cases in which both indices tend to produce close results are for lead (20.66 percent compared to 20.45 percent); zinc (25.73 percent compared to 25.04 percent); and tea (26.11 percent compared to 25.21 percent).

While the above differences may be readily attributed to the fact that the uncorrected coefficient of variation index does not acount for the trend, and so over estimates instability when the series display a significant trend, corrected instability indices are not without weaknesses.

By measuring instability as deviations from a trend, for example, instability falls by a small amount when the trend is estimated from a linear equation (i.e., GI) and by a larger amount when is estimated from a log-linear equation (i.e., EXPON). Also, absolute value formulations modify the effects of outliers while squaring accentuates their influence. Thus, the index (H) and the exponential index (EXPON), which are based on absolute value formulations, give, in general, the lowest instability. This might be explained in that the deviations have not been squared.

A noteworthy point is the reference to the values produced by index FI (the sum of the squared deviations from a linear trend). These are the highest values from all indices and clearly put in doubt its credibility, because they can be largely explained by the poor fit of the regression.

Table 3.3: Alternative Traditional Measures of Barter Terms of Trade Instability, 1900-82

Commodity	C.V.	Corr. C.V.	EPSILON	H	FI	GI	EXPON
Beverages	37.17 (7)	32.47 (5)	215.55 (5)	23.33 (5)	748.02 (6)	32.07 (5)	24.91 (6)
Cereals	22.69 (17)	17.88 (17)	122.86 (17)	13.74 (18)	276.83 (16)	17.77 (17)	14.39 (17)
Food	18.63 (19)	17.29 (19)	123.53 (16)	13.89 (17)	253.63 (19)	17.08 (19)	13.93 (19)
Non-food	48.63 (3)	25.97 (6)	176.72 (7)	19.76 (7)	508.76 (8)	25.65 (6)	18.17 (12)
Maize	25.68 (13)	21.63 (11)	147.58 (12)	16.08 (13)	353.63 (13)	21.36 (11)	18.03 (13)
Rice	28.39 (10)	24.43 (10)	165.99 (9)	18.28 (9)	474.87 (11)	24.13 (10)	19.03 (11)
Cotton	24.34 (16)	20.81 (12)	146.83 (13)	16.01 (14)	321.03 (15)	20.56 (12)	19.35 (10)
Wool	30.56 (9)	18.77 (16)	120.44 (19)	12.99 (19)	276.76 (17)	18.54 (16)	22.20 (7)
Rubber	103.65 (1)	51.89 (1)	342.17 (1)	55.64 (1)	4,992.7 (1)	51.25 (1)	38.74 (2)
Coffee	46.76 (5)	39.13 (4)	265.74 (3)	28.82 (4)	1,077.2 (5)	38.89 (3)	29.77 (4)
Cocoa	52.39 (2)	40.31 (3)	277.35 (2)	32.68 (2)	1,469.44 (4)	39.81 (4)	49.05 (1)
Tea	26.11 (11)	25.21 (8)	172.14 (8)	19.39 (8)	533.02 (7)	24.90 (8)	21.48 (8)
Sugar	48.19 (4)	43.06 (2)	261.58 (4)	29.66 (3)	1,520.65 (3)	42.53 (2)	35.78 (3)
Wheat	25.32 (15)	20.47 (13)	140.58 (15)	15.76 (15)	3,609.79 (2)	20.22 (14)	16.00 (16)
Copper	31.36 (8)	25.63 (7)	184.03 (6)	20.20 (6)	502.18 (9)	25.32 (7)	27.23 (5)
Tin	39.04 (6)	19.76 (15)	149.47 (10)	17.60 (10)	375.34 (12)	19.51 (15)	20.66 (9)
Lead	20.66 (18)	20.45 (14)	147.84 (11)	16.30 (11)	337.71 (14)	20.33 (13)	16.65 (15)
Zinc	25.73 (12)	25.04 (9)	146.43 (14)	16.19 (12)	499.65 (10)	24.73 (9)	17.56 (14)
Total Agriculture	25.59 (14)	17.39 (18)	122.13 (18)	13.90 (1)	261.22 (18)	17.17 (18)	14.02 (18)

Note: See text for definition of indices.
Numbers in parentheses are rankings in descending order.

In order to determine the degree to which various indices provide the same assessment of relative variability, the commodity rankings obtained with each of the indices were compared. As a summary measure of the degree of similarity between the rankings, the Spearman correlation coefficient has been used:

$$P = 1 - \frac{6\Sigma(d)^2}{N^3-N},$$

where d = difference in ranking

The value of this non-parametric coefficient varies from positive unity to negative unity. If the rank correlation is perfect, then all the **d**'s are zero and so the coefficient equals positive unity. If, on the other hand, the ranks are such that the first, second, third in one order correspond to the n+h, (n-1)th, (n-2)th, ... in the other, then P=-1; this means perfect dissimilarity in ranking between the two indices.

Table 3.4 displays the Spearman rank correlation coefficient of the seven indices for the 19 commodity prices of this study's sample. A first glance at these correlations reveals that the coefficients are positive and on the high side in all cases. From these cases, it can be argued that the present sample suggests an overall robustness of the measurement of instability through indices examined. This implies that the judgement on relative instability (e.g., the inter-commodity comparison of the same instability measure) is likely to be insensitive to the way that deviations are measured. For instance, selecting index GI or index FI, with or without the trend would not make much difference to the overall evaluation of relative instability across commodities.

Increased Instability in the Terms of Trade

The issue of increased instability in the terms of trade has not been extensively examined by researchers. To our knowledge, only one study, that of Hallwood (1982), specifically addressed the problem of instability in the terms of trade of primary producers.

Table 3.4: **Spearman Rank Correlation Coefficient Between Traditional Instability Indices of Barter Terms of Trade, 1900-82**

Indices	C.V.	Corr. C.V.	EPSILON	H	FI	GI
Corr. C.V.	0.804***					
EPSILON	0.788***	0.919***				
H	0.811***	0.931***	0.988***			
FI	0.688***	0.859***	0.788***	0.804***		
GI	0.793***	0.996***	0.928***	0.935***	0.837***	
EXPON	0.839***	0.818***	0.810***	0.804***	0.656***	0.814***

*** = Indicates significance at the 1 percent level.

In this study, Hallwood used the IMF's commodity price series as an index for primary product terms of trade and examined trends and instability in terms of trade over the 1957-80 period. As a measure of instability of terms of trade, he used the exponential index discussed in the previous section.

To tackle the question of increased instability, Hallwood split the 1957-80 period into two sub-periods, 1957-69 and 1970-80, finding that instability had increased sharply from an absolute annual average of 0.55 percent in 1957-69 to 1.83 percent in 1970-80. A test of the terms of trade instability in the pre-1939 period using the Lewis (1952) index also found that between 1871-1913, the average instability of the annual terms of trade, measured in terms of absolute deviations, was only 0.64 percent compared with 2.16 percent during the inter-war period.

However, as has been pointed out by Perkins (1984), the single measures of instability described earlier, and the one applied by Hallwood, provide information about the average variability in the period concerned and not on the tendency of instability to increase or decline over time.

If a uniform trend exists over an n-year period, then comparisons of any particular single measure used for sub-periods will depend on (i) the pattern of the deviations over time; and (ii) the way in which the total period is split. Therefore, if the objective is to detect any general, steady tendency toward greater or smaller variability over time, it may be misleading to draw policy conclusions on the basis of a simple comparison of instability indices in two sub-periods.

In order to cope with this problem, a simple method suggested by Johnston (1972) was applied. The method consists of computing a regression between the absolute value of the residual from the linear and/or the quadratic trend. The coefficient of this regression is then used to test the null hypothesis on the increase or decrease in variance over time. The results obtained are displayed in Table 3.5. [3/]

To interpret these results, the same statistics used for the analysis of the secular movements of the terms of trade are used, namely: (i) the first derivative (and the associated elasticity); (ii) the linear trend coefficient; (iii) the quadratic trend coefficient; and (iv) the number of years needed to reverse the sign of the first derivative.

As the table shows, in many cases the squared term of the trend is insignificant and therefore excluded from the regression. Even when it is included, its size is often sufficiently small for the main effect to still be represented by the linear term, even after several years. However, in the three equations where the square term is included—rice, rubber and tin—there appears to be a tendency to reverse the sign of the first derivative after a sufficient number of years.

As for the sign of the trend, the results are mixed. The instability of the terms of trade for beverages, food, rice, cocoa, tea, sugar, total agriculture, wool and lead, shows an overall persistent and sizeable increase. Instability, however, decreases for several individual commodities, notably maize, cereals, non-food, cotton, wheat, copper, tin, zinc, rubber, and coffee. The size of the trend coefficients, on the other hand, are, in all cases, very low.

Table 3.5: **Test of Increased Instability for Barter Terms of Trade, 1900-82**

Commodity	Trend	Trend Squared	$\bar{R}^2$	First derivative (elasticity)	Time of trend reversal (no. of yrs.)
Beverages	0.0002 (0.299)		-0.024	0.0002	
Cereals	-0.0002 (0.619)		-0.008	-0.0002	
Food	0.0004 (1.097)		0.002	0.0004	
Non-food	-0.0003 (0.475)		-0.022	-0.0003	
Maize	-0.0006 (1.093)		-0.015	-0.0006	
Rice	-0.0050 (2.532)***	0.00006 (2.685)***	0.061	0.0003	46
Cotton	-0.0002 (0.283)		-0.011	-0.0002	
Wool	0.0002 (0.302)		-0.024	0.0002	
Rubber	0.0044 (1.209)	-0.00010 (1.499)	0.015	-0.0005	22
Total agriculture	0.0005 (1.153)		0.004	0.0005	
Coffee	-0.0004 (0.617)		-0.008	-0.0004	
Cocoa	0.0016 (2.943)**		0.047	0.0016	
Tea	-0.00006 (0.097)		-0.025	0.00006	
Sugar	0.0025 (1.961)**		0.022	0.0025	
Wheat	-0.0005 (1.149)		0.004	-0.0005	
Copper	-0.0002 (0.442)		-0.023	-0.0002	
Tin	-0.003 (1.486)	0.00002 (1.033)	0.034	-0.001	75
Lead	0.0002 (0.508)		-0.009	0.0002	
Zinc	-0.0009 (1.568)		0.018	-0.0009	

*** = Indicates significance at the 1 percent level.
** = Indicates significance at the 5 percent level.

The analysis indicates that, in the period under consideration, there was a weak increase in instability in the NBTT. Rice appears to have become the most unstable single commodity over the 1900-82 period, followed in sequence by sugar, cocoa, food and total agriculture. From these commodities, however, only for rice, sugar and cocoa, is the coefficient significant at the five percent level.

For the commodities with decreasing instability, the coefficient is significant at 10 percent in all cases.

The next question to examine is whether or not there has been a structural shift in the parameters. This is done by introducing slope and intercept dummies and applying the same procedures as was done with the trends in the terms of trade. What follows is a brief discussion of the results obtained with the inclusion of dummy variables. Tables 3.6 and 3.7 summarize the results obtained.

Two break periods: 1900-50 and 1950-82

The hypothesis of parameter invariance, under the two break periods in question, cannot be rejected for copper, tin and lead.

It can be rejected, however, for sugar, rice and cotton, which have significant slope dummy coefficients. For the 1950-82 period BTT appear to have become more stable for sugar at an annual rate of 1.1 percent, for rice at 2.1 percent and for cotton at 0.29 percent.

Every 15-year breaks:

The Chow test rejects the hypothesis of structural stability in all cases. Overall, instability in the terms of trade shows a tendency to increase over time for six commodities: cereals, non-food, coffee, cocoa, wheat and wool.

Table 3.6: Time Breakdown: Instability in the Terms of Trade

	N₁				N₂				N₂¹				N₃				N₄				N₅			
	No. of time specific		Signific. trend		No. of time specific		Signific. trend		No. of time specific		Signific. trend		No. of time specific		Signific. trend		No. of time specific		Signific. trend		No. of time specific		Signific. trend	
	A	B	C	D	A	B	C	D	A	B	C	D	A	B	C	D	A	B	C	D	A	B	C	D
Beverages	0	0			1	1			2	1	−*		1	0			1	1			4	3	+***	
Cereals	0	0			0	0			0	1	+*		0	0			1	1			1	1		
Food	1	0	+*		1	1	+*		1	1			1	1			3	2	−**		3	3		
Non-food	0	0			1	1			0	1			1	0			1	1			0	0		
Coffee	0	0			0	0			0	0			0	1			2	1			1	2		
Cocoa	0	0			0	0			0	0			0	0			0	0			1	1		
Tea	0	0			0	0			0	0			1	1			0	0			0	0		
Sugar	1	1			0	0			0	0			1	1			0	1			1	0		
Wheat	0	0			0	0			0	0			1	0			1	1			0	0		
Maize	0	0	+*		0	0			0	1			1	1			1	1			0	0		
Rice	1	1	−*		4	3			1	1	*		1	1			3	1			1	1		
Cotton	1	1			0	1			0	0			1	1			0	1			1	1		
Wool	0	0			1	1			1	1			1	1			1	1			1	1		
Rubber	0	0			1	1			1	1	*		1	0			1	1			0	1		
Copper	0	0			0	0			0	0			1	1			0	0	*		2	1		
Tin	0	0			2	2	−**		0	0			0	0			1	1			1	1		
Lead	0	0			0	0			0	0			0	0			0	2			5	4	−***	
Zinc	0	0			1	0			0	1			0	0			1	2			1	1		
Total agriculture	1	0			2	0			0	0			0	0			1	1	−**		1	1		

N_1 = Two break periods: 1900–50, 1950–82.
N_2 = Historical period breaks: 1900–13, 1914–39, 1940–53, 1954–73, 1974–82.
N_2^1 = Historical period breaks: 1900–13, 1914–39, 1940–53, 1954–70, 1971–82.
N_3 = Every 20-year breaks.
N_4 = Every 15-year breaks.
N_5 = Every 10-year breaks.

A = Constant dummies.
B = Coefficient dummies.
C = Linear trend.
D = Quadratic trend.

*** = Indicates significance at the 1 percent level.
** = Indicates significance at the 5 percent level.
*   = Indicates significance at the 10 percent level.

Table 3.7: **Chow Test for Structural Breaks in the Instability of Terms of Trade**

Commodity	N_1	N_2	N_2^1	N_3	N_4	N_5
Beverages	***	***	***	***	***	***
Cereals	***	***	***	***	***	***
Food	***	***	***	***	***	***
Non-food	***	***	***	***	***	***
Total agriculture	***	***	***	***	***	***
Coffee	***	***	***	***	***	***
Cocoa	***	***	***	***	***	***
Tea	***	***	**	***	***	***
Sugar	***	***	***	***	***	***
Wheat	***	***	***		***	***
Maize	***	***	***	***	***	***
Rice	***	***	***	***	***	***
Cotton	***	***	***	***	***	***
Wool	***	***	***	***	***	
Rubber	***	***	***	***	***	***
Copper		***	***	***	***	***
Tin		***	***	***	***	***
Lead		***	***	***	***	***
Zinc	***	***	***	***	***	***

N_1 = Two break periods: 1900-50, 1950-82
N_2 = Historical break periods: 1900-13, 1914-39, 1940-54, 1955-73, 1974-82
N_2^1 = Historical break periods: 1900-13, 1914-39, 1940-54, 1955-70, 1971-82

N_3 = Every 20-year breaks.
N_4 = Every 15-year breaks.
N_5 = Every 10-year breaks.

*** Indicates significance at the 1 percent level.

Looking at the sub-periods, instability during 1900-15 increased for only food and agriculture. In the other sub-periods in which slope dummy coefficients were significant, the terms of trade became more stable over time. These included cereals, wheat, maize and lead during 1945-60; food, cotton, wool, rubber, lead, zinc and non-food during 1930-45; agriculture during 1900-15; and coffee for 1915-30.

Every 20-year breaks:

The hypothesis of parameter invariance is rejected in all but one case (wheat). The trend coefficient is positive in some cases and negative in others, but never significant.

For the period between 1960-82, the terms of trade became more stable for food, wheat and zinc. For the 1940-60 period, instability in the terms of trade increased for wool and copper, and for the 1900-20 period, only for zinc. Instability in the terms of trade decreased in the 1920-40 period for sugar, rice and cotton.

Historical break periods

The Chow test allows rejection of the hypothesis of parameter invariance for all commodities. This is true for both specifications applied (i.e., 1973 as a break year and 1970 as a break year). For the specification with 1973 as a break year, there were two commodities with significant slope coefficients: cereals and tin. For the former, instability over the entire 1900-82 period increased at an average rate of 0.2 percent, while, for the latter, instability declined by 0.2 percent.

For the 1973-82 period, the terms of trade became more unstable for beverages (3.5 percent) on average, food (1.44 percent), wool (2.6 percent) and tin (5.4 percent). For rice, however, the terms of trade became more stable at an annual average of 7 percent. For the 1955-73 period, the terms of trade became more stable for non-food (1 percent), and for rice (2.3 percent).

In the World War II and Korean War period (1940-53) there is evidence of increasing variability for wheat (1.7 percent) and rubber (3.4 percent). For the other commodities, there is no clear-cut increase or decrease in variability. This also applies for all commodities for the World War I and inter war period (1914-39).

Adjusting for productivity

As a final test, Table 3.8 reports the results of the same heteroscedasticity analysis applied to the SFTT for the agricultural commodities. These results are more consistent than the results for the BTT, in the sense that they show no evidence of a significant trend in instability except for sugar and maize. Furthermore, the sign of the trend coefficient is generally negative, except for rice, and tends to reverse the sign of the coefficient measure in the BTT regressions (Table 3.9).

Regarding the sub-period results, Tables 3.10 and 3.11 indicate that, by and large, productivity adjustment does not produce any major change in the pattern of instability from that observed for the BTT. The only main effects occurred are for the 15-year and 10-year breaks where the trend variable coefficients are statistically significant for rice and coffee.

Table 3.8: **Increased Instability for the Single Factorial Terms of Trade, 1900-82**

	Intercept	Trend	Trend squared	$\bar{R}^2$	First derivative	Time of trend reversal (no. of yrs.)
Coffee	0.272 (6.588)***	-0.0009 (-1.089)		0.002	-0.00080	
Cocoa	0.256 (6.600)***	-0.00008 (-0.097)		-0.140	-0.00008	
Tea	0.145 (5.186)***	-0.0005 (-0.727)		-0.006	-0.00050	
Sugar	0.328 (4.301)***	-0.009 (-2.090)**	0.0001 (2.519)**	0.071	-0.00080	45
Wheat	0.147 (6.867)***	-0.0006 (-1.399)		0.012	-0.00060	
Maize	0.339 (6.614)***	-0.006 (-2.152)**	0.0005 (1.400)	0.112	-0.00200	60
Rice	0.131 (4.666)***	0.0002 (0.355)		-0.011	0.00020	

*** = Indicates significance at the 1 percent level.
** = Indicates significance at the 5 percent level.
* = Indicates significance at the 10 percent level.

Table 3.9: **Comparison of Results of Instability Analysis**

	BTT		SFTT	
	Sign of first derivative	Time of trend reversal (no. of yrs)	Sign of first derivative	Time of trend reversal (no. of yrs)
Coffee	−		−	
Cocoa	+ **		−	
Tea	+		−	
Sugar	+ ***		− *	45
Wheat	−		−	
Maize	−		− *	60
Rice	− **	25	+	

*** = Indicate significance at the 1 percent level.
 ** = Indicate significance at the 5 percent level.
  * = Indicate significance at the 10 percent level.

Table 3.10: Time Breakdown: Instability in the Single Factorial Terms of Trade

	N_1					N_2					N_2^1					N_3					N_4					N_5				
	No. of time specific			Signific. trend		No. of time specific			Signific. trend		No. of time specific			Signific. trend		No. of time specific			Signific. trend		No. of time specific			Signific. trend		No. of time specific			Signific. trend	
	A	B	C	D		A	B	C	D		A	B	C	D		A	B	C	D		A	B	C	D		A	B	C	D
Coffee	0	0				0	0				0	0				0	0				1	1				2	3	+***	-*
Cocoa	0	0				0	0				0	0				1	1				1	1	-*			2	2		
Tea	0	0				0	0				0	0				0	0				0	0				0	1		
Sugar	1	1				0	0				0	0				0	0				1	1				1	1		
Wheat	0	0				0	0				0	0				1	1				0	0				1	1		
Maize	1	1	-***	+***		0	0				0	0				0	0				0	0				1	2		
Rice	1	1				4	3				1	1	-*			1	2				2	2	-**	+***		1	3		-**

N_1 = Two break periods: 1900–50, 1950–82.

N_2 = Historical period breaks: 1900–13, 1914–39, 1940–53, 1954–73, 1974–82.

N_2^1 = Historical period breaks: 1900–13, 1914–39, 1940–53, 1954–70, 1971–82.

N_3 = Every 20-year breaks.

N_4 = Every 15-year breaks.

N_5 = Every 10-year breaks.

A = Constant dummies.
B = Coefficient dummies.
C = Linear trend.
D = Quadratic trend.

*** = Indicates significance at the 1 percent level.
** = Indicates significance at the 5 percent level.
*   = Indicates significance at the 10 percent level.

Table 3.11: **Chow Test for Structural Breaks in the Trends of Single Factorial Terms of Trade**

Commodity	N_1	N_2	N_2^1	N_3	N_4	N_5
Coffee	**	**				
Cocoa		**				***
Tea		**			***	
Sugar		***	***	**		***
Wheat		***	***		***	
Maize		***	***			***
Rice						

N_1 = Two break periods: 1900-50, 1950-82.

N_2 = Historical break periods: 1900-13, 1914-39, 1940-53, 1954-73, 1974-82.

N_2^1 = Historical break periods: 1900-13, 1914-39, 1940-53, 1954-70, 1971-82.

N_3 = Every 20-year breaks.

N_4 = Every 15-year breaks.

N_5 = Every 10-year breaks.

*** = Indicates significance at the 1 percent level.
 ** = Indicates significance at the 5 percent level.
  * = Indicates significance at the 10 percent level.

Some Conclusions

The measurement of instability levels and trends over time is a necessary complement of the analysis of trend in the terms of trade of primary commodities. It appears that for economic and policy reasons, the relevance of the terms of trade problem depends on two critical questions: (i) Is there a systematic tendency to deprive primary producers of their share of the gains from trade through an unfavourable movement of relative prices? and (ii) Is this tendency reinforced and are its effects aggravated by instability?

Even though the tests developed in this chapter are only part of the analysis that is devoted to instability in this study, we can already conclude that our answer to the question in point (ii) is perhaps even more negative than to the question in point (i). The reason for such a conclusion is threefold: first, absolute instability measurers vary widely according to the index used. Even though they seem suitable, their order of magnitude is not above what can be expected from many random variables and from most price indices. Second, there is very little evidence of systematic increases in instability, and results to this effect vary widely according to the time period considered and the specification adopted. Third, results for the instability of the terms of trade adjusted for productivity also show mostly insignificant increases or decreases in instability over time, and reverse in most cases the results obtained for the BTT.

Notes

1/ It is interesting to note the differences between the various studies. The World Bank (1978), for example, reports copper as the most unstable in its four groups and coffee in the second most stable group. On the other hand, UNCTAD (1975) and Behrman (1977) report relatively great instability for copper in 1953 to 1972 and 1950 to 1975. These discrepancies might be explained by the fact that the World Bank study employed a moving average index, while UNCTAD used a trend estimated by regression.

2/ The log-variance index is defined as follows:

$$I = 100 \times \left(\text{antilog} \left[\frac{1}{N-1} \sum_{t=1}^{n-1} (\log \frac{X_{t+1}}{X_1} - m)^2 \right]^{1/2} \right)$$

where X_t = time series;

m = arithmetic mean of the algebraic differences between the logarithms of the successive pairs of Xs:

$$m = \frac{1}{N-1} \sum_{t=1}^{n-1} \log \left(\frac{X_{t+1}}{X_t} \right)$$

3/ An alternative test, which consists of the computation of Kendall's tau-statistic of absolute value of residuals from trend regressions, was also computed. The results are reported in Appendix III, Table A.3.1 for the 1900-82 period and in Table A.3.2 for the sub-periods.

CHAPTER IV

TERMS OF TRADE INSTABILITY: THE SPECTRAL ANALYSIS VIEW

Detection of Trends and Instability

The idea of instability seems to derive historically from the additive model of time-series analysis, according to which the variations over time of an economic variable can be decomposed into three basic mutually exclusive factors: trend, cycle and residual (Grenander and Rosenblatt, 1957). While the residual is the result of the specification of the other components, the concept of trends and cycles are not easy to define and to separate from each other.

If we view a time series as the result of several overlapping cyclical variations, a trend may be reasonably defined as a "long-term change in the mean" of the variable, but the difficulty with this definition is to decide what is meant by "long term". For a series of a given length, "long term" may be defined with reference to the length of the series, as, for example, a cycle with a period (i.e., difference between "peak" and "through") equal or greater than the length of the series (Granger, 1966). This definition, however, leaves unsettled the question of how long a time series to recognize a trend should be, since what may appear as a trend in a shorter series may be recognized as a mere short-term fluctuation in a longer one.

Because of the difficulty to separate the concepts of trends and cycles, spectral analysis appears as the most promising tool to investigate alternative definitions and measurements of instability. Without making any assumption on the shape and the number of the constituents of a time series, spectral analysis decomposes a "stationary" time series into a number of bands of different "frequency". A "stationary" series means the absence of a trend in the series mean and variance, while a given frequency band is defined as an identifiable cycle of a given average frequency. Since the frequency is inversely proportional to the period of the cycle (i.e., the difference between its "peak" and its "through") by a factor of $1/\pi$, a band of average frequency π/p, corresponds to movements with periods in the neighbourhood of period **p**, or, briefly, to an average cycle of period **p**.

Given the above definitions, spectral analysis classifies the different frequency bands in terms of their different contribution to the overall variance (called "power") of the time series. One of the basic tools of the analysis is the so called "power spectrum", which is simply the graph of variance against frequency. This graph shows a typical declining shape, because the lower frequency bands (the longer period movements) tend to account for the larger portion of the variability of the time series, while the higher frequency bands contribute gradually decreasing portions to the same variability.

Without any attempt to "smooth over" some of the frequencies, spectral analysis thus gives both an inventory of the fluctuations of a time series and a measure of their absolute and relative importance (the "power" of the spectrum). Given that a time series can be purged from its trend component in such a way that the resulting series respects the stationary assumptions, spectral analysis suggests that a measure of instability may be obtained through the variance of the components of a selected set of frequency bands.

Because the concept of instability refers to "unexpected" or "unpredictable" changes, however, it is by no means clear which frequency should be privileged and which weights, if any, should be given to the different bands. On one hand, if the time series were rendered completely stationary by the technique of trend removal used, one could take as a measure of instability the sum of the variance over all the remaining frequency bands. In this limiting case, the measure of instability chosen would coincide with the most commonly used measure of variability. On the other hand, because some of the frequency bands may be associated with somewhat predictable cycles (e.g., seasonal, annual or other) of known regularity, instability could be measured with the variance of the residual frequency bands, after the other regular cycles have been filtered out.

There is, however, no general reason why instability should be associated with higher frequency bands and lower frequency bands should be considered the expression of more regular or predictable phenomena. Seasonal fluctuations, for example, which are associated with lower frequency in the time series of many years, may be highly predictable. On the other hand, medium-term fluctuations, which may appear as trends in a short time series, may show much more irregular behaviour.

In order to produce a measure of instability, it is thus inevitable that subjective judgement be exercised, as to what characteristics of the fluctuations--amplitude or frequency--are relevant expressions of the underlying instability. This implies that decisions have to be made as to the frequency components that are to be included and to their weight. In making these decisions, the power spectrum may be helpful, since it will show the most relevant periodical movements as peaking in the correspondent frequency bands.

Before an index of instability can be defined through the procedure described, however, the main problem to be resolved is the removal of the trend. This problem can be viewed in a fashion that abstracts from the spectral view, as most of the empirical studies on the subject do. Alternatively, it can be viewed in a way that is essentially homogenous to the problem of detection of frequency bands of a given average length, as the spectral analysis literature proposes.

In the first case, the trend is removed by either regression analysis, most commonly in the semi-logarithmic form corresponding to an exponential trend, or by taking first differences of the original series. In the second case, the most appropriate method of trend removal is that of harmonic regression, which fits a low order Fourier polynomial to obtain least square estimates of the longer period (lower frequency) cycles of the time series.

In both cases, trend removal faces two main difficulties: on the one hand, since the trend may not be exponential or the frequency bands selected may not exhaust the long-term movements identifiable as trends, the residual may still contain trend elements. As a consequence, the residual may not exhibit the required stationarity and, moreover, the remaining portions of the trend may swamp in the spectrum of some of the low frequencies that are responsible for long-term instability. Because the trend component will generally account for the largest portion of the total variance of the series, this "leakage" effect will result in a typical spectrum peaking at the zero frequency "band", and smoothly decreasing for the next few frequency "band", thus possibly denying instability from long-run movements (Granger, 1966).

On the other hand, attempts to filter out the trend elements may result in an excessive removal of low-level frequencies and eliminate some of the bands corresponding to long-term instability. As a consequence, the spectrum would peak at the first low frequency not removed by the trend and suggest long-term instability.

In trend removal as in instability detection, therefore, the best approach appears to be a heuristic one, based on several different filters and definitions. Because spectral analysis is founded on statistical theory, this makes possible to apply significance tests to the alternative procedures selected, even though the statistical feasibility of the test does depend on the underlying model adopted.

Method of Analysis

As suggested in the preceding section, a definition of instability based on the variability of a set of frequency bands on a filtered stochastic process is favoured in this study. In order to use spectral analysis, specification must be made deductively as to what type of fluctuation is relevant for instability and thus to ensure that filtering is able to induce stationarity without disturbing those components of the time series that are of interest.

As mentioned, spectral analysis is essentially an analysis of variance technique in which a stationary time series is viewed as if it had been generated by a collection (or "spectrum") of independent sine curves, each with a different amplitude. The primary output of spectral analysis is a spectral density function that indicates the percentage of the overall variance of the time series that can be attributed to each frequency.

Because the sample spectrum of a series shows how total variance ("power") is distributed over frequency (or corresponding cycle lengths), it gives information as to the relative importance and statistical significance of one periodical movement vis-á-vis the others. Whether a cycle of (average) period (p) and frequency (f) is present in the series, can thus be tested by measuring its contribution to total variance in the series.

By focusing on cycles of "average" given frequency, spectral analysis allows one to separate classes of fluctuations, rather than swings of specific duration. Gelb (1979), for example, adopts the following classification:

Very high frequency	=	duration below 1 year
High frequency	=	duration from 1 to 2 years
Medium frequency	=	duration from 2 to 5 years
Low frequency	=	duration greater than 5 years

Given a classification of this type, a reasonable definition of instability can be given as the sum of the variances of the frequency components with duration t_0 to t_1. In fixing the cut-off point to determine the components to be included in the variance, we have two guidelines:

- A relative one, excluding components of duration longer than one half of the time series (Granger's definition of trend); and

- An absolute one, excluding components whose duration is above a reasonable upper bound (e.g., 10 to 50 years).

Before applying these guidelines to the measurement of instability in the terms of trade, however, one must:

- Test for stationarity of the series for all commodities; and

- Apply the appropriate filters to detrend those series that exhibit long-term movements in mean or variance.

In order to test for stationarity, the following statistics were computed:

- The Kendall's rank correlation tau-statistic;
- The Fisher's Kappa (FK) statistic; and
- The Bartlett's Kolmogorov-Smirnov (BKS) statistic.

While the first test is a simple comparison of rankings across variables and time, the last two statistics are based on the cumulative periodogram of the series, i.e., the distribution function of its cyclical components. Both FK and BKS can detect the presence of systematic periodical components, as opposed to non-systematic (or "random") ones. They can thus show evidence of non stationarity because of trends in mean and/or variance.

The results of the tests, reported in Table 4.1, show that one cannot reject the hypothesis of trendlessness, on the basis of the tau-statistic, only for tea, cocoa, copper, lead and zinc; while for all other series there appears to be significant rank correlation with time at the 1 percent significance level. As for FK and BKS, for all series, the stationarity hypothesis at the 1 percent confidence level was rejected.

Assuming that non-stationarity is due to trends in the mean values, the following transformation of the basic data was attempted:

a)   First differences. This transformation is capable of eliminating a linear trend from a stochastic process of the type:

$$Y_t = a + bt + u_t \qquad (1)$$

Table 4.1: Stationarity Tests on the Terms of Trade Series, 1900-1982

Commodity	Kendall's tau-statistic	Fisher's Kappa-test	Bartlett's test
Beverages	0.295***	12.920***	0.622***
Cereals	-0.457***	8.566***	0.589***
Food	-0.275***	8.147***	0.515***
Non-food	-0.678***	15.011***	0.764***
Total agriculture	-0.509***	15.117***	0.660***
Tea	0.022	12.340***	0.616***
Maize	-0.356***	6.894***	0.450***
Rice	-0.355***	9.933***	0.533***
Cotton	-0.284***	16.282***	0.557***
Sugar	-0.289***	9.863***	0.380***
Wheat	-0.440***	9.099***	0.608***
Cocoa	0.070	18.516***	0.658***
Coffee	0.391***	10.674***	0.626***
Wool	-0.442***	17.564***	0.575***
Copper	-0.022	19.915***	0.619***
Tin	0.516***	15.208***	0.649***
Rubber	-0.638***	16.626***	0.812***
Lead	0.062	7.932***	0.559***
Zinc	0.043	6.303***	0.399***

*** = Indicates significance at the 1 percent level.

where t is time, a and b are constant parameters and u_t a stochastic stationary residual. Applying the first difference operator we find:

$$\Delta Y_t = Y_t - Y_{t-1} = b + u_t - u_{t-1} \tag{2}$$

Thus, the resulting series Y_t is stationary if: (i) the trend affecting the original series is linear, and (ii) the residual u_t is itself stationary.

b) <u>Residuals from a least-square regression on time (and on time square where appropriate) corrected for autocorrelation.</u> This transformation is based on the assumption that the underlying stochastic process is both affected by an exponential trend and by autocorrelation in the residuals:

$$\log Y_t = a + gt + v_t \tag{3}$$

where g is the constant rate of growth, a dimensional parameter, and v_t a stochastic variable generated according to an auto-regressive scheme:

$$V_t = p_1 V_{t-1} + p_2 V_t + \ldots + p_n V_{t-n} + z_t \tag{4}$$

where z_t is a stationary residual and p_i is the coefficient of autocorrelation of the i-th order ($i = 1, 2 \ldots n$).

c) <u>Residuals from a mixed autoregressive and moving average process.</u> This transformation assumes that the non-stationarity of the series derives from the stochastic mechanism generating it, rather than from a simple linear or exponential trend. The fitting technique, known as (ARIMA) combines estimates from two basic models: the autoregressive scheme of order n:

$$V_t = \sum_{i=1}^{n} p_i V_{t-i} \quad \text{as in (4)}, \tag{5}$$

and the moving average scheme of order k:

$$Y_t = \sum_{j=1}^{k} m_j u_{t-j}^{k} \quad (6)$$

Estimates of (5) and (6) were obtained and additively combined, using the "portmanteau" test developed by Box and Pierce (1970) to measure the "lack-of-fitness" of several alternative specifications. The results are reported in Appendix IV, Table A.4.1.

d) <u>Residuals from a least-square harmonic regression</u>: This amounts to the estimation of the following equation:

$$(TOT)_t = \sum_{j=1}^{k} [(a_j \cos(\pi jt/n) + b_j \sin(\pi jt/n) + c] \quad (7)$$

where **t** is time, **n** is the sample size and **k** is the order of the polynomial. In this case, polynomials of order three were fitted (Harkness, 1968). The results obtained are reported in Appendix IV, Table A.4.2. Because in the former transformation in (7), a cycle is considered as a result of two series of mutually counterbalancing fluctuations of the same period, the order of polynomial is related to the period of the cycles removed by the relationship:

$$P_c (n/k) \cdot 2 \quad (8)$$

where P_c is the period of the c-th cycle removed. In the sample of 82 observations used in this study, this implies that the residuals from regression (7) with **k** = 3 will be free of all cycles of a period greater than 55 years: a result that is equivalent to trend removal according to Granger's definition (i.e., all cycles with a period above **n/2**). In order to test for stationarity, the residuals of the above transformation were subject to the Fisher's Kappa and the Bartlett's Kolmogorov-Smirnov (1955) tests. These tests are both based on the cumulative periodogram, defined as:

$$C(f_i) = \frac{\Sigma I(f_i)}{ns^2} \qquad (9)$$

where:
- f_i = frequency of the i-th component
- $I(f_i)$ = estimate of the power spectrum of frequency f_i
- s^2 = estimate of the total variance
- n = number of observations

Table 4.2 reports the results from the application of the statistical tests to stationarity. As can be seen, all versions produce stationary series. Only under the first-difference version are the rice and cotton series significantly non-stationary.

Empirical Results

In this section empirical evidence of magnitudes of instability measured by different detrending methods is presented. The analysis proceeds as follows: first, the variances of all components in the periodogram obtained from the above detrending methods are compared. Second, the variances over the prespecified frequency bands are estimated. In particular, three frequency bands are chosen:

- The high-frequency band, defined as $[(\pi/2), \pi]$;
- The medium-frequency band, defined as $[(\pi/5), (\pi/2)]$; and
- The low-frequency band, defined as greater than $[\pi/12]$.

Regarding the correlation between the instability measured by the different detrending procedures, Table 4.3 and Table 4.4 indicate that only the correlation between the log-linear version and the first-difference version for the medium-frequency band, is statistically insignificant at the 10 percent level. This implies that, in general, the relative magnitude of instability is not significantly affected by the version chosen. However, it is interesting to note some differences in specific

Table 4.2: Stationarity Tests Under Different Detrending Procedures, 1900-82

	First Differences			Log-Linear			ARIMA			Harmonic Version		
	Fisher's Kappa-Test	Bartlett's Test	Kendall	Fisher's Kappa-Test	Bartlett's Test	Kendall	Fisher's Kappa-Test	Bartlett's Test	Kendall	Fisher's Kappa-Test	Bartlett's Test	Kendall
Beverages	4.104	0.150	-0.038	3.864	0.187	-0.017	2.790	0.083	-0.022	3.303	0.125	-0.107
Cereals	3.669	0.129	-0.095	3.943	0.114	-0.053	4.354	0.120	-0.085	4.097	0.184	-0.061
Food	0.547	0.149	-0.069	4.385	0.193	-0.053	4.104	0.113	-0.077	4.222	0.134	-0.036
Non-food	3.921	0.146	0.002	3.073	0.172	-0.019	3.134	0.067	-0.027	4.072	0.116	0.071
Total agriculture	4.759	0.146	-0.053	4.646	0.197	-0.044	3.051	0.144	-0.085	4.486	0.108	0.014
Tea	3.427	0.128	-0.067	2.774	0.102	0.030	3.625	0.086	-0.075	4.056	0.128	-0.086
Maize	4.497	0.162	-0.099	4.103	1.140	-0.056	3.942	0.119	-0.118	3.336	0.079	-0.022
Rice	3.813	0.220*	-0.034	3.977	0.156	0.016	3.128	0.115	-0.047	3.867	0.161	0.027
Cotton	4.921	0.276**	-0.089	2.586	0.125	-0.059	2.552	0.054	-0.126	5.722*	0.105	-0.064
Sugar	4.223	0.203	-0.022	4.206	0.149	-0.046	2.803	0.087	-0.065	3.371	0.113	-0.039
Wheat	4.772	0.126	-0.034	5.700*	0.133	-0.057	5.633	0.111	-0.041	4.074	0.089	-0.038
Cocoa	3.128	0.201	0.015	2.769	0.095	-0.034	2.786	0.084	0.000	4.321	0.153	-0.106
Coffee	3.796	0.133	-0.0425	3.612	0.189	-0.013	3.027	0.069	-0.037	3.069	0.150	-0.077
Wool	4.433	0.160	-0.038	3.237	0.124	-0.020	2.939	0.106	-0.002	3.935	0.102	0.000
Copper	3.879	0.158	0.005	3.574	0.174	0.021	3.531	0.120	-0.019	3.696	0.142	0.054
Tin	2.339	0.105	0.009	3.884	0.156	-0.003	3.354	0.126	-0.032	3.831	0.164	0.024
Rubber	3.525	0.117	0.101	2.771	0.143	-0.044	2.947	0.061	0.053	3.896	0.198	0.104
Lead	3.084	0.103	-0.045	3.122	0.094	-0.040	3.606	0.066	0.010	3.663	0.156	-0.033
Zinc	2.959	0.160	-0.013	3.716	0.142	-0.010	2.729	0.068	0.165	3.273	0.067	0.059

** = Indicates significance at the 5 percent level.

* = Indicates significance at the 10 percent level.

cases. For instance, with the log-linear specification over the whole spectrum, rubber is ranked as the ninenteeth most unstable commodity; while with the first differences, and ARIMA versions, it is ranked as the third most unstable commodity. With the harmonic version it is ranked as the fourth most unstable commodity. Some discrepancies also occur for tin, non-food and wool.

An attempt was also made to compare traditional indices of instability with those obtained from spectral analysis. This is done by expressing the variance of the prespecified frequency bands in the spectrum in terms of a simple coefficient of variation. This transformation makes the variability derived from spectral analysis comparable to that obtained from the traditional instability indices discussed in the preceding chapter. In particular, the results derived from index (C.V) and index (GI) are directly comparable with these reported in Tables 4.5 to 4.8. As is evident from Table A.4.3 in Appendix IV, the Spearman rank correlation, is positive and significant at least at the 5 percent confidence level.

Table 4.3: **Spearman Rank Correlation between Different Detrending Procedures**

	Log-linear	Arima	Harmonic
a) Frequency over the whole spectrum:			
First difference	0.644***	0.993***	0.988***
Log-linear		0.629***	0.637***
ARIMA			0.986***
b) Frequency band 2-6 years:			
First difference	0.714***	0.964***	0.986***
Log-linear		0.653***	0.688***
ARIMA			0.989***
c) Frequency band 6-12 years:			
First difference	0.303	0.923***	0.811***
Log-linear		0.477**	0.532**
ARIMA			0.917***
d) Frequency band greater than 12 years:			
First difference	0.496**	0.929***	0.955***
Log-linear		0.584***	0.519**
ARIMA			0.913***

*** = Indicates significance at the 1 percent level.
 ** = Indicates significance at the 5 percent level.

Table 4.4: **Spearman Rank Correlation between Different Frequency Bands**

	Frequency Bands		
	6-12	12->	Whole spectrum
a) First difference			
2-6 years	0.819***	0.859***	0.970***
6-12 years		0.845***	0.904***
12-> years			0.903***
b) Log-Linear			
2-6 years	0.903***	0.904***	0.972***
6-12 years		0.820***	0.858***
12-> years			0.913***
c) ARIMA			
2-6 years	0.884***	0.918***	0.992***
6-12 years		0.823***	0.956***
12-> years			0.928***
d) Harmonic			
2-6 years	0.858***	0.822***	0.993***
6-12 years		0.764***	0.977***
12- >years			0.956***

*** = Indicates significance at the 1 percent level.
** = Indicates significance at the 5 percent level.

Table 4.5: **Variability over Frequency Interval of 2-6 Years (%)**

Commodity	First dif	Log linear	ARIMA	Harmonic
Beverage	52.732	33.170	48.489	43.578
Cereals	32.148	26.442	33.537	27.010
Food	33.253	30.214	31.259	26.592
Non-food	34.494	14.070	32.617	29.697
Tea	34.107	20.676	32.942	26.973
Maize	48.847	35.267	44.969	35.267
Rice	39.990	31.696	35.364	31.696
Cotton	31.688	17.620	26.795	23.205
Sugar	104.846	125.162	91.168	79.738
Wheat	10.668	30.919	34.403	28.225
Cocoa	75.325	60.998	68.486	60.764
Coffee	64.366	40.205	58.872	55.168
Wool	45.558	15.517	41.953	33.229
Copper	40.110	32.094	35.574	31.006
Tin	37.273	44.746	39.404	28.227
Rubber	61.559	12.513	62.646	52.586
Lead	30.590	24.506	29.663	25.760
Zinc	53.918	52.217	44.551	39.035
Total Agric.	26.667	22.384	26.054	22.202

Table 4.6: **Variability over Frequency Interval of 6-12 Years (%)**

Commodity	First dif	Log linear	ARIMA	Harmonic
Beverage	24.859	16.471	25.752	24.39
Cereals	21.822	16.541	20.132	15.59
Food	15.630	17.928	16.036	14.34
Non-food	23.151	8.485	19.544	16.79
Tea	15.573	10.728	15.036	15.57
Maize	28.500	23.986	27.131	21.37
Rice	26.011	19.211	22.183	17.82
Cotton	21.126	9.850	15.259	13.03
Sugar	41.052	78.039	46.726	49.89
Wheat	24.327	18.167	23.373	14.31
Cocoa	29.002	32.038	32.916	30.67
Coffee	33.377	20.193	32.041	30.88
Wool	22.596	8.276	25.078	19.70
Copper	22.367	18.263	20.298	19.05
Tin	20.214	29.982	20.713	20.71
Rubber	38.024	7.793	34.320	34.86
Lead	16.499	14.225	15.630	16.91
Zinc	26.866	30.696	22.388	21.47
Total Agric.	15.308	13.633	15.042	11.72

Table 4.7: **Variability over Frequency Interval of More than 12 Years (%)**

Commodity	First dif	Log linear	ARIMA	Harmonic
Beverage	19.796	19.604	25.605	24.553
Cereals	11.910	14.587	11.026	13.505
Food	10.757	17.566	12.421	14.343
Non-food	15.619	8.124	18.867	17.549
Tea	13.899	12.661	16.092	15.964
Maize	11.993	16.961	15.115	19.074
Rice	17.242	21.238	17.827	21.238
Cotton	11.012	10.563	14.103	14.610
Sugar	29.028	26.977	38.152	40.582
Wheat	14.705	16.527	13.065	15.549
Cocoa	22.655	37.945	31.591	34.191
Coffee	23.524	23.524	31.698	33.594
Wool	12.139	8.881	14.692	18.280
Copper	15.344	21.010	22.586	17.992
Tin	13.560	27.493	12.784	14.293
Rubber	33.745	7.889	34.188	35.378
Lead	13.732	14.944	16.290	17.126
Zinc	15.510	29.361	26.866	18.461
Total Agric.	10.636	13.633	11.371	13.333

Table 4.8: **Variability over The Whole Spectrum (%)**

Commodity	First dif	Log linear	ARIMA	Harmonic
Beverage	60.456	40.994	59.133	54.35
Cereals	39.374	33.537	39.503	33.08
Food	37.607	38.285	36.391	32.66
Non-food	43.102	17.832	41.495	37.22
Tea	39.104	30.947	37.053	34.04
Maize	56.178	44.400	53.160	44.01
Rice	48.978	41.624	43.901	40.75
Cotton	37.893	22.244	32.370	29.63
Sugar	113.782	157.421	106.298	99.40
Wheat	42.805	38.612	42.270	34.40
Cocoa	82.550	76.825	80.539	74.46
Coffee	74.974	49.683	72.254	69.74
Wool	50.997	19.275	49.615	41.48
Copper	47.085	41.314	45.603	39.24
Tin	43.355	58.412	45.425	36.16
Rubber	77.552	16.232	77.331	69.59
Lead	36.424	31.267	36.525	34.15
Zinc	60.737	65.502	55.746	46.74
Total Agric.	31.655	28.709	31.270	27.85

The following points can be made about Tables 4.5 to 4.8:

- Instability at medium frequencies is greater than at high frequencies. A result which is in conformity to that reported by Gelb (1979).

- The results show that there is a fair agreement between measurements of the spectral indices versus traditional ones in measuring instability. Because of the care taken in rendering the time series stationary and in checking the different frequency bands, making it less likely that they are affected by phenomena of over- or under-removal of the trend, the results of spectral analysis on the whole should be more accurate than the ones performed with traditional methods.

- With regard to the different possible definitions of instability, within the spectral context, the results obtained show that for most of the series, variance declines as one moves from longer periods to shorter periods. This result conforms to the typical shape of the economic time series noted, among others, by Granger (1966) and Gelb (1979).

- Within the framework of this analysis, however, this pattern of variance decline suggests that the highest measurement of instability does indeed coincide with the highest frequency of the occasional or unpredictable variations. However, the correlation between the variance of this frequency band and the variance of the other bands is so high that for most practical purposes the selection of one particular band to measure instability would not make much difference for the series analyzed.

Some Conclusions

The analysis of instability through spectral analysis offers a number of possibilities that are not available with a conventional approach. These possibilities include a more precise definition of trend, better tests of the stationarity of the residuals and the choice of alternative frequency bands to measure instability.

Perhaps the strongest result of the analysis, compared with this study's earlier results, concerns the presence of a trend in the series examined. The results of the tests, performed in various forms directly based to the examination of the spectrum, showed that one can reject for all series the hypotheses of "trendlessness" on the basis of two tests, and in the case of cocoa, lead, coffee and zinc, on the basis of one test. Furthermore, the latter test, based on Kendall's tau statistic, is quite significant and shows a negative trend for most commodities.

The meaning of this result, in the light of this study's detailed earlier trend analysis, is to be considered carefully. A negative linear trend component is neither necessary nor sufficient to prove a long-term tendency for the terms of trade to deteriorate. It does suggest, however, why Prebisch and others, based as they were on visual inspection of diagrams or first order measurements, did detect a negative trend in most primary commodity prices.

The same result, on the other hand, suggests that the adoption of a spectral analysis view in setting up a test for the existence of a negative trend brings the evidence clearly on the side of the claim. In other words, while an attempt to test the negative trend by measuring its linear and quadratic component fails to reject the hypothesis of trendlessness or of sign reversal, tests based on rank statistics, with no attempt to measure the size of the time effects, strongly uphold the hypothesis of a negative association between the terms of trade and the passing of time.

A second set of results concerns the measurements of instability. While in this study's earlier analysis the differences in the absolute values of the indicators of variability selected to measure instability were stressed, spectral analysis yields a further dimension in the form of the selection of a frequency band. The result of the consideration of this dimension is twofold: on the one hand, measurements of instability are obtained which are generally higher than those obtained with traditional analysis through a comparable indicator (the corrected coefficient of variation). On the other hand, the same measurements increase as one goes from the lower to the higher frequency bands. Since the peaks for relative variance are reached, in most cases, for the highest frequency band, it seems natural to conclude that it is for this band that the highest unexpected variation occurs. Thus, instability in primary commodities seems to be mainly a short-term (2-6 years) problem.

When the spectral indicators of instability are used to rank commodities, it finally emerges that the results show a high correlation with the results obtained with all traditional indicators. Thus, despite the differences in trend detection, absolute measurements and frequency specificity, spectral indicators tend to tell much the same story as traditional ones on variability differences among commodities.

CHAPTER V

BENEFITS AND COSTS FROM TRADE: THE CASE OF AGRICULTURAL EXPORT COMMODITIES

Introduction

The objective of this chapter is to analyze further the terms of trade issue from the point of view of the benefits and costs arising from trade in the export crops of developing countries. Because of data limitations, concentration is made on the study of export earnings from four major tropical commodities: cocoa, coffee, tea and sugar.

In order to obtain estimates of net gains from trade, a simple model of supply and demand is formulated; within this model a benefit-cost indicator of trade is defined. This indicator, which belongs to the class of measures based on the twin concepts of consumer and producer surplus, is shown to be a function of both the international and the domestic terms of trade and, therefore, dependent on domestic price policies as well as on the evolution of international markets.

Given this theoretical framework, first a review of the market situation and projects for each of the four commodities selected is presented. Then, using recent estimates of supply and demand elasticities, benefits and costs from trade by country are estimated. In order to obtain these estimates, gross benefits from trade (i.e., real export earnings or international income terms of trade), domestic BTT and net protection coefficients are computed. Combined with estimates of elasticity of demand and supply, these ingredients give the possibility of obtaining both the desired measure of net benefit and a meaningfull decomposition of its determinants.

The results of this analysis suggest two major conclusions. First, net benefits from trade for cocoa, sugar and tea have experienced a significant decline for the set of countries considered during the 1961-82 period. Only for coffee do they appear to have fluctuated around a near constant average. For the individual countries, however, the evidence of declines is sparser and less significant. Only four countries appear to have suffered significant real losses from movements in international prices, domestic price policies or exogenous shifts of different nature. Because of the considerable fluctuations involved, if any real loss has occurred, it has probably been compounded by instability.

Second, the analysis has shown that the domestic pricing policies followed by the producing countries as a group, have tended to depress domestic terms of trade and discourage production. The rise of the spread between domestic and international terms of trade appears broadly consistent, at the aggregate level, with the optimum tax prescription of the pure theory of trade. This behaviour, however, was probably effective in preventing welfare losses from static overproduction, but could not avoid the negative effects of other factors on the LDCs' terms of trade (e.g., productivity increases, commercial policies of industrial countries and negative consumption trends).

Terms of Trade and Cost-Benefit Analysis

The literature on terms of trade has been characterized by a sort of disregard of the concepts elaborated in parallel by the students of comparative advantage and project evaluation. In all probability, the reasons for the lack of communication between two streams of economic analysis so obviously related are mainly historical. The big debate on the deterioration of terms of trade started much before the cost-benefit concepts acquired any currency among theoretical economists. Furthermore, most of the terms of trade studies concern aggregate exchange ratios and can therefore be rigorously related to welfare economics concepts through index number theory in a national accounting framework. [1]

Partly as a consequence of this hiatus, the decline of international terms of trade faced by developing countries has become a dogma of the "structural" criticism levied by a number of economists, developing-country governments and international institutions against what is called "the present economic order". Paradoxically, in recent times, another group of economists and governments of developed countries, as well as sympathizing international institutions, have voiced the opposite contention that domestic terms of trade, arising from ill-guided market intervention policies, account for most of the evils facing agricultural production, export performance and growth in developing countries.

These two opposite claims, which appear at first to be highly contradictory, underline the lack of a comprehensive framework to capture welfare gains and losses from trade as a function of both domestic policies and international market conditions. On one hand, the argument based on the international terms of trade presumes identity or near identity between relative price changes and changes in welfare regardless of domestic policies. On the other hand, the contention that government induced distortions are responsible for welfare deterioration neglects both the exogenous changes in international prices and the effect domestic policies may have on their level.

A simple measure of the gains arising from export activities can be defined for a small country as the net social benefit.

$$W_i = P_i^x X_i - \sum_j P_j^m M_{ij}^x - \alpha \sum_k P_k Z_{ik}^x \tag{1}$$

where P_i^x = f.o.b. price of the i-th export good

P_j^m = c.i.f. price of the j-th import good

P_k = shadow price of the k-th domestic input

α = shadow exchange rate

X_i = quantity exported of the i-th good

M_{ij}^x = quantity used of the j-th importable input in the production of the quantity X_i of the i-th export good

Z_{ik}^x = quantity used of the k-th (non tradable) domestic input in the production of the quantity X_i of the i-th export good

In defining the shadow exchange rate, two different considerations are to be taken into account: (i) export and import prices differ from their corresponding domestic prices due to taxes, tariffs and other market distortions; and (ii) an appropriate set of deflators has to be specified to be able to compare the levels of net social benefit in two different time periods. Consideration (i) is at the base of the estimation method for shadow exchange rates in cost-benefit analysis, and thus requires no further elaboration. Consideration (ii), on the other hand, derives from the need to estimate "real" prices: a major task which in project evaluation is dealt with at the stage of estimating and forecasting shadow prices.

A simplifying assumption that permits a purchasing power parity definition of the shadow exchange rate is that domestic producers and international traders operate separately with two different sets of relative prices. Domestic producers operate under a set of prices P_i/P_c (i=1,2...n) where P_c is the price of a numeraire composite commodity (e.g., the basket of goods entering the consumer price index), while international traders use the ratios P_i^x/P_m, where P_m is an aggregate index of import prices.

Under the above hypotheses, the measure for net social benefit in (1) can be modified as follows:

$$W_i^* = \frac{W_i}{P_m} = \frac{P_i^x}{P_m} X_i - \sum_j \frac{P_j^m}{P_m} M_{ij}^x - \sum_k \frac{P_k}{P_c} Z_{ik}^x \qquad (2)$$

Expression (2) can be derived from expression (1) by taking the composite import good corresponding to P_m as numeraire (and thereby dividing both members of (1) by P_m) and by defining the shadow exchange rate as $\alpha = P_m/P_c$, that is, the purchasing power parity rate in terms of the two baskets of goods and related import and domestic prices.

Under the assumptions made, the net social benefit associated with the export X_i, is measured in (2) in terms of importables. It is thus possible to rewrite this expression using the terms of trade notation as follows:

$$W_i^* = BTT_i \quad X_i - C_i^x \qquad (3)$$

Net benefit = Barter terms of trade for the i-th commodity | Quantity exported | Cost of exporting X_i

If the technology is of the fixed coefficient type, expression (3) can be normalized dividing both of its members by the quantity exported X_i, thereby yielding:

$$w_i^* = W_i^*/X_i = BTT_i - c_i^x \qquad (4)$$

Net benefit per unit of exports | Barter terms of trade | Unit cost of exporting of X_i

As expression (4) shows, the BTT are only one component of the net benefits from the export activity, even in the case of input-output technology. An increase or decrease in the BTT, therefore, is only one source of potential change in welfare.

If technology is not of the fixed coefficient variety, on the other hand, expression (2) can be written as follows:

$$W_i^* = ITT_i - C_i^x \qquad (5)$$

Net benefit — Income terms of trade — Cost of exporting X_i

The use of ITT to measure the evolution of net benefits from export activities can thus be seen as a step forward from the use of BTT, in the sense that the underlying assumptions are somewhat weaker in the ITT case. However, under a fixed coefficient technology, a sufficient condition for the BTT to be an unbiased indicator of net benefits is that the unit cost of production remains constant over the period of comparison. Vice versa, when the technology is not of the input-output type, the ITT can be an unbiased indicator of net benefits only under the more stringent condition that no changes have occurred either in the unit costs or in the export volume.

In a similar way, the attempt to adjust for the increase/decrease in the productivity of one factor yields:

$$\frac{W_i^*}{Z_k} = SFTT_{ki} - \frac{C_i^x}{Z_k} \qquad (6)$$

Net benefit per unit of factor k — Single factorial terms of trade for the k-th factor — Cost of exporting per unit of factor k

where (6) has been derived from (2) dividing both members by Z_k and $SFTT_{ki}$ = BTT_i x (average productivity of factor k). Even in this case, the amended terms of trade variable, SFTT, turns out to be an unbiased indicator of net social benefit only under special circumstances on the composition and stationarity of production costs. In general, it will only be a component, and not necessarily a major one, of the evolution of net benefits from trade.

Measuring the Welfare Consequences of Terms of Trade Changes

A simple approach to measure the welfare level W_i^*, which has been widely used by trade specialists (see, for example, Bhagwati, 1965), is based on the concept of economic surplus. Earlier experimentation with trade measures based on this concept starts probably with Johnson (1958), and typically focuses on the welfare gains and losses caused by tariffs, taxes and other instruments of commercial policy. More recently, aggregate estimates based on a generalized concept of producer and/or consumer surplus (derived from duality theory) have been used to measure aggregate welfare gains and losses from trade. For example, Burgess (1974) estimated the welfare gains for the United States. Resulting from a decrease in import prices and analogous estimates were obtained by Kohli for Canada (1978), Australia (1983), and Switzerland (1982).

The relevant economic surplus for an export commodity is the sum of consumers' and producers' surplus. This sum, called net social payoff (NSP) by Samuelson (1952) in a seminal article, arises from the existence of an excess supply curve for the export good as shown in Figure 5.1.

Figure 5.1: Excess Supply Curve

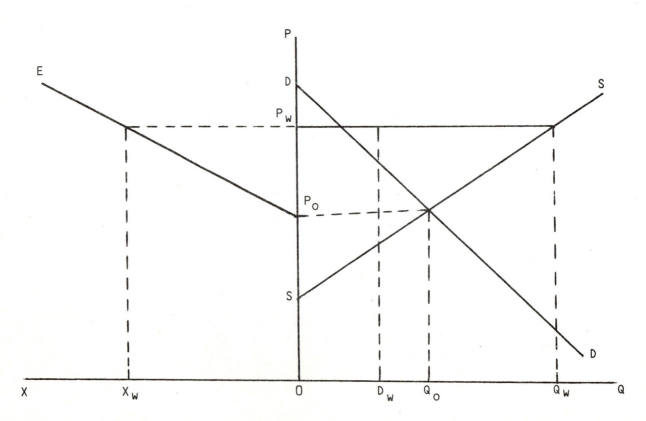

In the right hand quadrant of this figure a domestic market equilibrium with trade is shown as resulting from the intersection of the demand function DD and the supply function SS with the world price P_w. At this price, domestic supply equals Q_w, domestic demand equals D_w and the exportable surplus equals $Q_w - D_w$. This exportable surplus is reported in the left-hand quadrant of the figure, where the horizontal scale measures surplus quantities (i.e., production "net" of domestic consumption). An excess supply function $P_o E$ can thus be generated by varying the international price and reporting the surplus calculated according to the curves of the right quadrant into the left quadrant.

The excess supply curve has two interesting characteristics. First, its slope in any point is the difference between the slopes of the demand and supply function. Second, if it is read in its inverse form, it measures the marginal cost associated with each surplus quantity equal to X + D, that is, to the quantity exported augmented by the amount consumed. For this reason, the area under the excess supply curve measures the opportunity cost of producing the surplus. The area over the excess supply function on the other hand, measures the net economic surplus that would accrue to the country if the surplus production were sold at world price. This area equals the sum of producer and consumer surplus (i.e., the area between the supply function and the two prices P_o and P_w in the right quadrant).

In Figure 5.2, which reports a more general non-linear form of the excess supply function SS, the export level is shown at X_i^o in correspondence to domestic price P_i^o/P_o. Because the international price P_i^x/P_m is higher than P_i^o/P_c^o, the exporting country loses all the surplus (i.e., the potential NSP) relative to the area BS'S''. The actual NSP enjoyed by the country is thus the triangle AS'(P_i^o/P_c^o) plus the rectangle (P_i^o/P_c^o) S'B (P_i^x/P_m).

Algebraically, the general expression for the sub-optimal NSP indicated in Figure 5.2 is:

$$NSP = W = \int_A^{po} x(t)\, dt + (p^* - po)x^o \qquad (7)$$

where $po = P_i^o/P_c^o$, $p^* = P_i^x/P_m$, $x=X_i$, $x^o = X_i^o$

Figure 5.2: <u>Non-Linear Excess Supply Function</u>

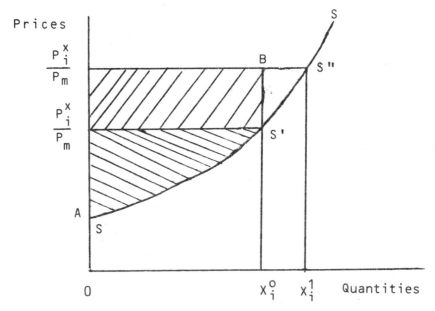

The simplest approximation to the measure in (7) is given by a linearization through the origin of the excess supply function x. Assuming $x = \lambda\, po$, after solving the integral and simplifying, yields:

$$W = \lambda\, po\, (p^* - \tfrac{1}{2} po) \qquad (8)$$

where λ = a constant

A better approximation is given by the exponential (double logarithmic) function $x_i = \lambda(po)^\varepsilon$, which yields:

$$W = \lambda(po)^\varepsilon \left(p^* - \tfrac{\varepsilon}{1+\varepsilon} po\right) \qquad (9)$$

where ε = elasticity of export supply

As extensive recent literature on the topic has shown, the area between the demand and the supply functions, which is measurable through (8) and (9), can be considered a good approximation of the benefits (costs) accruing to consumers and producers as a consequence of alternative price policies. [2/]

Expression (9) can be cast in terms of international (IBT) and domestic (DBT) barter terms of trade, by defining the "net" nominal protection coefficient, NNPC = DBT/IBT:

$$W = \lambda (NNPC)^\varepsilon \cdot (IBT)^{1+\varepsilon}(1 - \frac{\varepsilon}{1+\varepsilon} NNPC) = \lambda (DBT)^{1+\varepsilon} (\frac{1}{NNPC} - \frac{\varepsilon}{1+\varepsilon}) \qquad (10)$$

These latter two expressions define the welfare measure as dependent on two exogenous variables: the IBT and the NNPC. These two variables, however, are not unrelated to each other since the protection coefficient, which is essentially a policy variable, is influenced by the evolution of the BTT, while the terms of trade themselves must be ultimately affected by the policy decisions on domestic terms of trade and by the ensuing level of supply of the exporting countries.

Before proceeding to a more detailed exploration of this relationship, it is important to underline the twofold dependence of the welfare gain on both the exogenous variable and the policy variable. The interdependence between these two factors does not seem to have been fully realized, either in the controversy on the international terms of trade or in the recent discussion on domestic price policy. Differentiating partially with respect to IBT in (10), the following is obtained:

$$\frac{\partial (W)}{\partial (IBT)} = \lambda (1 + \varepsilon) (NNPC)^\varepsilon \cdot (IBT)^\varepsilon (1 - \frac{1}{1+\varepsilon} NNPC) \qquad (11)$$

The value of this expression is lower than zero if $NNPC > \frac{1+\varepsilon}{\varepsilon}$. This value represents an upper bound, in the sense that if domestic protection is pushed above such a threshold, a deterioration of the international terms of trade will improve country welfare.

In order to understand this result, which is quite important to identify benefits and costs due to domestic and international circumstances, note that expression (10), from which (11) derives, can be written as follows:

$$\dot{W} = (IBT) \cdot X \frac{(1 - \dot{X})}{1+ \varepsilon} = \frac{1}{1+\varepsilon}[IBT \cdot X - IBT \cdot X \cdot \dot{X}] \qquad (12)$$

where $\dot{X} = \varepsilon \frac{(po - p^*)}{p^*}$ is the percentage increase of domestic production due to protection.

The welfare generated by trade under protection is thus proportional to the export value at international prices (i.e., the so called "income terms of trade") minus the part of such value that protection has subtracted from other sectors of the economy. If the latter part is greater than the former, trade in commodity i is not beneficial. In these conditions, as ascertained by (11), a deterioration in international relative prices for the commodity in question will enhance a country's welfare by favouring the switching of resources to other sectors. 3/

Differentiating W in (10) with repsect to NNPC yields:

$$\frac{\partial (W)}{\partial (NNPC)} = \lambda \varepsilon (NNPC)^\varepsilon (IBT)^{1+\varepsilon} (\frac{1}{NNPC} - 1) \qquad (13)$$

This expression is less than zero if NNPC > 1, as predicted by the well-known free trade propositions. Note, however, the difference between the two conditions established by expressions (11) and (12): (i) if NNPC > $\frac{1+\varepsilon}{\varepsilon}$, exporting the commodity entails a net loss for the country since resources are forced into the sector via "net" protection, (ii) if NNPC > 1 (a weaker condition than the former one), trade may still be beneficial but welfare would rise by lowering the rate of protection.

If the net protection coefficient is less than unity, on the other hand, that is, if the commodity is anti-protected, expressions (11) and (13) can be used to measure respectively, the extent to which an improvement respectively, in the terms of trade or in the level of protection would improve the country welfare position. As expression (12) shows, negative or anti-protection implies a positive sign both for the benefits (the "income terms" of trade) and the costs (the value of resources that would flow into the sector should anti-protection decrease). The extent to which a terms of trade improvement would help or a deterioration hurt the country would thus depend, among other things, on the difference $|NNPC - \frac{\varepsilon}{1+\varepsilon}|$ or $|\dot{X} - 1|$. At the same time, the extent to which increase in protection would improve welfare would be directly a function of the difference $|1 - NNPC| \cdot \varepsilon$ or $|\dot{X}|$.

An additive decomposition of the welfare measure into a domestic and an international BTT effect, for any given level of protection can further be obtained by differentiating logarithmically expression (9):

$$\dot{W} = [\frac{\varepsilon(1+\varepsilon)(1-NNPC)}{1+\varepsilon(1-NNPC)}] \dot{DBT} + [\frac{1+\varepsilon}{1+\varepsilon(1-NNPC)}] \dot{IBT} \qquad (14)$$

where the dots indicate the logarithmic derivative.

Expression (14) shows that the percentage increase in welfare from trade depends positively on DBT and IBT if the relevant NNPC is less than one, i.e., if the commodity is "anti-protected". If the NNPC equals one, the increase in welfare depends only on the movement of the IBT. Finally, if the NNPC is greater than one, i.e., the commodity is "protected", the effect of a positive change in both DBT and IBT will be negative, i.e., welfare will show a negative correlation with movements in both DBT and IBT.

More than expression (13), expression (14) demonstrates that the IBT measure is an unreliable indicator of welfare changes unless it is considered in conjunction with domestic price policies and some measurement of resource opportunity costs (in this case the supply elasticity). Similarly, evaluation of domestic price policies, i.e., whether it is beneficial to raise or to lower domestic terms of trade depend on the same parameters.

The preceding results can be extended to the case of a large country by considering marginal revenues rather than prices in the international terms of trade:

$$R^* = p^* \left(1 - \frac{1}{|\eta|}\right) \qquad (15)$$

where R^* = marginal revenue
$|\eta|$ = absolute value of the elasticity of export demand facing the country with respect to $p^* = P_i^X/P_m$

This implies that for the individual country, the "optimum" NNPC can be defined as:

$$NNPC^* = \frac{p_o}{p^*} \frac{|\eta|}{|\eta| - 1} = NNPC \frac{|\eta|}{|\eta| - 1} \qquad (16)$$

Given these definitions, all the results obtained for the small country case apply to the large country with the proviso that IBT is substituted by R^* defined as in (15) and NNPC is substituted by NNPC*, defined as in (16).

The International Market for Tropical Commodities

Commodity trade presents two major trends for developing countries over the last 30 years: (i) a progressive decline in importance of agricultural raw materials both as a portion of world exports and of developing country exports; and (ii) a parallel increase of exports of fuels and manufactures. The fall in agricultural raw materials as a percentage of world exports (Table 5.1) is only matched by the fall in food and beverages. LDCs' share of world exports, during the 1965-82 period, fell by almost 50 percent for food and beverages, by 65 percent for agricultural raw materials and by 40 percent for minerals and metals (Table 5.2).

Table 5.1: **Product Composition of World Exports** [a]/
(%)

	1955	1960	1965	1970	1975	1981
Type of goods						
Food and beverages	21.8	19.4	18.4	14.7	13.2	11.3
Agricultural raw materials	12.9	10.8	8.1	5.8	3.9	3.5
Minerals and metals	12.2	13.0	12.2	12.7	9.7	7.6
Fuels	11.0	9.9	9.6	9.2	19.3	24.2
Total raw materials	57.9	53.1	48.3	42.4	46.1	46.6
(Total excluding fuels)	(46.9)	(43.2)	(38.7)	(33.2)	(26.8)	(22.4)
Manufactured products	40.5	45.7	50.1	55.5	52.0	52.0
TOTAL EXPORTS [b]/	100.0	100.0	100.0	100.0	100.0	100.0

[a]/ Based on export values in current U.S. dollar terms.

[b]/ Including products not otherwise classified and statistical discrepancies.

Source: UNCTAD, Handbook of International Trade and Development Statistics, various issues.

Table 5.2: **Product Composition of Developing Countries' Exports** [a]
(%)

Type of goods	1965	1970	1975	1980	1982
Food and beverages	43.2	36.3	32.2	23.4	21.9
Agricultural raw materials	13.8	13.2	7.5	6.5	4.8
Minerals and metals	13.6	18.9	11.9	10.1	8.2
Fuels	8.5	7.8	18.1	22.2	25.0
Total raw materials	79.1	76.2	69.7	62.2	59.9
(Total excluding fuels)	(70.6)	(68.4)	(51.6)	(40.0)	(34.9)
Manufactured products	14.0	23.3	29.6	36.0	38.5
TOTAL EXPORTS [b]	100.0	100.0	100.0	100.0	100.0

[a] Excluding OPEC countries.

[b] Including statistical discrepancies.

Source: UNCTAD, Handbook of International Trade and Development Statistics, various issues.

The decline in importance of commodity trade in the balance of payments of the _average_ developing country, however, does not imply that most traditional exporters have freed themselves from dependence on weak commodity markets. As Table 5.3 shows, the distribution of commodity exports is still highly concentrated, with almost 50 percent of the countries considered deriving more than 50 percent of their export earnings from the five most important raw materials.

Table 5.4 shows the importance of the four commodities considered in this study for the balance of trade of the developing countries that export the same commodities. For most of these countries the commodities in question account for a large, albeit declining share of export earnings. Despite the underlying process of diversification, the data collected in

Table 5.3: **Developing Countries' Export Earnings from Raw Materials (Sample of 69 Developing Countries)**

% of export earnings derived from all raw materials	Frequencies					
	1960		1970-72		1976-78	
	Simple	Cumulative	Simple	Cumulative	Simple	Cumulative
0-10	2	2	2	2	4	4
10-20	1	3	3	5	1	5
20-30	2	5	7	12	7	12
30-40	5	10	2	14	6	18
40-50	4	14	9	13	7	25
50-60	3	17	6	29	10	35
60-70	7	24	12	41	11	46
70-80	17	41	9	50	13	59
80-90	11	51	12	62	6	65
90-100	17	69	7	69	4	69

% of export earnings derived from the 5 most important raw materials	Frequencies					
	1960		1970-72		1976-78	
	Simple	Cumulative	Simple	Cumulative	Simple	Cumulative
0-10	2	2	2	2	4	4
10-20	1	3	3	5	2	6
20-30	2	5	7	12	8	14
30-40	7	12	3	15	6	20
40-50	3	15	11	26	7	27
50-60	5	20	9	35	9	36
60-70	6	26	9	44	11	47
70-80	19	45	11	55	14	61
80-90	10	55	7	62	4	65
90-100	14	69	7	69	4	69

Source: World Bank, <u>Commodity Trade and Price Trends</u>, various issues.

Table 5.4: **Percentage of Cocoa, Coffee, Tea and Sugar Exports Over Total Exports (f.o.b. Prices)**

Country	Commodity	\	\	Years	\	\	\
		1960	1965	1970	1975	1980	1984
Cameroon	: Cocoa	33.8	21.3	24.2	25.4	15.3	21.0
Ghana	: Cocoa	63.3	65.7	43.3	65.1	56.1	53.0
Côte d'Ivoire	: Cocoa	23.4	16.0	20.5	18.6	25.2	31.7
	: Coffee	50.1	37.9	33.0	24.1	20.5	17.7
	: Total	73.5	53.9	53.5	42.7	45.7	49.4
Nigeria	: Cocoa	21.7	15.9	15.0	3.7	0.9	2.2
Dominican Republic	: Sugar	46.0	46.0	48.6	63.0	29.8	32.0
	: Cocoa	8.0	5.0	8.9	2.8	5.3	7.3
	: Total	54.0	51.0	57.5	65.8	35.1	39.3
Brazil	: Cocoa	5.5	1.7	2.8	2.5	1.4	0.9
	: Tea	0.1	0.1	0.1	0.1	0.1	0.1
	: Coffee	56.2	44.3	34.3	9.9	12.3	9.5
	: Sugar	4.5	3.6	4.6	11.2	4.7	1.4
	: Total	66.3	54.7	46.8	23.7	18.5	11.9
Ecuador	: Cocoa	14.8	10.6	10.0	4.3	1.3	3.7
Kenya	: Tea	8.3	10.0	13.2	10.6	12.1	16.8
	: Coffee	19.1	17.5	20.3	15.8	20.6	21.8
	: Total	27.4	27.5	33.5	26.4	32.7	38.6
Malawi	: Tea	–	27.7	21.7	17.7	12.5	18.1
Tanzania	: Tea	1.8	2.2	2.3	2.9	4.2	4.7
Argentina	: Tea	0.2	0.5	0.5	0.5	0.3	0.6
Bangladesh	: Tea	–	5.9	10.9	4.5	4.4	9.8
India	: Tea	18.9	13.2	9.7	6.6	7.0	6.1
Indonesia	: Tea	3.3	2.4	1.6	0.7	0.5	1.0
	: Coffee	1.6	4.5	6.0	1.4	3.0	2.5
	: Total	4.9	6.9	7.6	2.1	3.5	3.5

Table 5.4 (cont).

Country	Commodity	\multicolumn{6}{c}{Years}					
		1960	1965	1970	1975	1980	1984
Sri Lanka	: Tea	59.7	62.1	71.1	49.1	40.3	45.9
Ethiopia	: Coffee	52.1	66.4	59.8	31.9	64.2	58.6
Uganda	: Coffee	34.5	41.3	50.9	76.4	94.7	86.9
Colombia	: Coffee	71.4	63.8	63.5	46.1	59.8	48.7
El Salvador	: Coffee	65.5	50.8	52.2	32.9	63.4	55.4
Mexico	: Coffee	8.1	6.6	6.7	6.5	2.7	1.8
Mauritius	: Sugar	89.7	90.9	88.4	81.4	63.4	48.5
Philippines	: Sugar	23.8	16.6	16.3	25.3	9.6	4.4
Thailand	: Sugar	-	0.5	0.6	11.8	2.2	2.8
Guyana	: Sugar	45.3	26.5	27.1	48.6	31.9	36.1

\- = Indicates that the amount is negligible or nil

Source: FAO, <u>Trade Yearbook</u>, various issues.

the table suggest that commodity trade remains an important source of export earnings and that dependence on international commodity markets is still an issue of concern to developing countries.

Given these premises, the analysis is made by examining in some detail the performance of cocoa, tea, coffee and sugar, for the major exporters, using as the basic framework the model specified in the preceding sections.

Cocoa

Cocoa beans are exclusively produced by developing countries with 74 percent of the 1982/84 production concentrated in five countries: Brazil, Côte d'Ivoire, Ghana, Nigeria and Cameroon (Table 5.5). Production within these main producers, once strongly concentrated in Ghana and Nigeria (which in 1964/1966 detained a share respectively of 34 percent and 18 percent of the world market), has undergone a redistribution in favour of Brazil and Côte d'Ivoire. These two countries accounted in 1982/84 respectively for 22 percent and 27 percent of world production, against 12 and 10 percent, correspondingly, for 1964/66. Ghana and Nigeria shares, however, fell to 11 percent and 9 percent of the total.

Table 5.5: **Cocoa Production by Main Countries** a/

Country	Production			Shares in world total			Exponential growth rates
	1964/1966	1974/1976	1982/1984	1964/1966	1974/1976	1982/1984	1964-84
	('000 m.t.)			(%)			(%/yr)
Brazil	162	252	359	11.8	16.9	21.7	4.59
Colombia	17	27	39	1.2	1.8	2.4	5.10
Ecuador	46	77	66	3.4	5.2	4.0	1.87
Dominican Rep.	31	34	41	2.3	2.3	2.5	1.35
Cameroon	86	100	111	6.3	6.7	6.7	0.99
Côte d'Ivoire	137	235	441	10.0	15.8	26.7	7.26
Ghana	459	370	179	33.5	24.8	10.8	-4.56
Nigeria	250	198	140	18.2	13.3	8.5	-3.09
WORLD TOTAL	1372	1490	1654	100.0	100.0	100.0	1.12

a/ Cocoa beans.

Source: FAO, *Production Yearbook*, various issues.

Performance differences among the major producers are due to a variety of causes, the most prominent of which seems to be the differences in real producer prices (Table 5.6). These differences have been the consequence of direct taxation policies as well as of differences in the movements of exchange and inflation rates.

Table 5.6: **Trends in Real Cocoa Producer Prices in Major Producing Countries** a/

(%/yr.)

Country	1960-80	1960-70	1970-80
Brazil	5.6	-0.8	14.1
Côte d'Ivoire	-0.1	-4.8	2.1
Ghana	-5.0	-6.1	-8.9
Nigeria	-0.3	-4.0	0.7
Cameroon	-2.3	-3.6	-2.0
WORLD b/	4.4	2.5	8.6

a/ Producer prices deflated by the consumer price indices of the various countries.

b/ U.S. import unit values deflated by the manufactured exports unit value.

Source: Akiyama and Duncan 1982 (Table 2).

In addition to movements in real prices, which explain most of the fall in production in Ghana and Nigeria during the 1960s and 1970s, and much of the increase in Côte d'Ivoire and Brazil during the 1970s, producer subsidies and direct investment in research and extension appear to also be a factor of differential producer performance. Brazil and Cameroon, in particular, have benefited from the expansion of hybrid plantings and the diffusion of modern methods of cultivation, in both cases sponsored or supported by government policies.

World cocoa production shows a pattern of seven- to ten-year cycles of increasing production-cum-decreasing prices and stagnant production-cum-increasing prices (Figure 5.3). These cycles in turn are due to adjustment lags by producers and to the tree-crop plantation cycle.

Figure 5.3: World Production — COCOA
(1000 mt)

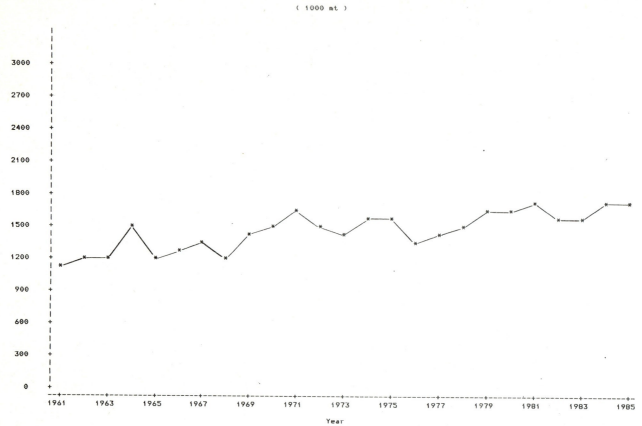

Source : FAO — Production Yearbook, various issues.

International Prices — COCOA a)
Yearly average (U.S. cents/kg)

Legend :   * $ current prices
           — 1980 $ constant prices

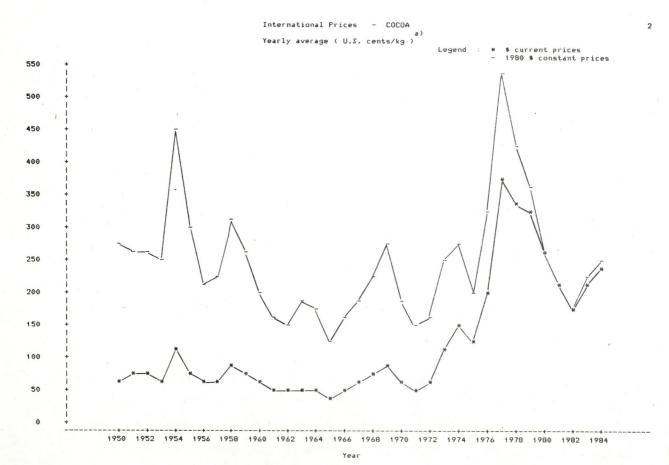

a) ICCO — average prices New York and London
Source : World Bank — Commodity Trade and Price Trends (1986 ed.).

Traditional varieties of cocoa trees start producing only five years after planting and production increases continuously up to the 11th year, after which yields tend to decline unless proper care is taken of the trees and increasing quantities of fertilizer and pesticides are used. Hybrid varieties, on the other hand, show higher yields, shorter gestation periods (three years) and shorter cycles, with peak production at the seventh year and a much sharper tendency to yield declines after 10-15 years.

Because domestic consumption of cocoa in developing countries is very low, most of the cocoa produced is exported. Domestic supply conditions in LDCs are, therefore, the almost exclusive determinant of export supply, while domestic demand conditions in DCs shape world demand for cocoa exports. The evolution of processing costs of cocoa in developing countries relative to the industrialized ones, however, has determined in recent years a trend toward a significant shift in the way cocoa production is traded. This trend, which clearly emerges from Tables 5.5 and 5.7, implies that an increasing amount of cocoa beans is ground in LDCs mostly by foreign producers. As a consequence, trade statistics contain an increase in the real value of cocoa exports, which is largely accounted for by the higher value added incorporated in the product, rather than by increases in the income terms of trade.

In order to measure the evolution of cocoa supply, it is necessary to use a model that takes into account (i) the tree-crop nature of the basic produce, (ii) its cyclical behaviour, and (iii) the evolution of the quality of the product exported.

Because most of the producing countries retain a relatively large share of the market, it is also necessary to take into account the elasticity with respect to price of the export demand function faced by each of them. This elasticity permits estimating the NNPC* adjusted for the "large" country case as in equation (15).

Table 5.7: **Cocoa Exports by Main Countries**

Country	Exports			Shares in world total			Exponential growth rates
	1964/ 1966	1974/ 1976	1982/ 1984	1964/ 1966	1974/ 1976	1982/ 1984	1964-84
	('000 m.t.)			(%)			(%/yr)
Brazil							
Cocoa beans	93	145	135	8.0	12.4	10.9	2.16
Cocoa pdcts.	22	72	144	5.5	8.5	11.0	11.87
Total	115	217	279	7.4	10.7	11.0	5.50
Colombia							
Cocoa beans	–	–	2	–	–	0.2	
Cocoa pdcts.	–	5	2	–	0.6	0.2	41.72 a/
Total	–	5	4	–	0.3	0.2	
Ecuador							
Cocoa beans	33	43	32	2.8	3.7	2.6	-4.41
Cocoa pdcts.	1	19	32	0.3	2.2	2.4	34.22
Total	34	62	64	2.2	3.1	2.5	3.31
Dominican Rep.							
Cocoa beans	25	24	35	2.2	2.1	2.8	1.02
Cocoa pdcts.	4	2	3	1.0	0.2	0.2	1.30
Total	29	26	38	1.9	1.3	1.5	0.92
Cameroon							
Cocoa beans	74	77	85	6.4	6.6	6.9	0.51
Cocoa pdcts.	11	25	13	2.7	2.9	1.0	0.73
Total	85	102	98	5.4	5.1	3.8	2.00
Côte d'Ivoire							
Cocoa beans	125	190	334	10.8	16.3	27.0	6.20
Cocoa pdcts.	8	35	62	2.0	4.1	4.7	14.02
Total	133	225	396	8.5	11.1	15.5	6.58
Ghana							
Cocoa beans	429	321	178	37.0	27.5	14.4	-4.77
Cocoa pdcts.	38	38	13	9.4	4.5	1.0	-5.33
Total	467	359	191	29.8	17.8	7.5	4.99
Nigeria							
Cocoa beans	233	205	138	20.1	17.5	11.2	-2.85
Cocoa pdcts.	–	18	19	–	2.1	1.5	3.86 a/
Total	233	223	157	14.9	11.0	6.2	2.51
WORLD							
Cocoa beans	1161	1169	1235	100.0	100.0	100.0	0.24
Cocoa pdcts.	404	850	1314	100.0	100.0	100.0	6.56
TOTAL	1565	2020	2549	100.0	100.0	100.0	2.64

a/ 1967-84.

– = Indicates that the amount is negligible or nil.

Source: FAO, <u>Trade Yearbook</u>, various issues.

Table 5.8 summarizes the estimates of export supply and demand elasticities with respect to prices that were chosen to be used in this study. Supply elasticities are generally taken from the study of Akiyama and Duncan (1982), while country demand elasticities are obtained by dividing the world demand elasticity, taken from the same study, by the average world export share of each country. The underlying data on cocoa supply include not only cocoa grindings (as a proxy for cocoa consumption), but also other cocoa products (cocoa butter, powder, paste and cake). Because world demand is strongly inelastic (-0.30), producing countries can follow either a "selfish" strategy by imposing an optimum tariff, or they can try cooperatively to restrict world production with a quota system.

Table 5.8: **Cocoa Export Price Elasticities**

Country	Supply	Demand c/
Cameroon	0.590 b/	-4.545
Ghana	0.126 b/	-2.083
Côte d'Ivoire	0.590 b/	-1.840
Nigeria	0.113 b/	-2.679
Dominican Republic	0.550 a/	-14.286
Brazil	0.540 b/	-2.752
Ecuador	0.540 b/	-11.538
WORLD DEMAND b/		-0.300

a/ Own estimates.

b/ Akiyama and Duncan (1982). They relate to price elasticity of supply.

c/ World demand elasticity divided by the average market share (1964/66, 1974/76 and 1982/84 averages were computed and then the median of the three was selected).

Table 5.9, which presents data analyzing the price strategy followed by cocoa producers, clearly shows two points. First, the NNPC for cocoa, measured as a ratio of domestic and the international terms of trade, is smaller, even though often not significantly different than the uncorrected coefficient (NPC), which is measured as a ratio of domestic and border prices converted at the official exchange rate for all countries except Nigeria. For Ghana, there appears to be a large discrepancy between the parity exchange rate (based on the ratio between import prices and domestic consumer prices) and the official rate. This difference signals the large overvaluation of the cedi during the years considered. For Nigeria, on the other hand, there appears to have been a slight undervaluation.

Table 5.9: **Cocoa: Net Nominal Protection Coefficients (NNPC) with and without the Adjustment for Market Share, and Nominal Protection Coefficients (NPC), 1961-82**

Country	NNPC	"Optimum" NNPC	NNPC with the adjustment (NNPC/Optimum)	NPC	NPC with the adjustment (NPC/Optimum)
Cameroon	0.457 (0.126)	0.780	0.586	0.458 (0.127)	0.587
Ghana	0.444 (0.222)	0.520	0.854	0.935 (1.257)	1.798
Nigeria	0.388 (0.119)	0.627	0.619	0.282 (0.108)	0.449
Brazil	0.614 (0.288)	0.637	0.964	0.652 (0.158)	1.024
Côte d'Ivoire	0.417 (0.114)	0.457	0.912	0.500 (0.117)	1.094
Ecuador	0.817 (0.152)	0.913	0.895	0.907 (0.173)	0.993
Dom. Rep.	0.611 (0.141)	0.930	0.657	0.917 (0.276)	0.986
TOTAL	0.536 (0.225)	0.571	0.939	0.667 (0.538)	1.168

Note: Figures in parentheses are standard deviations.

Second, for five out of seven countries (the exceptions being Cameroon and Nigeria), there is no significant difference between the "optimum" NNPC corresponding to the "selfish" strategy and the average uncorrected NPC. The corrected NNPC, on the other hand, is significantly different from the optimum in five out of seven cases. Thus, most countries seem to have chosen an optimum "selfish" strategy, but at the same time they were affected by a kind of "currency illusion".

Table 5.10 shows the estimates of the percentage changes of benefits from trade according to the decomposition indicated in expression (14). Overall, the results show that both the benefit changes and its components are: (i) negative, (ii) of varying size and (iii) not significantly different to zero. These characteristics are generally confirmed at the country level, where, however, there appear to be two cases of positive effects of domestic policies. [5/] The results are also confirmed by trend analysis (see Appendix V) of the benefit levels, computed according to equation (16) and its components.

Table 5.10: **Cocoa: Decomposition of Benefits from Trade**

(mean % change/yr.)

Country	Benefits from trade	DBT effect	IBT effect
Cameroon	-0.922 (6.953)	0.244 (1.427)	-1.166 (6.460)
Ghana	-1.168 (5.977)	-0.566 (0.457)	-0.601 (5.853)
Nigeria	-0.409 (6.991)	-0.052 (0.299)	-0.357 (6.903)
Brazil	-11.289 (12.319)	-1.528 (7.123)	-9.762 (13.884)
Côte d'Ivoire	-4.814 (8.179)	0.102 (0.483)	-4.916 (8.377)
Ecuador	-2.884 (8.433)	-1.184 (0.742)	-1.700 (8.294)
Dominican Rep.	-4.667 (10.669)	-1.294 (1.975)	-3.372 (9.266)
TOTAL	-3.773 (3.274)	-0.617 (1.077)	-2.156 (3.277)

Note: Figures in parentheses are standard errors.

Coffee

As in the case of cocoa, coffee production is concentrated in developing countries largely because of ecological requirements. The market structure includes a number of countries with vastly different market power. The predominant traditional producing countries are in Latin America, with Brazil the largest single producer, although Africa's production has been rapidly growing. Latin America's share of world production has been declining, from about 66 percent in 1964/66 to about 61 percent in 1974/76, mainly due to the falling trend of Brazil's production since the early 1960s. On the other hand, during the same period, Africa's share has increased from 27 percent to 29 percent and the Far East's share from 6 percent to 8 percent. However, in 1980/84 Africa's share of world production has fallen to 23 percent, while Latin America's share has increased to 65 percent (Table 5.11). Brazil's production still continues to be the crucial influence on world coffee production and the main determinant of world coffee prices as well.

Coffee trees mature in 10 to 12 years and begin bearing a substantial crop in about four to five years. Output diminishes after 20 years. The crop cycle combined with an inelastic demand introduces a supply lag that is posited to substantially contribute to cyclical price fluctuations in this market. Weather conditions and the last year's crop are the main determinants of the crop size.

Most of the producing countries export virtually all the coffee they grow (Table 5.11 and Table 5.12). Among the few where domestic consumption is substantial are: Brazil, Ethiopia, India, Indonesia and Mexico. Consumption by producing countries shows no significant trend for the 1961-80 period.

Owing to competition from other beverages such as soft drinks, juices and tea, growth rates of consumption in coffee importing countries declined substantially in the 1970s compared with the 1960s.

Table 5.11: **Coffee Production, by Economic Regions and Main Countries**

Econ. region/ country	Production			Shares in World total			Exponential Growth rates
	1964/ 1966	1974/ 1976	1982/ 1984	1964/ 1966	1974/ 1976	1982/ 1984	1964-84
	('000 m.t)			(%)			(%/yr)
Developing market econ.	4529	4284	5242	99.7	99.7	99.5	1.38
Latin America	2835	2632	3416	66.4	61.2	64.9	1.38
Brazil	1513	1088	1321	35.4	25.3	25.1	-0.21
Colombia	484	489	819	11.3	11.4	15.6	3.30
Mexico	167	220	269	3.9	5.1	5.1	2.10
Guatemala	113	152	161	2.7	3.5	3.1	2.48
El Salvador	118	153	156	2.8	3.6	3.0	1.66
Africa	1150	1249	1185	26.9	29.1	22.5	0.00
Ethiopia	150	168	221	3.5	3.9	4.2	1.91
Uganda	159	178	181	3.7	4.1	3.4	-0.99
Kenya	46	72	95	1.1	1.7	1.8	4.75
Côte d'Ivoire	249	258	201	5.8	6.0	3.8	-0.31
Far East	256	361	589	6.0	8.4	11.2	5.18
India	65	88	129	1.5	2.1	2.5	4.18
Indonesia	132	171	259	3.1	4.0	4.9	4.43
Near East	6	4	4	0.1	0.1	0.1	-1.27
WORLD TOTAL	4272	4299	5267	100.0	100.0	100.0	1.39

Source: FAO, Production Yearbook, various issues.

Table 5.12: **Coffee Exports, by Economic Regions and Main Countries** a/

	Exports			Shares in World total			Exponential Growth Rates
Econ. Region/ country	1964/ 1966	1974/ 1976	1982/ 1984	1964/ 1966	1974/ 1976	1982/ 1984	1964-84
	('000 m.t)			(%)			(%/yr)
Developing market econ.	2858	3371	3838	98.8	96.5	96.8	1.18
Latin America	1804	1959	2383	62.1	56.1	60.1	1.00
Brazil	905	757	953	31.1	21.7	24.0	-1.27
Colombia	352	425	559	12.1	12.2	14.1	2.82
Mexico	90	138	151	3.1	4.0	3.8	3.21
Guatemala	93	125	137	3.2	3.6	3.5	2.50
El Salvador	102	146	154	3.5	4.2	3.9	2.12
Africa	878	1142	969	30.2	32.7	24.4	0.24
Ethiopia	75	60	88	2.6	1.7	2.2	0.33
Uganda	155	186	151	5.3	5.3	3.8	-1.18
Kenya	45	72	97	1.6	2.1	2.5	4.71
Côte d'Ivoire	190	280	235	6.5	8.0	5.9	1.64
Far East	157	230	435	5.4	6.6	11.0	5.27
India	27	52	74	0.9	1.5	1.9	6.15
Indonesia	88	126	254	3.0	3.6	6.4	6.45
Near East	9	4	4	0.3	0.1	0.1	-5.47
WORLD TOTAL	2907	3493	3967	100.0	100.0	100.0	1.33

a/ Coffee green.

Source: FAO, Trade Yearbook, various issues.

Figure 5.4: World Production — COFFEE
(1000 mt)

Legend : * World
          + Brazil

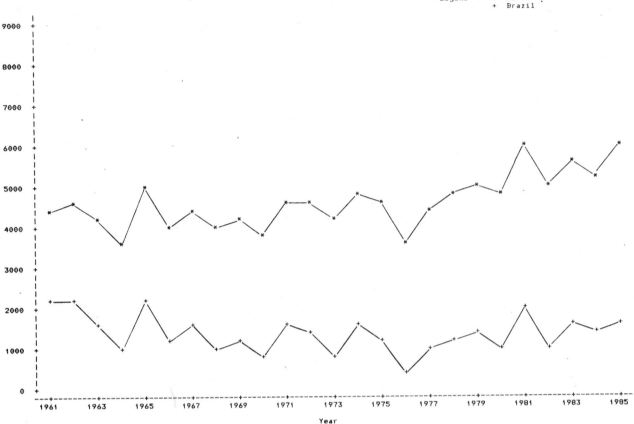

Source : FAO-Production Yearbook, various issues.

International Prices — COFFEE
Yearly average (U.S. cents/kg) a)

Legend : * $ current prices
          - 1980 $ constant prices

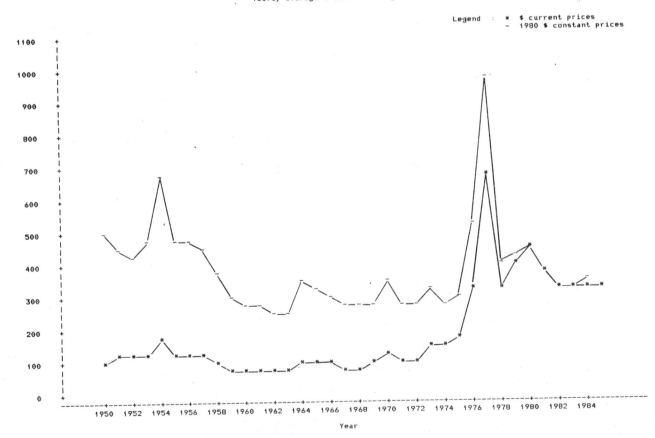

a) ICO quotations for Unwashed Arabica — BRAZILIAN
Source : World Bank — Commodity Trade and Price Trends (1986 ed.).

Table 5.13 displays the estimates of export supply and demand elasticities which are used to calculate benefits from trade. Supply elasticities are generally taken from the study of Akiyama and Duncan (1982), while country demand elasticities are obtained by dividing the world demand elasticity, taken from the same study, by the average world export share of each country.

Table 5.13: **Coffee Export Price Elasticities**

Country	Supply	Demand c/
Brazil	1.768 a/	-0.958
Colombia	0.960 b/	-1.885
El Salvador	0.560 b/	-5.764
Mexico	1.413 c/	-6.053
Ethiopia	0.882 c/	-10.454
Côte d'Ivoire	0.730 b/	-3.538
Kenya	0.415 c/	-10.952
Uganda	1.226 c/	-4.339
Indonesia	1.080 b/	-6.389
WORLD		0.230

a/ Elasticity of demand equal to -0.14 used (Akiyama & Duncan, 1982).

b/ Akiyama & Duncan (1982). They refer to price supply elasticity.

c/ World demand elasticity divided by the average market share (1964/66, 1974/76 and 1982/84 averages were computed and then the median of the three was selected).

Table 5.14: **Coffee: Net Nominal Protection Coefficients (NNPC) with and without the Adjustment for Market Share, and Nominal Protection Coefficients (NPC), 1961-82**

Country	NNPC	"Optimum" NNPC	NNPC with the adjustment (NNPC/Optimum)	NPC	NPC with the adjustment (NPC/Optimum)
Côte d'Ivoire	0.405 (0.099)	0.717	0.565	0.516 (0.104)	0.720
Kenya	0.602 (0.181)	0.909	0.662	0.962 (0.043)	1.058
Brazil	0.378 (0.214)	negative	negative	0.427 (0.221)	negative
Ethiopia	0.392 (0.080)	0.904	0.434	0.522 (0.091)	0.577
Colombia	0.445 (0.065)	0.469	0.949	0.515 (0.116)	1.098
El Salvador	0.618 (0.176)	0.827	0.747	0.730 (0.137)	0.881
Indonesia	0.375 (0.418)	0.843	0.445	0.282 (0.329)	0.334
Uganda	0.049 (0.027)	0.770	0.064	0.247 (0.082)	0.321
Mexico	0.064 (0.014)	0.835	0.077	0.073 (0.016)	0.087
TOTAL	0.399 (0.261)	0.706	0.565	0.505 (0.288)	0.715

Note: Figures in parentheses are standard deviations.

Table 5.14 shows that NPCs are larger in mean than NNPCs for all countries except Indonesia. For this country, the import parity exchange rate incorporated in the NNPC measure appears to exceed the official evaluation of foreign exchange by a small factor of about 2.3.

As Table 5.15 shows, the evolution of the benefits from trade is negative for almost all countries. As in the case of cocoa, the average annual change in welfare and its components is not significantly different from zero at the 95 percent confidence level. It is also rather small (less than 5 percent) for most countries with a few exceptions. Again, these results are confirmed by trend analysis (see Appendix V).

Table 5.15: **Coffee: Decomposition of Benefits from Trade**
(Mean % change/year)

Country	Benefits from trade	DBT effect	IBT effect
Côte d'Ivoire	-4.296 (6.505)	0.797 (1.00)	-3.499 (6.749)
Kenya	-5.537 (8.477)	-0.166 (0.742)	-5.371 (7.955)
Brazil	1.862 (11.697)	1.966 (11.284)	-0.134 (1.150)
Ethiopia	-4.512 (10.308)	-0.801 (1.447)	-3.711 (8.605)
Colombia	-3.723 (11.436)	-1.473 (0.881)	-2.250 (11.790)
El Salvador	-0.992 (9.723)	-1.303 (1.181)	0.311 (9.540)
Indonesia	-47.925 (44.444)	-32.149 (25.128)	-15.776 (22.120)
Uganda	-4.953 (9.679)	-10.714 (7.175)	5.761 (7.165)
Mexico	-1.149 (11.686)	-1.416 (7.764)	0.267 (5.456)
TOTAL	-6.571 (4.901)	-4.266 (2.736)*	-2.305 (3.096)

Note: Figures in parentheses are standard errors.

* = Indicates significance at the 10 percent level.

Sugar

Unlike coffee, sugar beets can be adequately grown in a variety of climatic environments, including those of most major consumers. This precludes total producer dominance and potentialy encourages domestic subsidies and other protectionist policies.

Sugar is unique among agricultural products in being a crop both of the tropics (sugar cane) and of the colder parts of the temperate areas (sugar beets). Developed countries dominate in the production of sugar beets and developing countries in the production of sugar cane. Approximately 60 percent of sugar comes from sugar cane and 40 percent from sugar beets. The developed countries account for about 45 percent of world production, but because their per capita consumption is higher, their share of world consumption is around 55 percent. This implies that there is net flow of sugar from developing to developed countries. As Table 5.17 shows, except for the EEC and Oceania, the largest exporters are developing countries, with Latin America accounting for more than half, Cuba and Brazil being the major producers. As for the other developing regions, India is the main producer in Asia, while African production is insignificant.

In most years since 1960 world production has exceeded consumption. In the 23 years from 1960 to 1983 there were only seven years with a production deficit, caused by crop failures in one or more major producers. Since the mid-1970s, there has been a tendency to overproduction: production rose by an annual average of 3 percent between 1964-84 to 100 million tons, while consumption rose by an annual average of only 2 percent to 90 million tons.

World sugar prices have been more volatile than prices of any other agricultural commodity. In recent years, however, they have fallen sharply because of the unprecedented large global surpluses built up (Figure 5.5). These surpluses are attributable to major structural changes in the world market resulting from EEC and U.S. policies.

Table 5.16: **Sugar Production, by Economic Regions and Main Countries** a/

Econ. region/ country	Production			Shares in World total			Exponential Growth rates
	1964/1966	1974/1976	1982/1984	1964/1966	1974/1976	1982/1984	1964-84
	('000 m.t.)			(%)			(%/yr)
Developed market econ.	18575	23990	28213	29.5	30.2	28.2	2.49
EEC	8491	11182	14515	13.5	14.1	14.5	3.34
Oceania	2115	3000	3407	3.4	3.8	3.4	2.60
U.S.A.	4870	5745	5243	7.7	7.2	5.2	0.43
South Africa	1268	1909	2120	2.0	2.4	2.1	2.55
Developing market econ.	28285	40979	53659	44.9	51.5	53.6	3.59
Far East	6279	10464	16524	10.0	13.2	16.5	5.66
India	3379	4742	8183	5.4	6.0	8.2	5.18
Indonesia	678	1037	1670	1.1	1.3	1.7	5.22
Philippines	1548	2572	2489	2.5	3.2	2.5	2.98
Thailand	252	1273	2516	0.4	1.6	2.5	15.12
Taiwan	950	806	676	1.5	1.0	0.7	-0.88
Near East	1394	2541	3825	2.2	3.2	3.8	5.04
Africa	1967	2951	3931	3.1	3.7	3.9	3.65
Mauritius	629	655	659	1.0	0.8	0.7	0.00
Latin Amer.	18303	24743	28936	29.0	31.1	28.9	2.63
Argentina	1116	1480	1597	1.8	1.9	1.6	3.11
Brazil	4324	6867	9407	6.9	8.6	9.4	4.68
Colombia	483	933	1291	0.8	1.2	1.3	3.38
Guyana	290	331	259	0.5	0.4	0.3	-0.90
Peru	811	965	558	1.3	1.2	0.6	-1.93
Cuba	5029	6251	7944	8.0	7.9	7.9	2.50
Dominican R.	700	1229	1256	1.1	1.5	1.3	3.12
Mexico	2024	2761	3010	3.2	3.5	3.0	1.75
Centrally planned econ.	16180	14588	18320	25.7	18.3	18.3	0.49
E. Europe	4268	4250	4978	6.8	5.3	5.0	0.90
USSR	9462	7594	8282	15.0	9.6	8.3	-1.16
Asian C.P.E.	2450	2743	5060	3.9	3.5	5.1	4.32
WORLD TOTAL	63040	79557	100191	100.0	100.0	100.0	2.60

a/ Sugar raw centrifugal.

Source: FAO, Production Yearbook, various issues.

Table 5.17: **Sugar Exports, by Economic Regions and Main Countries** [a/]

Econ. region/ country	Exports			Shares in World total			Exponential Growth rates
	1964/ 1966	1974/ 1976	1982/ 1984	1964/ 1966	1974/ 1976	1982/ 1984	1964-84
	('000 m.t.)			(%)			(%/yr)
Developed market econ.	3155	5625	9566	17.3	24.7	32.1	6.67
EEC	1408	2547	5851	7.7	11.2	19.6	9.35
Oceania	1233	1928	2471	6.8	8.5	8.3	3.55
U.S.A.	3	111	202	–	0.5	0.7	36.38
South Africa	471	827	741	2.6	3.6	2.5	2.15
Developing market econ.	11892	15919	19036	65.1	69.7	63.9	2.59
Far East	1671	3044	3626	9.1	13.3	12.2	5.67
India	327	846	536	1.8	3.7	1.8	3.83
Indonesia	71	–	–	0.4	–	–	
Philippines	1038	1327	1038	5.7	5.8	3.5	0.90
Thailand	64	721	1669	0.4	3.2	5.6	32.19
Taiwan	829	495	230	4.5	2.2	.8	-5.99
Near East	145	55	350	0.8	0.2	1.2	-0.39
Africa	1286	1325	1673	7.0	5.8	5.6	1.09
Mauritius	575	573	579	3.2	2.5	1.9	-0.07
Latin Amer.	8501	11242	13001	46.5	49.3	43.7	2.22
Argentina	54	374	547	0.3	1.6	1.8	14.71
Brazil	672	1771	2847	3.7	7.8	9.6	8.43
Colombia	82	135	266	0.5	0.6	0.9	3.97
Guyana	280	301	226	1.5	1.3	0.8	-1.27
Peru	407	382	90	2.2	1.7	0.3	-16.60
Cuba	4569	5666	6976	25.0	24.8	23.4	2.35
Dominican R.	573	977	896	3.1	4.3	2.9	2.32
Mexico	509	197	5	2.8	0.9	–	
Centrally planned econ.	3232	1278	1184	17.7	5.6	4.0	-6.21
E. Europe	1269	519	663	6.9	2.3	2.2	-4.55
USSR	704	80	213	3.9	0.4	0.7	-9.54
Asian C.P.E.	1258	679	309	6.9	3.0	1.0	-6.14
WORLD TOTAL	18279	22823	29786	100.0	100.0	100.0	2.75

[a/] Sugar raw centrifugal and sugar refined in terms of raw sugar

– = Indicates that the amount is negligible or nil

Source: FAO, *Trade Yearbook*, various issues.

Figure 5.5: World Production and stocks - SUGAR
(1000 mt)

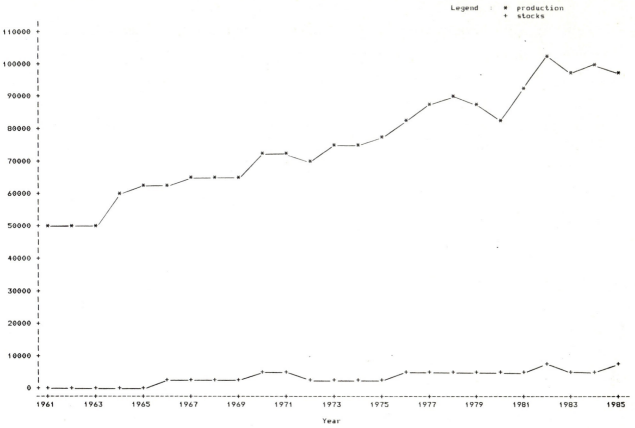

Source : FAO - Production Yearbook, various issues.

International Prices - SUGAR
Yearly average (U.S. cents/kg) a)

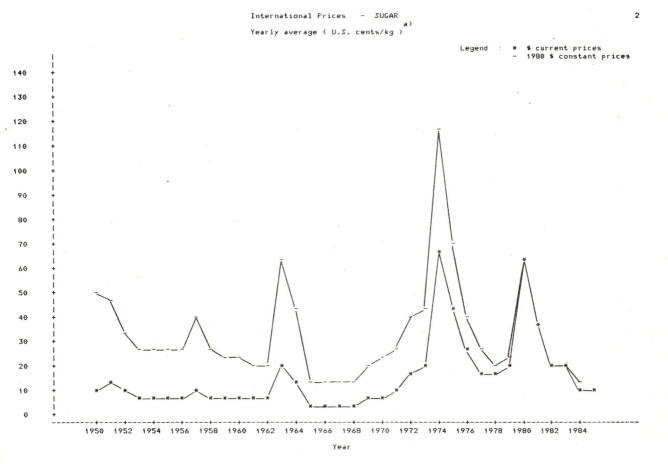

a) World Raw - International Sugar Council
Source : World Bank - Commodity and Trade Price Trends (1986 ed.)

In most net-exporting countries, retail prices show little relationship with the world market price of sugar, and the response of domestic consumption to changes in the international price is negligible. However, for net-importing countries, which cannot easily insulate their retail prices from international price movements, a clear price response exists. Faster growing consumption in LDCs has been due to faster growth in population and income and higher income and price elasticities. On the contrary, in DCs per capita production has not led to higher per capita consumption.

Although sugar is produced in virtually every country and consumed worldwide, production is insulated from market considerations and is related more to political and socio-economic factors. About one-fifth of the sugar trade occurs under special arrangements which insulate it from the free market.

Domestic sugar policies can be distinguished into two broad types: protectionist and defensive. Protectionist policies can take the form of guaranteed prices and import duties and quotas. Such policies assist producers mainly in developed countries to maintain or increase production beyond economically efficient levels. Due to its price support policies, the EEC has become the second largest exporter accounting for almost the entire growth in the world market since the mid-1970s.

The defensive policies, on the other hand, are mainly confined to developing countries aiming at maintaining their shares in the export markets for sugar. These policies try to control domestic supply within the framework of a commodity agreement, through a system of quotas and export taxes.

The overall tendency of world production to exceed consumption is best illustrated by the consideration of price changes. Since 1960, the price level in real terms has been below the average level in 16 out of the 24 years (Figure 5.5). Due to insulation of the major sugar beet producers from world price movements, and partly due to the perennial nature of sugar cane, the response in production to the recent decline in world sugar prices was marginal.

As Table 5.18 shows, the values of the export supply elasticities for sugar appear to be higher than the other primary commodities. Furthermore, the export demand elasticities facing the exporters are also rather high, mainly because export shares for this commodity are relatively small as a large amount of exports originate from developed countries. As a consequence, the "optimum" NNPC for most exporters is near unity, while the actual degree of protection appears to vary considerably in access countries (Table 5.19). All countries appear to be in pursuit of strategies of production control with net rates of protection much below unity. For two of the countries considered, however (Mauritius and Guyana), the anti-protectionist policies are entirely the result of the overvaluation of the exchange rate.

Table 5.18: **Sugar Export Price Elasticities**

Country	Supply	Demand
Mauritius [a]	1.090	-20.000
Philippines [d]	1.256	-8.690
Dominican Republic [d]	1.256	-16.129
Brazil [c]	0.799	-6.410
Guyana [a]	1.700	-38.462
Thailand [e]	2.397	-15.625
WORLD [b]		-0.500

[a] Taken from U. Koester, and P.M. Schmitz (1982).
[b] Berhman, J. (1977).
[c] It was assumed that $e^D=0$ and $e^S=0.25$ (as used in de Vries, 1979).
[d] Own estimates.
[e] Own estimates using e^D and e^S from de Vries (1979).

Table 5.19: **Sugar: Net Nominal Protection Coefficients (NNPC) with and without the Adjustment for Market Share, and Nominal Protection Coefficients (NPC), 1961-82**

Country	NNPC	"Optimum" NNPC	NNPC with the adjustment (NNPC/Optimum)	NPC	NPC with the adjustment (NPC/Optimum)
Mauritius	0.823 (0.932)	0.950	0.866	2.190 (2.390)	2.293
Thailand	0.355 (0.199)	0.936	0.379	0.546 (0.232)	0.583
Brazil	0.433 (0.255)	0.844	0.513	0.459 (0.174)	0.544
Guyana	1.976 (2.866)	0.974	2.029	2.133 (2.783)	2.190
Philippines	0.304 (0.129)	0.884	0.344	0.500 (0.160)	0.566
Dominic. Rep.	0.248 (0.049)	0.938	0.264	0.375 (0.092)	0.400
TOTAL	0.694 (1.373)	0.921	0.754	1.039 (1.684)	1.128

Note: Figures in parentheses are standard deviations.

Table 5.20 shows the results of domestic policies and of international price changes on welfare and its components. Compared to cocoa and coffee, the welfare changes appear to be larger. As for the other commodities, however, they are insignificant. The results seem to indicate, and this is confirmed by trend analysis (see Appendix V), that it is the IBT that is the leading cause of the deterioration registered.

Table 5.20: **Sugar: Decomposition of Benefits from Trade**
(mean % change/yr.)

Country	Benefits from trade	DBT effect	IBT effect
Mauritius	4.589 (17.329)	4.264 (14.186)	0.325 (6.882)
Thailand	-3.647 (17.981)	-0.196 (9.013)	-3.451 (17.014)
Brazil	-10.102 (13.855)	1.838 (3.424)	-11.940 (12.434)
Guyana	32.218 (18.663)	26.556 (16.669)	5.662 (6.527)
Philippines	-7.610 (9.389)	0.041 (3.875)	-6.569 (7.157)
Dominican Republic	2.266 (13.380)	0.139 (6.311)	2.127 (8.251)
TOTAL	4.244 (5.852)	5.465 (4.148)	-2.046 (4.202)

Note: Figures in parentheses are standard errors.

Tea

Tea is a perennial crop giving its first yield about two or three years after planting. Depending on the location, its cycle ranges from seven to nine years. Tea production is widely spread over the geographic regions. Nevertheless, the developing countries, particularly India, and Sri Lanka, are the dominant producing countries.

Tea may be broadly classified into two types, depending on whether the tea leaves are fermented (black tea) or unfermented (green tea). The black tea constitutes about three-quarters of all tea produced. Virtually all the tea grown in LDCs (except for Taiwan and Indonesia) is black tea.

The share of the traditional producers, India and Sri Lanka, dropped from 34 percent and 21 percent, respectively, in 1964/66 to 29 percent and 9 percent, respectively, in 1982/84. The African producers, on the other hand, increased their share from 7 percent to 11 percent, mainly due to area expansion (Table 5.21).

Although production in LDCs grew at 3 percent a year, their exports expanded only about 1.9 percent largely because domestic consumption rose faster than production in key Asian countries (Table 5.22).

Tea price movements can be characterized as being relatively stable and secularly declining (Figure 5.6). The relative stability may be attributed to the characteristics of the crop and its marketing structure. Tea is not affected much by seasonality, since most producers can pluck throughout the year. Also, tea importing, blending and packaging is mainly concentrated in a few transnational firms, whose oligopolistic nature is a stabilizing factor in the world market.

Table 5.21: **Tea Production, by Economic Regions and Main Countries**

	Production			Shares in World total			Exponential Growth rates
Econ. region/ country	1964/ 1966	1974/ 1976	1982/ 1984	1964/ 1966	1974/ 1976	1982/ 1984	1964-84
	('000 m.t.)			(%)			(%/yr)
Developed market econ.	83.8	103.6	103.6	7.7	6.7	5.0	1.32
Japan	81.4	100.3	98.1	7.5	6.5	4.7	1.14
Developing market econ.	824.6	1095.6	1364.1	75.7	71.1	65.9	2.95
Far East	701.1	816.0	947.0	64.4	52.9	45.8	1.84
India	371.6	496.1	597.8	34.1	32.2	28.9	2.83
Sri Lanka	223.0	204.9	191.7	20.5	13.3	9.3	-0.79
Indonesia	75.3	79.6	106.9	6.9	6.2	5.2	2.45
Bangladesh	27.8	31.9	45.0	2.6	2.1	2.2	3.03
Near East	27.0	75.0	132.9	2.5	4.9	6.4	8.89
Turkey	15.3	52.6	94.2	1.4	3.4	4.6	10.38
Africa	74.5	153.4	220.1	6.8	10.0	10.6	6.16
Kenya	21.8	57.4	110.4	2.0	3.7	5.3	9.77
Malawi	13.6	26.0	36.0	1.2	1.7	1.7	5.69
Uganda	9.1	18.6	3.6	0.8	1.2	0.2	-8.32
Mozambique	11.2	14.9	18.0	1.0	1.0	0.9	2.40
Tanzania	5.8	13.1	16.2	0.5	0.8	0.8	6.16
Latin America	21.9	46.3	55.5	2.0	3.0	2.7	4.96
Argentina	15.1	34.0	38.4	1.4	2.2	1.9	4.55
Brazil	5.3	7.3	10.4	0.5	0.5	0.5	5.06
Centrally planned econ.	108.2	343.0	601.1	16.6	22.2	29.1	7.03
China	99.5	214.2	403.9	9.1	13.9	19.5	8.19
USSR	51.4	86.4	145.7	4.7	5.6	7.0	6.29
WORLD TOTAL	1088.6	1542.2	2068.8	100.0	100.0	100.0	3.73

Source: FAO, Production Yearbook, various issues.

Table 5.22: **Tea Exports, by Economic Regions and Main Countries**

Econ. region/ country	Exports			Shares in World total			Exponential Growth rates
	1964/ 1966	1974/ 1976	1982/ 1984	1964/ 1966	1974/ 1976	1982/ 1984	1964-84
	('000 m.t.)			(%)			(%/yr)
Developed market econ.	25.9	57.2	57.8	4.0	6.9	5.8	3.27
Japan	3.4	2.9	2.5	0.5	0.4	0.3	1.13
Netherlands	0.2	21.2	14.2	0.1	2.6	1.4	8.36
U.K.	18.4	25.3	28.8	2.9	3.1	2.9	2.61
Developing market econ.	554.4	674.7	764.0	86.0	82.0	77.1	1.89
Far East	467.7	490.9	508.5	72.5	59.6	51.3	0.58
India	196.4	220.9	204.6	30.5	26.8	20.6	0.48
Sri Lanka	210.3	195.8	181.2	32.6	23.8	18.3	-0.89
Indonesia	32.4	47.9	72.6	5.0	5.8	7.3	5.08
Bangladesh	22.9	22.2	32.6	3.6	2.7	3.3	2.13
Near East	3.2	10.2	3.5	0.5	1.2	0.4	-0.32
Turkey	1.9	3.9	0.5	0.3	0.5	0.1	-8.97
Africa	69.9	140.6	195.3	10.8	17.1	19.7	5.92
Kenya	25.8	56.9	98.4	4.0	6.9	9.9	8.27
Malawi	13.6	26.7	37.7	2.1	3.2	3.8	5.88
Uganda	6.5	15.1	1.3	1.2	1.8	0.1	-12.35
Mozambique	10.7	14.1	15.4	1.7	1.7	1.6	1.39
Tanzania	5.2	10.7	14.5	0.8	1.3	1.5	6.14
Latin America	13.5	28.5	50.0	2.1	3.5	5.0	7.39
Argentina	11.3	22.2	40.3	1.8	2.7	4.1	7.05
Brazil	2.1	5.1	8.8	0.3	0.6	0.9	8.02
Centrally planned econ.	64.5	91.2	169.6	10.0	11.1	17.1	5.80
China	32.4	50.7	123.4	5.0	6.2	12.5	8.07
USSR	10.6	15.1	24.2	1.6	1.8	2.4	4.59
WORLD TOTAL	644.8	823.1	991.4	100.0	100.0	100.0	2.44

Source: FAO, Trade Yearbook, various issues.

Figure 5.6: World Production – TEA
(1000 mt.)

Source : FAO-Production Yearbook, various issues.

International Prices – TEA
Yearly Average (U.S. cents/KG)[a]

Legend : * $ current prices
− 1980 $ constant prices

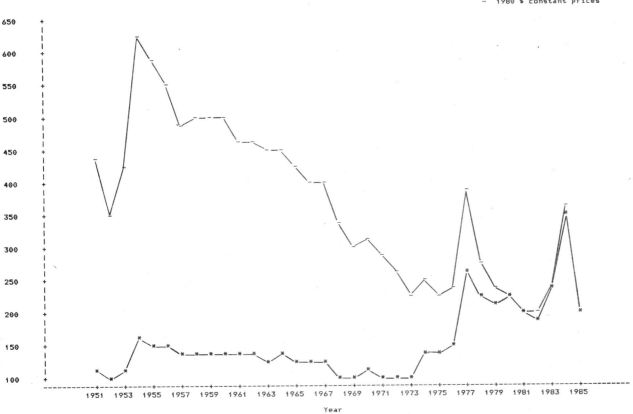

a) Average All Tea – London Auction
Source : World Bank – Commodity trade and price Trends (1986 ed.).

Nearly 80 percent of world tea exports are re-exports from industrialized countries. Traditionally, a large proportion of the tea sold in the world market has been purchased by a handful of tea wholesaling firms through London auctions, and these firms have blended and re-exported these teas to other countries.

As Table 5.23 shows, tea export supply elasticities appear to be generally below unity, but vary widely from country to country. Kenya, Malawi and Brazil show relatively large elasticities exceeding the unit level. Export demand elasticities, on the other hand, tend to be relatively large because of the small shares of the market covered by most country exports. Only for India and Sri Lanka, the two largest world producers, is export demand elasticity in the neighbourhood of one.

Table 5.23: **Tea Export Price Elasticities**

Country	Supply	Demand
Indonesia	0.050 [c]	-4.310
Kenya	1.399 [a]	-3.623
Malawi	2.245 [a]	-7.813
Tanzania	0.197 [a]	-19.231
Argentina	0.595 [a]	-9.259
Brazil	1.509 [a]	-4.667
Bangladesh	0.685 [a]	-7.578
India	0.489 [c]	-0.933
Sri Lanka	0.406 [a]	-1.050
WORLD [b]		-0.25

[a] Own estimates.

[b] It is taken from Berhman (1977) and refers to the average of developed and developing countries.

[c] Calculated using supply & demand elasticities from Choeng-Hoy Chung (1979).

The consequences of the elasticity distribution can be observed in Table 5.24, which shows that the two larger exporters produce far too much tea and tend to depress overall prices by failing to apply restrictions to their export supplies. Small producers, however, appear to be sufficiently close to an optimum tariff policy, at least in the sense that the optimum falls between the adjusted and the unadjusted NPC.

Table 5.24: **Tea: Net Nominal Protection Coefficients (NNPC) with and without the Adjustment for Market Share, and Nominal Protection Coefficients (NPC), 1961-82**

Country	NNPC	"Optimum" NNPC	NNPC with the adjustment (NNPC/Optimum)	NPC	NPC with the adjustment (NPC/Optimum)
Indonesia	0.658 (0.182)	0.768	0.857	0.764 (0.178)	0.995
India	0.226 (0.094)	negative	negative	0.432 (0.044)	negative
Kenya	0.644 (0.209)	0.724	0.889	1.025 (0.078)	1.416
Bangladesh	0.658 (0.261)	0.868	0.789	1.023 (0.260)	1.179
Brazil	0.515 (0.127)	0.786	0.655	0.612 (0.184)	0.779
Sri Lanka	0.199 (0.123)	0.048	4.416	0.642 (0.113)	13.375
Malawi	0.904 (0.302)	0.872	1.037	0.947 (0.211)	1.086
TOTAL [a]	0.531 (0.299)	0.521	0.930	0.763 (0.264)	1.336

Note: Figures in parentheses are standard deviations.
[a] Excludes India.

As Table 5.25 demonstrates, even though average percentage changes in the benefits from trade appear to be always negative and sizeable, they are not statistically significant at a reasonable degree of confidence, except for Brazil. Domestic price policies have negative effects everywhere except in Sri Lanka. The IBT effect, on the other hand, is always negative.

Table 5.25: **Tea: Decomposition of Benefits from Trade**
(mean % change/year)

Country	Benefits from trade	DBT effect	IBT effect
India	-3.249 (4.568)	-0.721 (3.028)	-2.528 (2.145)
Indonesia	-1.892 (7.917)	-0.036 (0.056)	-1.756 (7.581)
Kenya	-30.481 (18.951)	-2.099 (2.996)	-28.383 (19.283)
Bangladesh	-18.507 (16.492)	-3.272 (2.832)	-15.235 (18.358)
Brazil	-18.741 (8.597)**	-6.702 (3.573)	-12.039 (7.057)
Sri Lanka	-8.067 (15.033)	13.828 (12.140)	-21.895 (16.605)
Malawi	-95.644 (81.557)	-48.898 (34.555)	-45.746 (50.656)
TOTAL	-22.299 (10.056)**	-5.012 (4.294)	-17.287 (7.397)**

Note: Figures in parentheses are standard errors.

** = Indicates significance at the 5 percent level.

Overall Considerations

In a broader context, the trends in the gains from trade are in part the consequence of trade policies and any deterioration can be interpreted as a failure to enact an optimum tax or to restrict production accordingly. As Table 5.26 shows, however, the analysis suggests that production of primary commodities from developing countries has been restricted as required by the pure theory of trade arguments and that departures from the optimal policy should have caused changes in the distribution of the benefits among countries rather than overall declines in welfare.

Table 5.26: **Net Nominal Protection Coefficients (NNPC) with and without the Adjustment for Market Share, and Nominal Protection Coefficients (NPC), 1961-82**

Commodity	NNPC	"Optimum" NNPC	NNPC with the adjustment (NNPC/Optimum)	NPC	NPC with the adjustment (NPC/Optimum)
Cocoa	0.536 (0.225)	0.571	0.939	0.667 (0.538)	1.168
Coffee	0.399 (0.261)	0.706	0.565	0.505 (0.288)	0.715
Sugar	0.694 (1.373)	0.921	0.754	1.039 (1.684)	1.128
Tea a/	0.531 (0.299)	0.521	0.930	0.763 (0.264)	1.336

Note: Figures in parentheses are standard deviations.
a/ Excludes India.

In support of the above conclusion, the results presented in Table 5.26 do suggest three main arguments: (i) the optimum NNPC is never significantly different from either the corrected or the uncorrected NPC; (ii) it tends to fall between the two; and (iii) the variance of the NPCs is small, despite the large instability affecting the benefit changes and its components (Table 5.28).

Given these indications, the statistical results presented in Tables 5.27, 5.28 and 5.30 show some evidence of deterioration in the welfare and terms of trade position and stability of developing countries for cocoa, tea and sugar. For tea, in particular, the concentration of production in India and Sri Lanka makes unavoidable a certain overall deterioration, since these countries fail to discourage production to the extent requested by their large share of the market.

The above results are, nevertheless, partial, in the sense that they take no account of the shifts of either the supply functions (mainly productivity) or the demand functions (mainly income and tastes). Even though they are mixed with positive changes, the measurable and sizeable negative changes reported in Tables 5.27, 5.28 and 5.30 can be interpreted as the likely effect of these shifts. In other words, one can conjecture that the overall policy of LDCs appears to be effective in contrasting the reduction of gains from trade that would follow from an expansion along the supply curve. The same policy, however, is unable to prevent productivity increases and changes of taste to transfer some welfare over to consuming countries.

In the case of sugar, the explanation is more complex, since the negative trend in the international terms of trade is mostly due to the high protection that the EEC offers to its producers. Restriction of production in LDCs, therefore, has mainly the effect of preventing a larger fall of world prices and reducing the cost of protectionist policies in the industrial countries.

While the aggregate results are somewhat stronger for the trends in welfare and terms of trade, the instability results (Tables 5.29 and 5.30) at the commodity level, confirm the picture of high instability without significant trends obtained in the earlier analysis. [6/] Compared with earlier measures (see, for example, Table 3.3), the size of the instability indices is much larger, probably as a result of the shorter time period encompassed by the series examined here. Finally, from the tests of increased instability (Table 5.30), we can conclude that for tea there has been a significant declining trend, while no trend is detectable for the other commodities.

Table 5.27: **Decomposition of Benefits from Trade**
(mean % change/year)

Commodity	Benefits from trade	DBT effect	IBT effect
Cocoa	-3.773 (3.274)	-0.617 (1.077)	-2.156 (3.277)
Coffee	-6.571 (4.901)	-4.266 (2.736)*	-2.305 (3.096)
Sugar	-4.244 (5.852)	5.465 (4.148)	-2.046 (4.202)
Tea	22.299 (10.056)**	-5.012 (4.294)	-17.287 (7.397)**

Note: Figures in parentheses are standard errors.

** = Indicates significance at the 5 percent level.

* = Indicates significance at the 10 percent level.

Table 5.28: **Trends in the Benefits from Trade and its Components**
(annual % variation) a/

Commodity	Benefits from Trade	DBT	IBT
Cocoa	-0.039 (0.008)***	0.009 (0.007)	0.011 (0.015)
Coffee	0.039 (0.033)	-0.042 (0.016)***	0.025 (0.029)
Sugar	-0.103 (0.030)***	0.129 (0.027)***	-0.029 (0.026)
Tea	-0.047 (0.024)*	-0.059 (0.023)**	-0.098 (0.021)***

Note: Figures in parentheses are standard deviations.

*** = Indicates significance at the 1 percent level.
** = Indicates significance at the 5 percent level.
* = Indicates significance at the 10 percent level.

a/ Computed from log-linear trend equations and weighted by the export share of each country.

Table 5.29: **Instability Levels of Benefits from Trade and its Components**

Commodity	Benefits from trade	DBT	IBT
Cocoa	14.014	14.239	26.205
Coffee	107.692	107.693	107.690
Sugar	38.220	28.759	23.832
Tea	54.624	65.674	91.469

Table 5.30: **Trends in Instability of Benefits from Trade and its Components** a/
(annual % variation)

Commodity	Benefits from trade	DBT	IBT
Cocoa	0.012 (0.004)***	0.005 (0.004)	0.020 (0.008)**
Coffee	-0.032 (0.019)	0.006 (0.003)*	0.042) (0.016)**
Sugar	0.031 (0.022)	-0.003 (0.007)	0.008 (0.009)
Tea	-0.009 (0.015)	-0.012 (0.012)	0.020 (0.012)

Note: Figures in parentheses are standard deviations.

*** = Indicates significance at the 1 percent level.
 ** = Indicates significance at the 5 percent level.
  * = Indicates significance at the 10 percent level.

a/ Computed from log-linear trend equations and weighted by the export share of each country

Notes

1/ See, for example, Krueger and Sönnenschein (1967).

2/ See, in particular, Willig (1976), Hausman (1981) and Kohli (1984).

3/ A similar result was obtained in a "pure trade" context by Batra and Pattanak (1970), who assume, however, immobility of factors of production and a wage differential.

4/ Price elasticities of exports supply and demand have been calculated with the formula:

$$\frac{s \cdot e^S - e^D}{s - 1}, \text{ where } s = \text{degree of self-sufficiency;}$$

$$e^S = \text{price elasticity of domestic supply;}$$

$$e^D = \text{price elasticity of domestic demand.}$$

5/ In all cases but one (Brazil), the benefit changes are less than 5 percent a year.

6/ See Chapters III and IV and Appendix V.

CHAPTER VI

CONCLUSIONS AND POLICY IMPLICATIONS

Some General Remarks

It is difficult to systematize conclusions from this study, because of the difficulty of the issues involved and the sheer size of the statistical results examined. The basic problem explored was the question of the secular trend of the terms of trade of primary commodities. In confronting this issue, a variety of statistical means were used and applied to each commodity and within a truly secular set of data.

Since the beginning of the study, however, it soon became clear that it was not possible to avoid some of the other major issues surrounding the problem of the trend in the terms of trade. The most important of these issues were: (i) the theoretical questions on definitions and measures; (ii) the size and the trends in instability; and (iii) the link between international terms of trade, domestic price policies and welfare.

These three problems were, in turn, the object of separate sub-studies, even though in each of them the question of the existence of a long-term trend rise emerges as the central issue to be decided upon by empirical evidence.

Are there any general conclusions to be drawn from this difficult journey through these issues? Keeping in mind that most empirical results add to knowledge by showing the lack of corroboration of prior hypotheses, this work does warrant three major conclusions.

First, there is no basis to believe that a general deterioration has occurred in the welfare position of developing countries because of a declining trend in relative prices of primary commodities. On one hand, the weight of primary commodities in LDC trade has drastically decreased, but also, more cogently, there is no evidence that a combination of price declines, high and increasing instability and ill-conceived domestic policies has caused a significant decline in LDC welfare.

Second, there is, however, every reason to suspect that a "selective" deterioration has affected some commodities, and some LDCs for specific sub-periods. Support for this hypothesis is provided by the fact that terms of trade of primary commodities tend to deteriorate slightly over the longer period considered, and considerably more in some of the sub-periods. In a context of high instability, it is reasonable to conclude that such a deterioration has hampered the country's welfare position and that full recovery has been prevented by other aggravating factors: (i) deteriorating macro-economic performances; (ii) domestic price policies; (iii) lack of coordination among producing countries; and (iv) perhaps insufficient international credit for short-term, stabilising purposes.

Third, the commodities whose supply is controlled by commodity agreements tend to fare better than the others, in the sense that the terms of trade do not fall and sometimes show significant increases, and in the sense that instability of prices and welfare is lower. On the other hand, commodities such as sugar, where producers (in the EEC) follow policies that encourage the expansion of supply, show both significant decreases in prices and welfare and comparatively higher instability.

These conclusions, however, are to be understood within the framework of the conceptual and methodological limitations surrounding the very question of the "declining" trend. The results obtained, in fact, show the ambiguities that empirical research on these issues inevitably face. To begin with, the very concept of terms of trade is subject to controversy, as is its measurement and implications. Giving a clear definition of a "trend" and specifying an effective statistical measure is also by no means an easy job. Examining systematically questions related to sub-periods, upswings and downswings, different functional forms, stability and instability, requires so many different tests, and yields such a large set of results, that one is often overwhelmed by the sheer size of the information obtained and by the multiplicity of its possible different meanings.

A general impression that the many statistical results present to the reader, is that the null hypothesis dominates, i.e., the statistical tests utilized do not permit rejection of the various hypotheses advanced: that terms of trade have been declining, that they fall more in the downswings, that they rise in the upswings, that instability has been increasing, etc. This impression corresponds broadly to the main result of the analysis, which shows both that there is some justification in suspecting a negative bias in the movement of international trade of primary commodities and that the evidence is insufficient to warrant firm conclusions on the matter.

From a policy point of view, it is perhaps interesting that for the limited case of the four tropical crops considered, this study's analysis tends to, at least partially, exonerate the LDCs from the charge of pursuing irrational domestic policies and exploiting agricultural producers. The results show that both agricultural taxation and overvalued exchange rates have gone in the right direction in restricting production of tropical crops, thereby avoiding much larger falls in terms of trade and welfare.

Have the Terms of Trade of Primary Commodities Been Falling?

On a purely qualitative basis, this study confirms the original observation by Prebisch and others that international barter terms of trade (BTT) of primary commodities have a tendency to deteriorate. This conclusion is broadly supported by four sets of results: (i) the prevalence of negative coefficients in the log-linear relationships between BTT and time; (ii) the constant and almost always dominant presence of a negative coefficient in the log-quadratic relationships between the same variables; (iii) the prevalence of negative signs in the trend equations fitted in the sub-periods; and (iv) the negative signs of the trends fitted to obtain stationary residuals for spectral analysis.

The same conclusion, however, would be highly misleading if read without a number of qualifications: the measured tendency to decline, in fact, is: (i) small in size; (ii) statistically significant at the lowest confidence level; (iii) in most cases, reversing itself given a sufficiently large number of years; and (iv) erratic in sign and size if considered over a small number of years.

While meaningfull measures of income terms of trade for a sufficiently long number of years for the entire international market could not be obtained, SFTT were estimated (i.e., barter terms corrected for land productivity) for all primary agricultural commodities. The results of the analysis of these series often showed opposite tendencies compared to the IBT series. Agricultural productivity also proved to be a more successful explanatory variable for the IBT series than the linear or the quadratic trend variable. Moreover, the sign of the linear trend was often reversed once productivity was introduced in the equation used to explain the IBT or SFTT time behaviour.

These results are in line with the objections moved to the original finding by Prebisch on the partial irrelevance of the IBT measure and on its likely dependence on the evolution of productivity. A separate piece of analysis also shows that the claim originally advanced by Prebisch as to the asymmetry of the upswings and downswings in primary commodity prices can be clearly rejected within a truly (near)-secular perspective.

The statistical conclusions reached, however, should be interpreted with caution, because of the inherent methodological difficulties associated with the main question examined. Because the existence of a trend is not linked to the specification of a structural model, the lack of statistical significance is ambiguous. It can be interpreted as a failure to reject the null hypothesis, either because the alternative hypothesis (i.e., that there is a declining trend) is false, or because the simple, unstructured models used are inadequate for the task. Similarly, the measurement of large instability could be interpreted as evidence of lack of fitness of the models used rather than as reflections of truly unstable prices.

On the other hand, more "structural" models would not necessarily help, since their explanatory power would simply absorb portions of the trends or the fluctuations of the dependent variables into the independent ones. One would then ask whether or not the terms of trade are declining, or whether or not they are unstable, <u>after</u> the effects of certain influencing variables have been netted out. As the reader can clearly see, this is an entirely different question and it is not the one addressed in this study.

The weak trends found make it more likely that the findings of high instability are due to model specification and vice versa that the high instability found makes it more likely that the trends measured are real, even if they are not highly significant from a statistical point of view. As seen in Chapter IV, trend removal may artificially reduce or amplify the instability measured, while, in turn, instability over the low frequency range can easily be confused with a trend.

The Benefits from Trade

Because neither BTT nor SFTT can be considered satisfactory proxies for welfare movements, benefits from trade have to be estimated taking into account both DBT and IBT for each producing country. This conclusion caused a significant departure in the last part of this study from its original scheme of analysis, which was characterized by concern for (i) all primary commodities, except oil; (ii) the years 1900-82; and (iii) the LDCs as a group.

Because of data limitations and the country-level nature of the questions asked, estimates were developed of the gains from trade for four main primary commodities of agricultural origin and for each of their main exporters among the developing countries.

Despite the significantly different context, the results of this analysis confirmed the earlier results in all important respects. First, a clear pattern of losses from trade emerged for almost all countries. However, as before, this finding was not supported by statistical significance except in a few cases. Furthermore, in most countries the size of the yearly changes was very small and fluctuated widely between years. Again, as in the earlier analysis, instability was large and also increasing. Decomposition of the benefits from trade also showed that it was impossible to place the blame for the welfare decline on IBT or on domestic policies. Most of the time the average effect of domestic and international terms of trade changes were similarly small and statistically insignificant. When larger, they often tended to offset each other. As for welfare, they were both subject to wide yearly fluctuations.

Somewhat unexpectedly, the level of domestic protection accorded by most countries to the four primary commodities considered was often not far from its theoretical optimum if both market shares and world demand elasticities were taken into account. On average, there was no significant difference between the domestic price level and its optimum, as calculated on the basis of the pure theory of trade optimum tariff formula. Therefore, it appears that producers of the four crops considered did what they could to prevent terms of trade from deteriorating, but there was a partial redistribution of gains within the LDC group and, in part, in the case of sugar, between LDCs and DCs.

The Question of Instability

As mentioned earlier, most of the results outlined are at least partly a consequence of the rather large variability of the series involved and of the inability of the trend hypothesis to explain a significant portion of such a variability. These findings bring up two questions regarding instability: (i) Is it especially large for primary commodities? and (ii) Has it been increasing over time?

The main difficulty in answering the first question is that no clear term of comparison exists to decide "how large is large" in the case of terms of trade, welfare and the like. However, a careful analysis of instability, according to several indicators, produced measures of instability large in comparison with the mean values of the series and to similar measures of different variables. This was especially so if the most unpredictable, short-term frequency band was used for the measurement.

Moreover, the analysis of welfare changes, while revealing high instability as well, also showed how the instability of DBT and IBT tended to offset each other, thereby reducing the fluctuations of the real income that each country derives from trade.

Has instability been increasing over time? The answer is no for the long term, even though it is subject to the same caveats exposed for the answer to declining trend issues. However, for the shorter, more recent period of time, and the four tropical commodities considered in the last part of this study, instability appears to have been increasing for some countries.

Clearly, asking whether instability has been increasing is tantamount to asking whether it is possible to detect a significant positive trend in the instability measure selected. The difficulties, however, are compounded, as we are looking at a second degree trend, the trend of a residual around a trend. Therefore, while we did obtain sparse evidence on selected instability increases, we feel that it is insufficient to warrant firm conclusions.

Policy Implications

The policy implications of this analysis are difficult to draw, for the same reasons that made a clear cut answer to the statistical tests attempted difficult. Nevertheless, since policy actions drive rather on expediency than rigour, one can be less cautious in formulating prescriptions than in claiming scientific results.

From a policy point of view, the questions: (i) Have the terms of trade of primary commodities been deteriorating in the past 80 years? (ii) Has their instability been large? and (iii) Has it been increasing? should all be reformulated by considering whether developing countries have reason to be concerned about such issues. In other words, is the statistically weak evidence uncovered politically significant?

If the results obtained in this analysis are reviewed in the framework of these general questions, the answer is positive. Despite the smallness and reversals, the tendency to decline over extended periods of time is undeniable for the terms of trade of many primary commodities. The fact that this tendency is combined with large, short-term instability makes the policy concerns even more justified.

Even though limited to only four commodities, the country level results are even more significant in the policy context. These results point to an overall welfare loss for developing countries during the period 1965-82, due to a deterioration of their terms of trade, and at the same time indicate a significant instability in the performance of individual countries. In the same period of time, in other words, while all LDCs were losing in the aggregate, some of them were losing less than others and some were gaining.

The explanation of these different performances is not simple, since quality, market and productivity factors play an important role that is only partly reflected in the different barter prices. One major factor, however, is constituted by price and foreign exchange policies. In fact, the countries that sustained the burden of restricting production by imposing low domestic prices and overvalued exchange rates, appear clearly to have the merit of having prevented a larger fall in the terms of trade. Unwittingly, these countries have suffered losses in favour of the countries that have done less than their share in restructuring production or have even encouraged its expansion.

The need for concerted action on the part of LDCs appears thus to be dominant, with respect to the need to rationalize domestic markets by reducing state intervention. The present situation could deteriorate further if the largely fortuitous mechanism that has prevented excessive supply growth were to be broken by an unchecked liberalization of prices and exchange rates.

The policy prescriptions deriving from the above considerations are plain and reflect the position that most LDCs have long been taking in international forums. First, developing countries should be actively concerned about deteriorating terms of trade and instability. They should study the characteristics of their own markets and carefully predispose a domestic policy response, avoiding blunt and inappropriate instruments, such as overvalued exchange rates.

Second, LDCs should strive to take effective group actions, both to give a consistent framework to domestic policies without unwilling transfers of welfare and implicit free-ridership, and to increase market power towards large industrial purchasers, and protected producers in industrial countries.

Finally, these two policies, the domestic and the collective, are not independent of each other, since the failure to enforce appropriate domestic policies would make collective action impossible, while conversely, the lack of a collective agreement would suggest different, and perhaps selfish, domestic responses. The possibility of following rational domestic policies for primary commodities and exchange rates thus hinges on the capacity that the producers will display in achieving a sufficient degree of consensus among themselves and with their trading partners in the developed countries.

APPENDIX I

GRAPHS

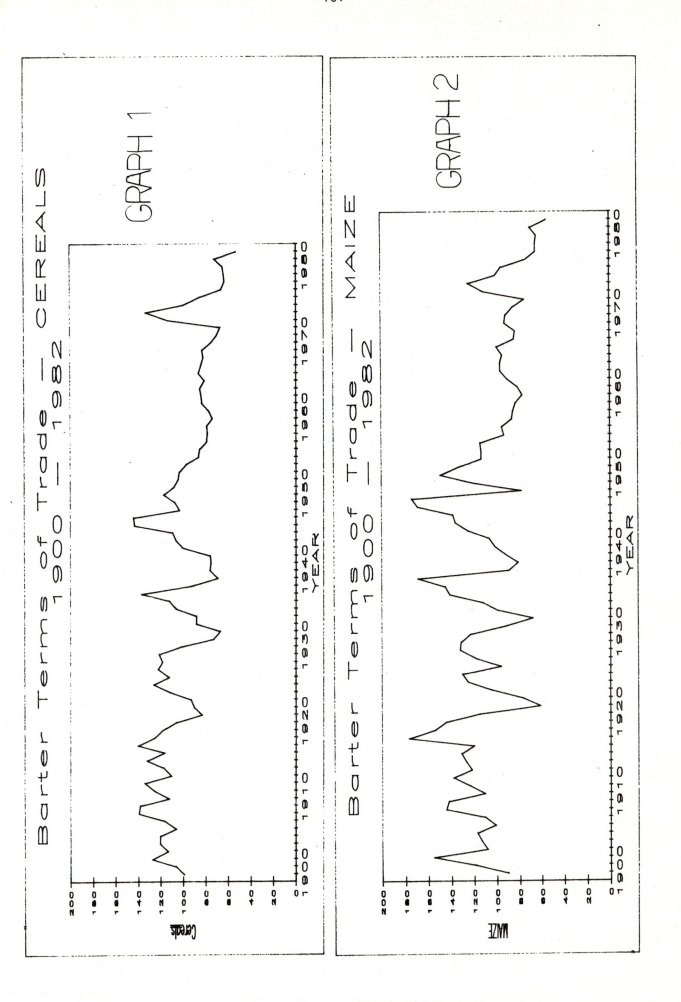

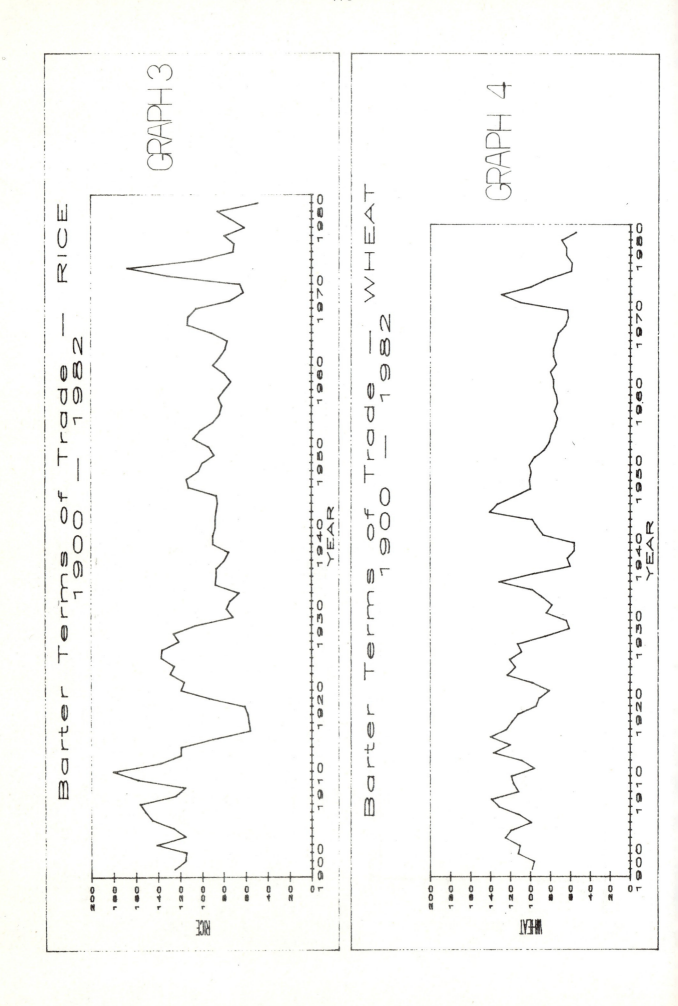

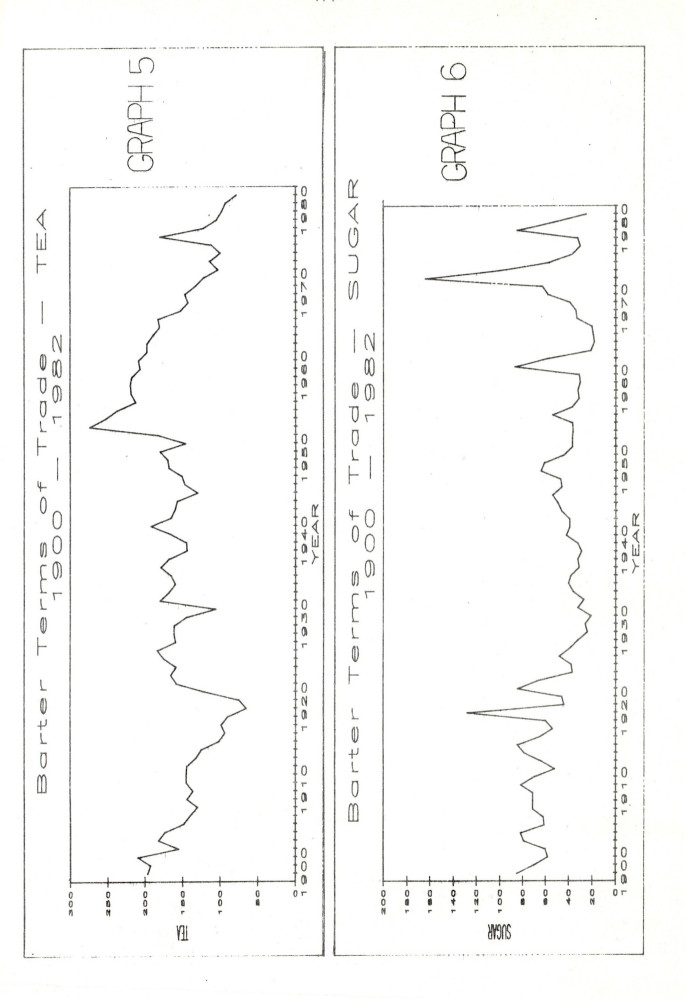

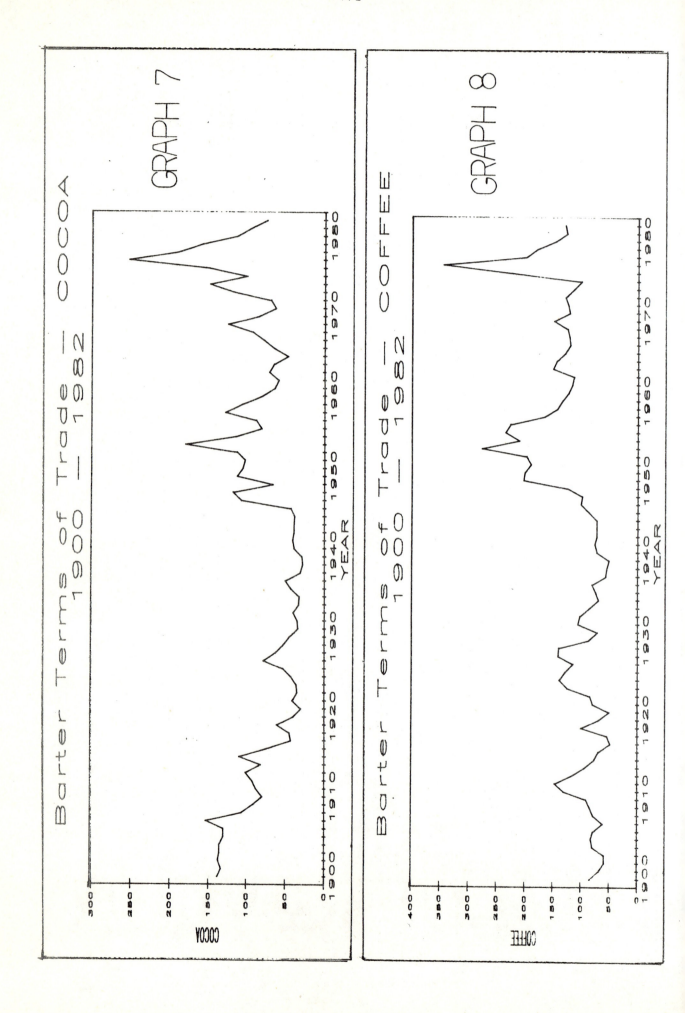

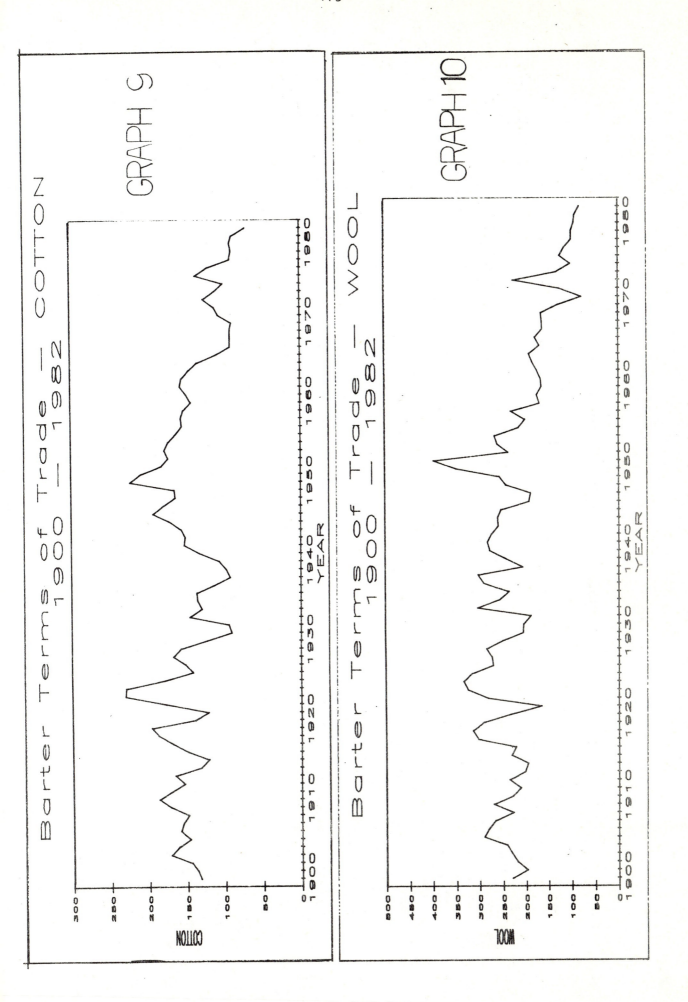

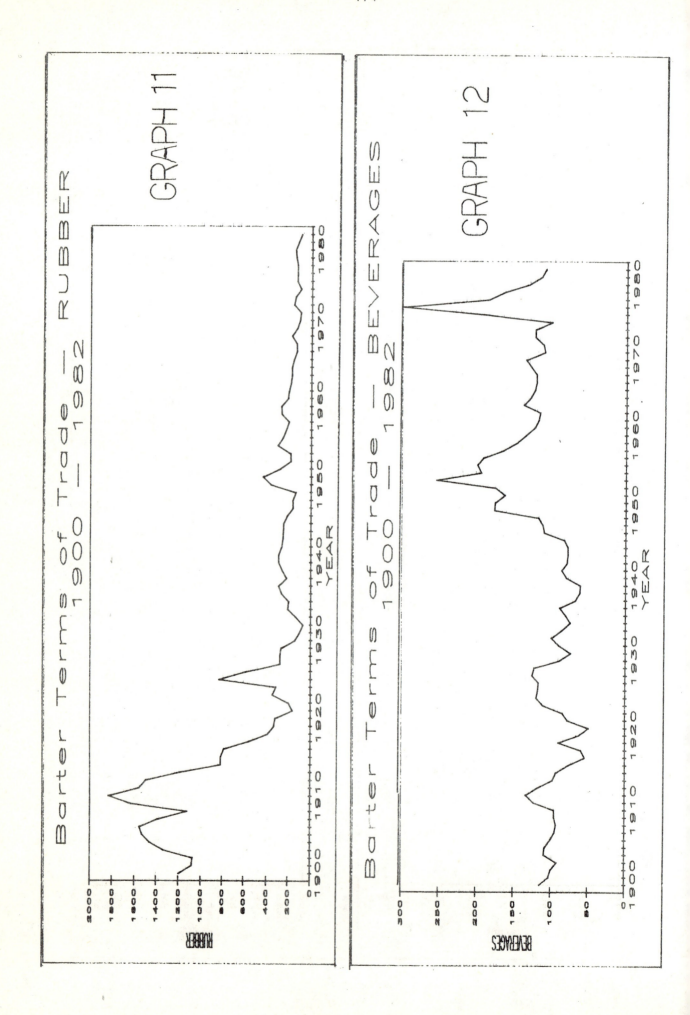

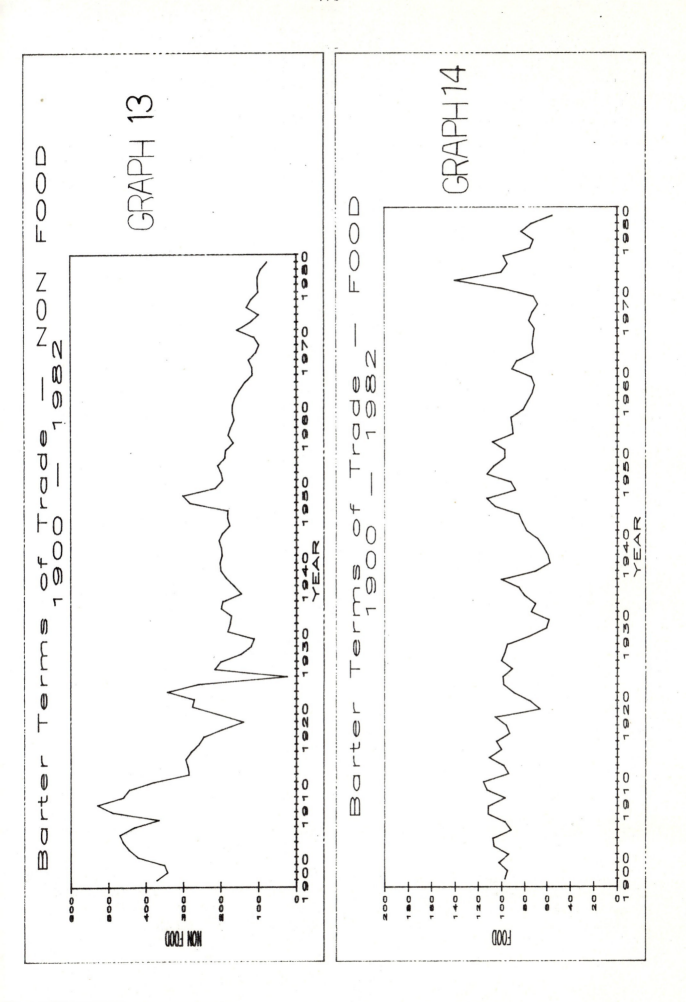

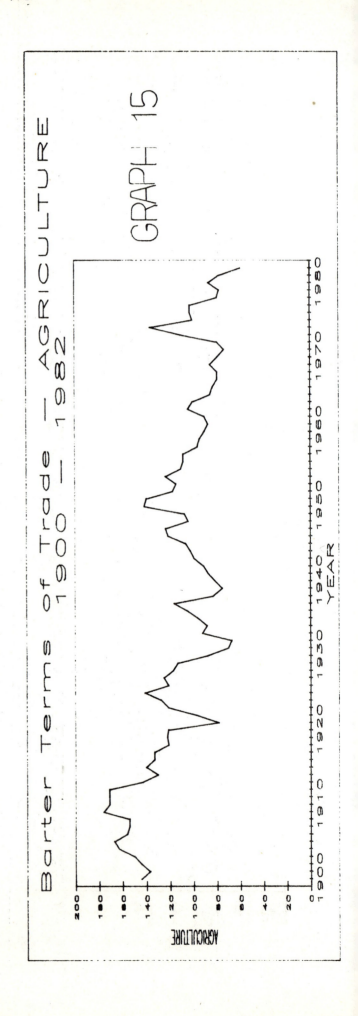

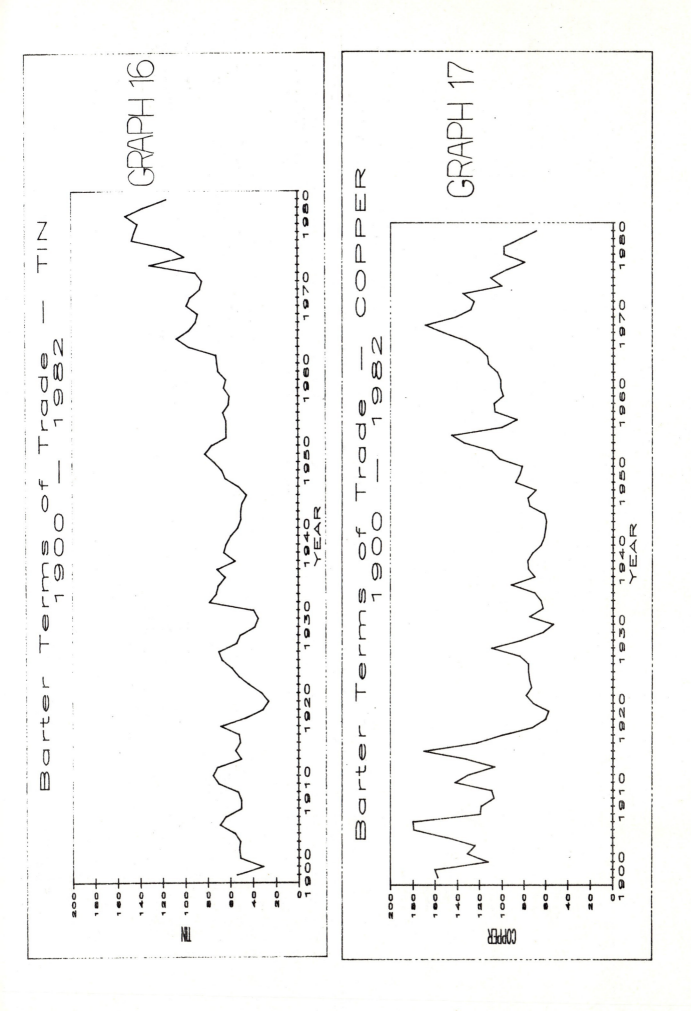

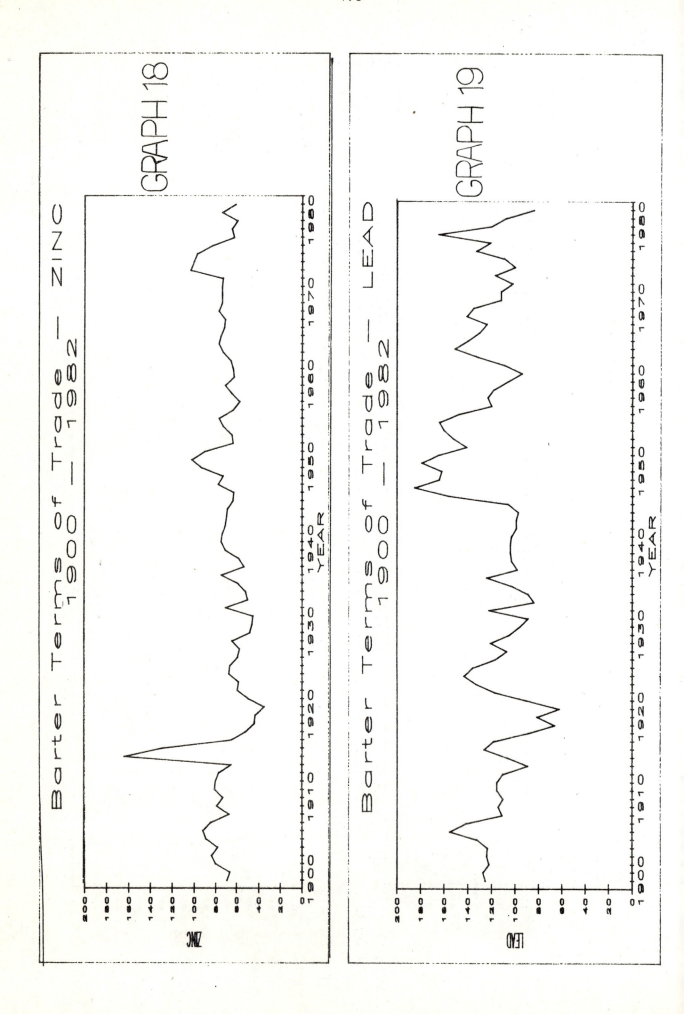

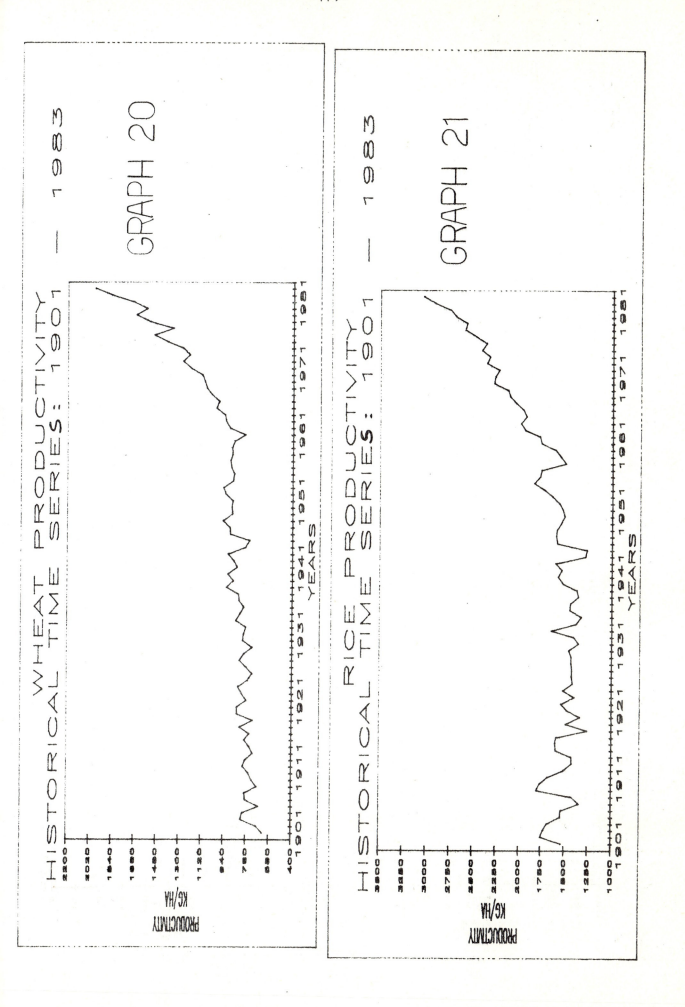

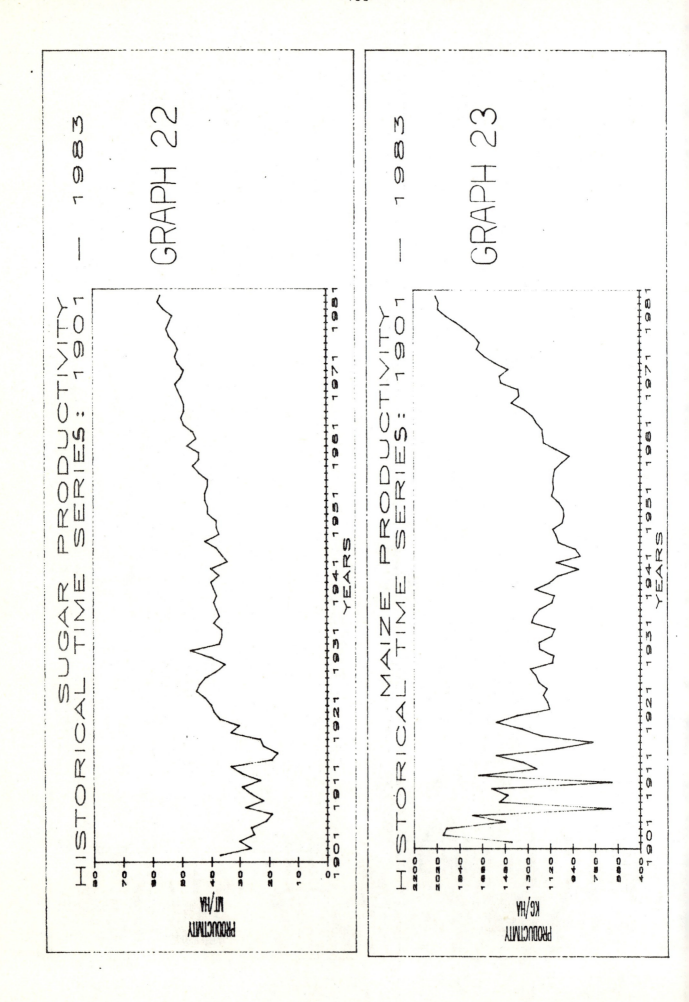

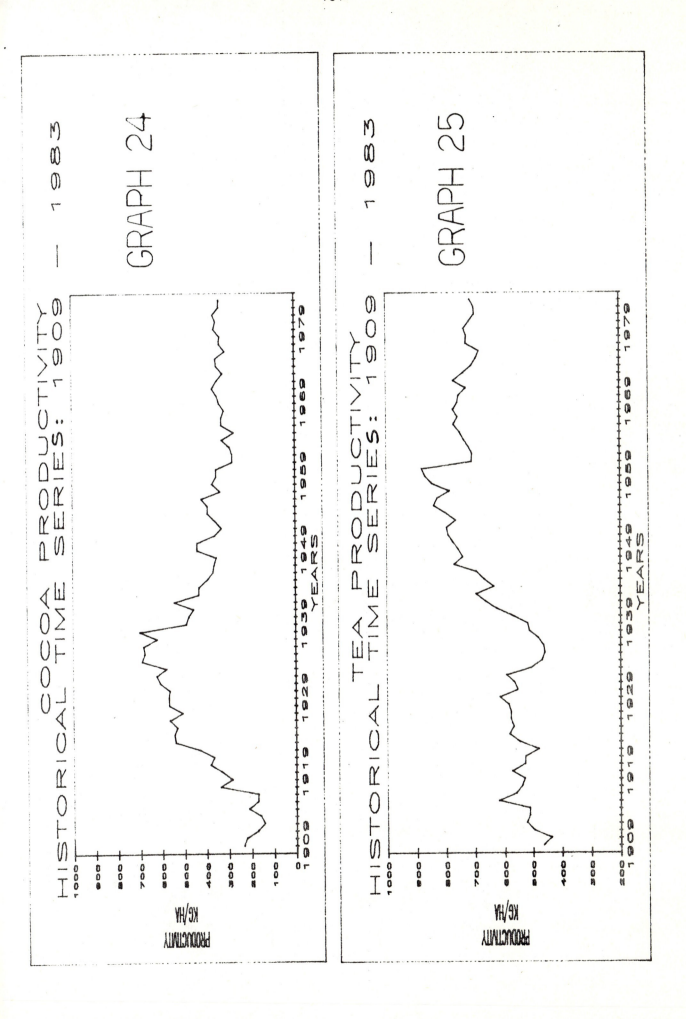

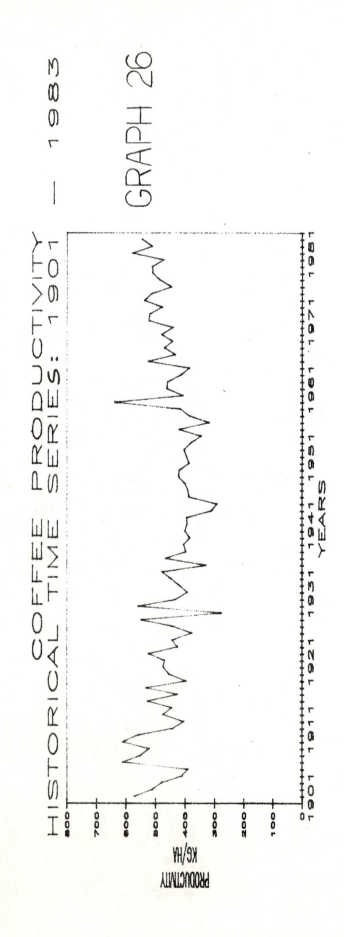

APPENDIX II

NOTES ON TIME SERIES OF PRODUCTIVITY

Sources:

1901-46

International Institute of Agriculture, International Yearbook of Agricultural Statistics. From 1901, figures of yields refer to particular countries, either important in production or good in data collection. Starting in 1920, totals for continents have been calculated. In arriving at totals, an attempt has been made to take into account all the countries by filling in the gaps by means of conjectural estimates. However, certain countries have been left out of the totals because most of the figures were lacking or because it was difficult to make even rough estimates of missing data.

1947-60

FAO, Yearbook of Food and Agricultural Statistics. The same methodology used in the case of the data of the Institute of Agriculture has been applied during this period. In general, however, more data were available.

1961 onwards

All figures come from FAO ESS tabulations and include all countries of the group "Total Developing Countries".

Commodities:

Wheat

In the first period of the century (1901-19), India and Argentina accounted for about 90 percent of the total production of developing countries. Since 1920, India and Argentina still remained the main producing countries, with 76 percent of production; but a small group of countries such as Algeria, Egypt and Morocco have contributed about 10 percent of production of total developing countries. In more recent years, the weight of India and Argentina has been around 28 percent while other countries such as Pakistan and Turkey have accounted for about 18 percent and China alone has accounted for about 35 percent.

Rice

In the period 1901-09, only data from India were available; from 1910 to 1920, other countries contributed in calculating the yield, but the India weight is by far the largest. From 1920, all developing countries have been considered, but still India accounts for about 60 percent of production. In more recent years, the weight of India has decreased to around 20-25 percent of total weight, while China has reached about 38 percent of total weight.

Maize

From 1901 to 1909, figures refer particularly to Argentina. From 1910 to 1920, besides Argentina, Egypt contributed to the yield for about one third of the total. In the period 1921-45, the contribution of Brazil and Mexico was very important, even though all developing countries are included. In more recent years, the contribution of the three main Latin American countries was about 19 percent of the total, while China increased its weight to 38 percent of the total.

Sugar cane

This time series is limited for lack of data of the two major producing countries—Cuba and Brazil—in the period 1901-30. The series is essentially built up with Argentina yields till 1930, Cuba and Brazil yields prevailing over the years 1931-51, and Cuba yields missing again from 1952 to 1960. From 1961, all developing country yields are included, but Brazil and China together account for about 40-43 percent of the total.

Coffee

The main producing country is Brazil, which during the 1920s and 1930s produced ten times more than Colombia and twenty times more than Guatemala. Even though Colombia increased its production in the following years, this series reflects mainly Brazil's yield because statistics for Colombia are limited to quantity data. In more recent years, Brazil and Colombia together accounted for 45 percent of all developing country production.

Cocoa

The main producing country is Ghana with a production which is double that of Brazil. Therefore, the series, when data were available, reflect the trends of these two countries. In recent years, another African country, the Côte d'Ivoire, has overtaken Ghana and has become the main cocoa-producing country. These two African countries, plus Nigeria and Brazil, contribute together 70 percent of total production.

Tea

The tea time series is very homogeneous because there is data for India and Sri Lanka from 1909 (plus Indonesia from 1951), continuously till 1960. India's weight predominates. In more recent years, Asian countries, including China, have represented 92 percent of total production.

Productivity Time Series, 1901-83

	Maize a/	Wheat b/	Rice c/	Sugar cane d/	Coffee e/	Cocoa f/	Tea g/
				m.t./ha			
1901	1.425	0.628	1.530	36.69	0.570	...	...
1902	1.972	0.673	1.750	25.66	0.510	...	...
1903	1.945	0.799	1.720	29.80	0.480	...	...
1904	1.482	0.783	1.680	25.29	0.410	...	...
1905	1.734	0.659	1.540	26.11	0.390	...	...
1906	0.637	0.764	1.530	21.28	0.610	...	...
1907	1.525	0.770	1.340	19.35	0.550	...	...
1908	1.458	0.675	1.420	28.36	0.520	...	...
1909	1.586	0.713	1.798	21.89	0.610	...	...
1910	0.626	0.740	1.758	25.67	0.560	0.235	0.463
1911	1.687	0.784	1.678	29.28	0.441	0.223	0.436
1912	1.229	0.765	1.510	22.52	0.404	0.173	0.495
1913	1.336	0.707	1.423	29.34	0.474	0.143	0.523
1914	1.547	0.734	1.428	33.46	0.445	0.160	0.512
1915	1.082	0.774	1.593	18.80	0.525	0.212	0.511
1916	0.782	0.733	1.600	16.72	0.425	0.171	0.621
1917	1.195	0.812	1.588	22.13 F	0.531	0.170	0.561
1918	1.342	0.707	1.258	23.24	0.396	0.338	0.540
1919	1.549	0.834	1.488	32.63	0.453	0.287	0.531
1920	1.381	0.837	1.339	30.15	0.473	0.330	0.575
1921	1.126	0.760	1.474	36.93	0.469	0.383	0.530
1922	1.143	0.799	1.537	38.80	0.523	0.367	0.528
1923	1.174	0.828	1.399	40.00 F	0.425	0.429	0.478
1924	1.145	0.754	1.516	42.11	0.443	0.540	0.549
1925	1.211	0.716	1.419	45.05	0.376	0.546	0.584
1926	1.234	0.767	1.428	43.74	0.440	0.532	0.569
1927	1.278	0.816	1.424	41.81	0.548	0.566	0.579
1928	1.101	0.783	1.433	37.69	0.275	0.508	0.578
1929	1.091	0.717	1.431	34.90	0.558	0.568	0.586
1930	1.204	0.790	1.459	39.52	0.433	0.569	0.616
1931	1.209	0.784	1.353	46.57	0.392	0.564	0.555
1932	1.106	0.765	1.408	37.03	0.419	0.607	0.566
1933	1.080	0.845	1.643	36.29	0.448	0.624	0.593
1934	1.267	0.813	1.382	36.40	0.478	0.579	0.506
1935	1.248	0.784	1.325	38.57	0.329	0.690	0.466
1936	1.204	0.821	1.447	36.63	0.466	0.678	0.456
1937	1.106	0.828	1.440	37.86	0.397	0.685	0.460
1938	1.086	0.921	1.358	39.25	0.404	0.621	0.478
1939	1.240	0.868	1.375	37.90	0.384	0.700	0.512
1940	1.124	0.911	1.522	39.10	0.400	0.488	0.519
1941	1.058	0.838	1.574	39.56	0.392	0.478	0.570
1942	0.891	0.865	1.534	36.85	0.395	0.456	0.624
1943	1.069	0.910	1.601	39.88	0.310	0.544	0.661
1944	0.876	0.773	1.281	34.31	0.290	0.433	0.696
1945	0.915	0.740	1.264	36.23	0.386	0.431	0.634
						0.395	0.667

	Maize a/	Wheat b/	Rice c/	Sugar cane d/	Coffee e/	Cocoa f/	Tea g/
				m.t./ha			
1946	1.052	0.894	1.583	37.84	0.390	0.368	0.693
1947	1.069	0.898	1.599	41.91	0.400	0.362	0.771
1948	1.098	0.952	1.587	37.17	0.421	0.352	0.741
1949	1.021	0.879	1.543	37.95	0.419	0.439	0.756
1950	1.009	0.884	1.507	38.46	0.386	0.440	0.774
1951	1.015	0.873	1.529	41.02	0.395	0.361	0.790
1952	1.048	0.930	1.564	40.54	0.403	0.330	0.796
1953	1.106	0.950	1.636	42.43	0.380	0.359	0.765
1954	1.089	0.873	1.725	41.94	0.345	0.392	0.798
1955	1.098	0.864	1.839	41.44	0.420	0.392	0.838
1956	1.089	0.888	1.774	41.23	0.318	0.420	0.826
1957	1.079	0.896	1.757	44.12	0.384	0.334	0.785
1958	1.024	0.878	1.499	45.55	0.416	0.371	0.845
1959	0.963	0.883	1.550	44.24	0.637	0.352	0.869
1960	1.068	0.861	1.607	44.28	0.406	0.352	0.881
1961	1.170	0.778	1.760	47.94	0.460	0.279	0.709
1962	1.178	0.900	1.779	45.37	0.458	0.280	0.707
1963	1.182	0.932	1.947	45.84	0.413	0.291	0.720
1964	1.226	0.944	1.998	48.64	0.384	0.326	0.737
1965	1.260	1.011	1.935	50.27	0.523	0.273	0.751
1966	1.324	0.987	1.971	48.56	0.432	0.327	0.771
1967	1.423	1.048	2.051	48.89	0.469	0.327	0.757
1968	1.365	1.087	2.112	49.79	0.441	0.316	0.772
1969	1.372	1.106	2.136	50.89	0.479	0.338	0.757
1970	1.505	1.125	2.278	52.30	0.440	0.348	0.753
1971	1.518	1.216	2.270	49.73	0.521	0.369	0.729
1972	1.449	1.279	2.225	49.17	0.518	0.350	0.771
1973	1.555	1.225	2.359	51.37	0.476	0.321	0.738
1974	1.638	1.279	2.326	51.75	0.536	0.349	0.708
1975	1.698	1.400	2.417	50.50	0.512	0.354	0.693
1976	1.674	1.510	2.364	51.50	0.446	0.310	0.682
1977	1.720	1.356	2.479	53.97	0.485	0.336	0.728
1978	1.788	1.547	2.596	54.65	0.508	0.333	0.725
1979	1.856	1.656	2.574	54.12	0.511	0.360	0.735
1980	1.941	1.568	2.693	53.15	0.471	0.351	0.717
1981	2.007	1.677	2.752	56.32	0.577	0.364	0.698
1982	2.001	1.849	2.916	57.50	0.511	0.337	0.700
1983	2.024	1.983	3.046	56.76	0.545	0.335	0.714

F = FAO estimate.
... = not available.

Country coverage:

a/ 1901-08 Argentina
   1909-20 Argentina, Chile, Uruguay, Algeria, Egypt, Tunisia
   1921-60 Total developing countries
   1961-83 Total developing countries (FAO-ESS tab.)

b/ 1901-20 India, Korea, Algeria, Egypt, Morocco, Tunisia, Mexico, Argentina, Chile, Uruguay
   1921-60 Total developing countries
   1961-83 Total developing countries (FAO-ESS tab.)

c/ 1901-08 India
   1909-20 India, Indonesia, Sri Lanka, Philippines, Egypt, Guyana
   1921-60 Total developing countries
   1961-83 Total developing countries (FAO-ESS tab.)

d/ 1901-20 Argentina
   1921-30 Argentina, Trinidad, Mexico
   1931-51 Argentina, Trinidad, Mexico, Cuba, Brazil
   1952-60 Argentina, Trinidad, Mexico, Brazil
   1961-83 Total developing countries (FAO-ESS tab.)

e/ 1901-12 Brazil
   1913-23 Brazil, Guatemala
   1924-32 Brazil, Guatemala, Colombia
   1933-46 Brazil, Guatemala
   1947-60 Brazil
   1961-83 Total developing countries (FAO-ESS tab.)

f/ 1901-19 Trinidad and Tobago
   1920-37 Trinidad, Brazil, Ghana
   1938-43 Brazil, Mexico, Ghana, Côte d'Ivoire
   1944-56 Brazil, Mexico
   1957-60 Brazil, Mexico, Trinidad, Côte d'Ivoire
   1961-83 Total developing countries (FAO-ESS tab.)

g/ 1909-50 India, Sri Lanka
   1951-60 India, Indonesia, Sri Lanka
   1961-83 Total developing countries (FAO-ESS tab.)

Table A.2.1: **Terms of Trade During Downswing Periods**

	Intercept	Trend	$\bar{R}^2$
Beverages	−0.131 (0.887)	0.006 (1.660)	0.024
Cereals	0.159 (3.373)***	−0.005 (4.379)***	0.350
Food	−0.040 (0.398)	−0.003 (1.397)	−0.002
Non-food	1.272 (7.810)***	−0.015 (4.237)***	0.348
Total agric.	0.330 (2.691)**	−0.007 (2.646)**	0.143
Coffee	−0.345 (2.966)***	0.011 (3.999)***	0.333
Cocoa	−0.270 (0.726)	−0.001 (0.118)	−0.070
Tea	0.568 (4.014)***	−0.003 (1.017)	−0.033
Sugar	−0.505 (2.334)**	−0.009 (1.777)*	0.037
Wheat	0.121 (2.032)*	−0.006 (4.153)***	0.321
Maize	0.196 (2.398)**	−0.004 (2.178)**	0.054
Rice	0.219 (2.072)**	−0.005 (2.056)**	0.069
Cotton	0.471 (3.358)***	−0.004 (1.318)	0.009
Wool	1.066 (7.635)***	−0.008 (2.636)***	0.142
Rubber	2.194 (5.551)***	−0.030 (3.504)***	0.255

Table A.2.1: (cont.)

	Intercept	Trend	$\bar{R}^2$
Copper	0.086 (0.448)	-0.004 (0.935)	-0.039
Tin	-0.991 (15.114)***	0.012 (7.789)***	0.661
Lead	0.081 (1.159)	0.002 (1.015)	0.010
Zinc	-0.540 (7.195)***	0.002 (1.318)	0.024

*** = Indicates significance at the 1 percent level.
 ** = Indicates significance at the 5 percent level.
  * = Indicates significance at the 10 percent level.

Table A.2.2: **Terms of Trade During Upswing Periods**

	Intercept	Trend	$\bar{R}^2$
Beverages	-0.222 (1.328)	0.007 (2.094)**	0.045
Cereals	0.277 (3.171)***	-0.007 (4.256)***	0.240
Food	0.015 (0.180)	-0.003 (2.131)**	0.048
Non-food	1.492 (16.805)***	-0.018 (10.271)***	0.670
Total agric.	0.447 (5.676)***	-0.008 (5.376)***	0.345
Coffee	-0.434 (2.272)**	0.011 (2.983)***	0.119
Cocoa	-0.224 (0.651)	-0.0005 (0.071)	-0.041
Tea	0.362 (2.135)**	-0.0001 (0.026)	0.000
Sugar	-0.439 (2.424)**	-0.006 (1.809)*	0.025
Wheat	0.237 (2.079)**	-0.008 (3.498)***	0.166
Maize	0.348 (3.711)***	-0.007 (3.689)***	0.185
Rice	0.174 (1.284)	-0.006 (2.382)**	0.067
Cotton	0.611 (5.066)***	-0.007 (2.864)***	0.108
Wool	1.186 (8.244)***	-0.011 (4.070)***	0.223
Rubber	2.519 (13.176)***	-0.031 (8.334)***	0.569

Table A.2.2: (cont.)

	Intercept	Trend	$\bar{R}^2$
Copper	0.124 (0.587)	-0.003 (0.755)	-0.028
Tin	-0.823 (5.682)***	0.010 (3.748)***	-0.264
Lead	(0.128) (1.170)	0.001 (0.350)	-0.038
Zinc	-0.274 (2.404)**	-0.001 (0.549)	-0.035

*** = Indicates significance at the 1 percent level.
 ** = Indicates significance at the 5 percent level.
  * = Indicates significance at the 10 percent level.

Table A.2.3: **Regression Results for Productivity (Equation 2)**

	Intercept	Trend	DY	DYC	$\bar{R}^2$
Wheat	8.460 (72.04)***	0.180 (5.81)***	0.110 (2.18)**		0.283
Rice	9.233 (90.69)***	0.118 (4.40)***	0.226 (4.990)***		0.299
Maize	9.241 (77.08)***	0.020 (0.650)	0.265 (4.64)		0.185
Cocoa	6.984 (23.70)***	0.324 (3.80)***	-0.555 (5.27)***	0.285 (4.05)***	0.333
Coffee	8.664 (129.14)***	-0.094 (4.57)***	0.215 (5.140)***		0.259
Tea	3.082 (13.41)***	0.310 (4.85)***	-0.184 (3.27)***		0.236
Sugar	5.463 (44.01)***	0.118 (2.98)***	0.196 (2.26)**	0.058 (0.80)	0.307

*** = Indicates significance at the 1 percent level.
 ** = Indicates significance at the 5 percent level.
  * = Indicates significance at the 10 percent level.
 DY = Dummy year.
 DCY = Dummy country.

Table A.2.4: **Regression Results for the Single Factorial Terms of Trade (Equation 3)**

	Intercept	Trend	Trend Squared	DY	DYC	$\bar{R}^2$
Wheat	17.332 (70.76)***	-0.112 (0.67)	0.100 (2.86)***	0.127 (1.35)		0.293
Rice	14.315 (50.21)***	-0.103 (0.530)	0.016 (0.460)	0.236 (2.540)**		0.043
Maize	14.043 (56.06)***	0.130 (0.780)	-0.037 (1.300)	0.149 (2.250)**		0.096
Cocoa	16.535 (5.24)***	-3.131 (1.580)	0.545 (1.820)*	-0.519 (1.780)*	0.016 (0.10)	0.047
Coffee	13.329 (33.77)	-0.638 (2.060)**	0.152 (2.350)**	0.001 (0.004)		0.033
Tea	7.627 (3.20)***	0.465 (0.31)	-0.008 (0.04)	-.283 (-1.550)		0.040
Sugar	9.963 (34.144)***	-0.056 (0.596)		0.387 (1.913)*	-0.179 (1.024)	-0.003

*** = Indicates significance at the 1 percent level.
** = Indicates significance at the 5 percent level.
* = Indicates significance at the 10 percent level.

APPENDIX III
TESTS OF INCREASED INSTABILITY

Table A.3.1: **Kendall's Tau Test of Increased Instability for Barter Terms of Trade, 1900-82**

	Beverages	Cereal	Food	Non-food	Maize	Rice	Cotton	Wool	Rubber	Total Agriculture
Time	-0.017	-0.143*	0.053	-0.046	-0.092	-0.060	-0.031	-0.029	-0.090	0.096

	Coffee	Cocoa	Tea	Sugar	Wheat	Copper	Tin	Lead	Zinc
Time	-0.102	0.179**	-0.002	0.127*	-0.193***	-0.044	-0.101	0.056	-0.121

*** = Indicates significance at the 1 percent level.

** = Indicates significance at the 5 percent level.

* = Indicates significance at the 10 percent level.

Table A.3.2: **Heteroscedasticity Test of Increased Instability:**

Kendall's Tau Test

	Ten years	Fifteen years	Twenty year	Break periods a/	Historical periods b/	Historical periods c/
Beverages	0.019	-0.088	0.033	0.012	-0.009	0.029
Cereals	0.068	-0.100	-0.113	-0.106	-0.108	-0.108
Food	0.052	-0.019	0.192***	0.044	0.013	0.013
Non-Food	-0.066	0.009	-0.135*	-0.102	-0.078	-0.096
Total Agriculture	0.049	0.024	0.087	0.081	-0.047	-0.065
Cocoa	0.199***	0.140*	0.239***	0.120	0.155**	0.115
Coffee	0.001	-0.059	-0.027	-0.106	-0.088	-0.083
Tea	-0.074	-0.041	-0.059	0.047	-0.111	-0.084
Sugar	0.225***	0.067	0.178**	0.127*	0.155**	0.155**
Wheat	-0.065	-0.109	-0.086	-0.145**	-0.058	-0.058
Maize	-0.084	-0.119	-0.034	-0.087	-0.121	-0.121
Rice	-0.067	0.008	0.000	-0.033	-0.030	-0.003
Cotton	-0.064	-0.018	-0.093	-0.115	-0.086	-0.119
Wool	-0.12	-0.102	-0.104	-0.083	-0.106	-0.077
Rubber	-0.190***	-0.099	-0.071	-0.098	-0.134*	-0.097
Copper	-0.169**	-0.094	-0.041	-0.031	-0.090	-0.081
Tin	-0.096	-0.182**	-0.104	-0.149**	-0.218***	-0.079
Zinc	-0.109	-0.041	-0.047	-0.109	-0.087	-0.021

a/   1900-50; 1950-82
b/   1900-13, 1914-39, 1940-54, 1955-70, 1971-82
c/   1900-13, 1914-39, 1940-54, 1955-73, 1974-82

*** = Indicates significance at the 1 percent level.
 ** = Indicates significance at the 5 percent level.
  * = Indicates significance at the 10 percent level.

APPENDIX IV
REGRESSION RESULTS USED IN SPECTRAL ANALYSIS

Table A.4.1: **ARIMA Model Specifications for Terms of Trade, 1900-82**

		AR1	MA1	AR2	MA2	Box-Pierce Portmanteau test a/	Fisher's Kappa test	Bartlett's Kolmogorov-Smirnov statistics
Beverages	ARMA (1,2)	0.989 (46.01)***	0.056 (.50)		0.202 (1.78)	14.19 (21)	2.262	0.060
Cereals	ARMA (1,1)	0.983 (44.88)***	-0.048 (0.43)			11.21 (22)	4.323	0.125
Food	ARMA (2,2)	0.915 (1.31)	-0.19 (0.03)	0.077 (0.11)	0.168 (1.42)	11.96 (20)	4.542	0.109
Non-food	ARIMA (1,1,2)	0.279 (.76)	0.186 (0.53)		0.297 (2.75)***	12.55 (21)	2.985	0.081
Total agriculture	ARMA (2,2)	0.842 (1.85)*	-0.137 (0.30)	0.143 (0.32)	0.085 (0.74)	10.31 (20)	5.035	0.132
Tea	ARMA (2,2)	1.741 (4.02)***	0.823 (1.84)*	-0.742 (1.74)*	0.019 (0.13)	10.09 (20)	2.633	0.075
Maize	ARMA (1,2)	0.991 (57.50)***	0.115 (1.04)		0.241 (2.17)**	20.27 (21)	3.942	0.119
Rice	ARMA (1,2)	0.986 (46.23)***	-0.144 (1.31)		0.336 (3.06)***	12.28 (21)	3.128	0.115
Cotton	ARIMA (2,1,2)	0.428 (2.25)**	0.185 (0.88)	-0.444 (2.38)**	0.129 (0.61)	11.33 (20)	2.552	0.054
Sugar	ARMA (2,2)	0.975 (2.41)***	0.302 (0.78)	0.014 (0.03)	0.299 (1.55)*	10.85 (20)	4.010	0.092

Table A.4.1: (cont.)

		AR1	MA1	AR2	MA2	Box-Pierce Portmanteau Test [a]	Fisher's Kappa test	Bartlett's Kolmogorov-Smirnov statistics
Wheat	ARMA (2,1)	0.414 (0.45)	-0.633 (0.73)	0.556 (0.61)		11.37 (21)	5.355	0.117
Cocoa	ARMA (1,2)	0.974 (30.89)***	0.058 (0.49)		0.192 (1.62)*	11.08 (21)	3.261	0.107
Coffee	ARMA (1,2)	0.990 (31.27)***	0.042 (0.37)		0.269 (2.39)**	12.61 (21)	2.377	0.050
Wool	ARIMA (2,2,1)	-0.116 (1.01)	0.907 (17.19)***	-0.301	(2.65)***	16.09	2.939 (21)	0.106
Copper	ARIMA (2,1,1)	0.413 (0.80)	0.480 (0.94)	-0.069 (0.16)	0.181 (0.38)	12.98 (20)	3.531	0.120
Tin	ARIMA (2,2,2)	-0.187 (0.19)	0.590 (0.61)	-0.114 (0.66)	0.187 (0.22)	9.48 (20)	3.354	0.126
Rubber	ARIMA (1,1,2)	0.042 (0.04)	-0.046 (0.05)		0.122 (0.86)	17.01 (21)	2.947	0.061
Lead	ARIMA (2,1,1)	0.836 (7.29)***	1.000 (57.63)***	-0.108	(0.94)	9.73	3.606 (21)	0.066
Zinc	ARIMA (1,1,2)	0.400 (2.26)**	0.754 (4.06)***		0.263 (1.41)	11.14 (21)	2.729	0.068

*** = Indicates significance at the 1 percent level.
** = Indicates significance at the 5 percent level.
* = Indicates significance at the 10 percent level.
[a] = Numbers in parentheses are degrees of freedom.

Table A.4.2: Estimation Results of the Harmonic Version (corrected from autocorrelation)

	Intercept	COS1	COS2	COS3	SIN1	SIN2	SIN3	$\bar{R}^2$
Beverages	1.820 (0.729)	-0.298 (0.569)	-0.610 (0.259)	-0.162 (0.465)	-1.161 (0.278)	0.010 (0.016)	0.294 (0.385)	0.039
Cereals	-1.230 (1.154)	-0.085 (0.393)	1.976 (1.993)*	0.199 (1.459)	3.686 (2.073)**	0.317 (1.248)	-0.551 (1.772)*	0.249
Food	-0.394 (0.403)	-0.101 (0.500)	1.175 (1.281)	0.159 (1.215)	2.106 (1.290)	0.212 (0.892)	-0.295 (1.010)	0.049
Non-food	-3.279 (1.251)	-0.096 (0.180)	5.424 (2.224)**	1.336 (3.972)***	9.198 (2.104)**	1.524 (2.439)**	-1.437 (1.879)*	0.733
Total Agriculture	-0.812 (0.908)	-0.127 (0.621)	1.828 (1.955)*	0.375 (2.892)***	3.191 (1.907)*	0.467 (1.946)*	0.467 (1.589)	0.495
Coffee	2.736 (0.870)	-0.658 (0.999)	-1.597 (0.537)	0.247 (0.564)	-2.705 (0.514)	0.289 (0.370)	0.671 (0.698)	0.045
Cocoa	-1.333 (0.640)	-0.253 (0.587)	2.543 (1.301)	0.294 (1.049)	3.666 (1.054)	0.196 (0.385)	-0.805 (1.290)	0.208
Tea	3.970 (2.141)**	1.034 (2.684)**	-2.392 (1.372)	-0.342 (1.361)	-4.009 (1.294)	-1.328 (2.922)***	0.733 (1.312)	0.264
Sugar	-0.561 (0.430)	-0.080 (0.300)	1.104 (0.910)	0.119 (0.705)	1.776 (0.817)	0.216 (0.694)	-0.273 (0.716)	0.081

Table A.4.2: (Cont.)

	Intercept	COS1	COS2	COS3	SIN1	SIN2	SIN3	$\bar{R}^2$
Wheat	-0.681 (0.577)	0.104 (0.431)	1.422 (1.293)	0.210 (1.384)	2.670 (1.356)	0.351 (1.247)	-0.358 (1.037)	0.196
Maize	-1.898 (1.506)	-0.167 (0.645)	2.614 (2.243)**	0.244 (1.549)	4.962 (2.365)**	0.395 (1.332)	-0.790 (2.178)**	0.231
Cotton	2.084 (1.266)	-0.225 (0.661)	-0.999 (0.648)	0.419 (1.913)*	-1.170 (0.426)	0.477 (1.192)	0.483 (0.985)	0.200
Wool	1.920 (0.832)	0.517 (1.108)	-0.324 (0.152)	0.143 (0.495)	0.449 (0.117)	0.011 (0.020)	0.064 (0.097)	0.508
Rubber	-23.638 (2.023)**	-0.709 (0.290)	29.316 (2.655)***	5.381 (3.319)***	47.096 (2.409)**	6.446 (2.224)**	-8.292 (2.323)**	0.626
Copper	-0.896 (0.792)	0.394 (1.716)*	1.973 (1.880)*	-0.087 (0.608)	3.145 (1.668)*	-0.426 (1.592)	-0.417 (1.276)	0.485
Tin	-0.476 (0.578)	-0.542 (3.195)***	1.332 (1.730)*	0.091 (0.839)	1.973 (1.435)	0.345 (1.733)*	-0.445 (1.820)	0.571
Lead	0.487 (0.317)	-0.057 (0.178)	0.648 (0.448)	0.151 (0.716)	1.176 (0.458)	-0.029 (0.077)	-0.182 (0.390)	0.016
Zinc	-1.570 (1.775)*	-0.317 (1.771)*	2.162 (2.642)**	0.243 (2.191)**	3.783 (2.568)**	0.366 (1.754)*	-0.620 (2.439)**	0.121

*** = Indicates significance at the 1 percent level.
** = Indicates significance at the 5 percent level.
* = Indicates significance at the 10 percent level.

Table A.4.3: Spearman Correlation Coefficient between Traditional Instability Indices and Indices Based on the Spectrum for BTT, 1900-82

Indices based on the spectrum	C.V.	CORR.CV	EPSILON	Traditional indices H	FI	GI	EXPON
Harmonic	0.632***	0.681***	0.561**	0.540**	0.437*	0.693***	0.682***
Log-Linear	0.730***	0.810***	0.735***	0.749***	0.668***	0.810***	0.798***
ARIMA	0.634***	0.680***	0.558**	0.529**	0.469*	0.687***	0.687***
First dif.	0.647***	0.686***	0.554**	0.528	0.449*	0.693***	0.682***

*** = Indicates significance at the 1 percent level.
** = Indicates significance at the 5 percent level.
* = Indicates significance at the 10 percent level.

APPENDIX V

ESTIMATES OF DEGREE OF CURRENCY OVERVALUATION AND OF TRENDS AND INSTABILITY IN THE BENEFITS FROM TRADE AND ITS COMPONENTS

In order to estimate parity exchange rates, identification was made for each country of the initial year of the process that led the country inflation rate to diverge progressively from the international inflation rate. The results of this analysis are summarized in Tables A.5.1 and A.5.2.

Table A.5.1: **Base Years Used in Estimating Parity Exchange Rates**

Africa		Asia		Latin America	
Cameroon	1975	Bangladesh	1981	Brazil	1975
Ethiopia	1975	Sri Lanka	1981	Colombia	1980
Ghana	1970	India	1981	Ecuador	1970
Côte d'Ivoire	1982	Indonesia	1967	El Salvador	1976
Kenya	1981	Philippines	1981	Dominican Rep.	1981
Malawi	1980	Thailand	1981	Guyana	1976
Mauritius	1971			Mexico	1980
Nigeria	1965 a/				
Uganda	1967				

a/ Shadow exchange rate.

Table A.5.2: **Degree of Currency Overvaluation (NNPC/NPC), 1961-82**

Africa		Asia		Latin America	
Cameroon	0.998	Bangladesh	0.669	Brazil	0.942
Ethiopia	0.751	Sri Lanka	0.310	Colombia	0.864
Ghana	0.475	India	0.523	Ecuador	0.901
Côte d'Ivoire	0.834	Indonesia	0.861	El Salvador	0.847
Kenya	0.628	Philippines	0.608	Dominican Rep.	0.666
Malawi	0.955	Thailand	0.650	Guyana	0.926
Mauritius	0.376			Mexico	0.877
Nigeria	1.376				
Uganda	0.198				

Table A.5.3: **Trends in the Benefits from Trade and its Components: Country Results**

A. COCOA

	WELFARE		DBT		IBT	
	Trend	Quadratic trend	Trend	Quadratic trend	Trend	Quadratic trend
Cameroon	-0.299 (1.874)*		0.025 (4.104)***		0.027 (2.698)**	
Côte d'Ivoire	-0.103 (0.617)		0.002 (0.425)		0.017 (1.489)	
Brazil	-0.164 (1.055)		0.049 (2.595)**		0.124 (1.685)	-0.005 (1.741)*
Ghana	0.126 (1.935)*	-0.005 (1.845)*	0.022 (0.574)	-0.004 (2.238)**	0.021 (2.106)**	
Dominican Republic	0.037 (1.287)		0.008 (0.441)		0.021 (1.310)	
Ecuador	-0.166 (1.778)		-0.004 (0.265)		0.008 (0.520)	
Nigeria	0.024 (1.049)		0.012 (1.727)		0.024 (1.967)*	
TOTAL	-0.039 (5.005)***		0.009 (1.422)		0.001 (0.783)	

B. COFFEE

	WELFARE		DBT		IBT	
	Trend	Quadratic trend	Trend	Quadratic trend	Trend	Quadratic trend
Mexico	-0.077 (0.709)		0.005 (0.332)		0.009 (0.799)	
Côte d'Ivoire	0.258 (1.606)		-0.011 (4.753)***		-0.002 (0.137)	
Brazil	-0.112 (0.700)		0.172 (3.490)***	-0.007 (3.195)***	-0.010 (0.819)	
Colombia	-0.154 (0.894)		0.001 (0.133)		0.009 (1.091)	
El Salvador	0.0002 (0.008)		0.052 (4.699)***		0.009 (1.031)	
Uganda	0.235 (1.572)		0.067 (1.865)*		0.025 (2.705)**	
Kenya	-0.139 (1.008)		0.010 (0.693)		-0.019 (1.826)*	
Indonesia	0.462 (1.678)		-0.150 (2.988)***		0.052 (4.294)***	
Ethiopia	-0.002 (0.065)		0.088 (2.022)*	-0.004 (2.230)**	0.004 (0.422)	
TOTAL	0.039 (1.165)		-0.042 (2.603)***		0.025 (0.860)	

C. TEA

	WELFARE		DBT		IBT	
	Trend	Quadratic trend	Trend	Quadratic trend	Trend	Quadratic trend
Indonesia	0.310 (1.422)		-0.008 (0.573)		-0.010 (1.062)	
Malawi	-0.129 (5.789)***		0.006 (0.724)		-0.051 (11.304)***	
Brazil	0.211 (1.258)		0.099 (2.867)**	-0.006 (3.762)***	0.023 (1.090)	-0.003 (3.878)***
Kenya	-0.077 (0.547)		-0.029 (4.914)***		-0.062 (7.579)***	
Sri Lanka	-0.189 (1.405)		-0.085 (3.223)***	0.005 (4.076)***	-0.057 (10.267)***	
India	-0.086 (2.465)**		-0.008 (0.573)		-0.055 (7.660)***	
Bangladesh	0.277 (1.798)*		-0.059 (2.214)**		-0.085 (2.709)**	
TOTAL	-0.047 (1.095)*		-0.059 (2.284)***		-0.098 (4.574)***	

D. SUGAR

	WELFARE		DBT		IBT	
	Trend	Quadratic trend	Trend	Quadratic trend	Trend	Quadratic trend
Mauritius	-0.242 (1.427)		0.161 (5.273)***		0.003 (0.216)	
Thailand	-0.205 (1.606)		-0.052 (2.079)*	0.003 (3.059)***	0.200 (2.755)**	-0.009 (2.978)***
Brazil	-0.121 (0.97)		0.023 (1.829)*		0.124 (1.576)	-0.007 (2.004)*
Guyana	0.193 (1.490)		-0.089 (1.175)	0.011 (3.351)***	-0.0008 (0.086)	
Philippines	0.003 (0.029)		0.003 (0.172)		0.076 (1.840)*	-0.005 (3.046)***
Dominican Republic	0.185 (2.496)**	-0.009 (2.861)**	-0.010 (0.987)		0.082 (2.024)*	-0.004 (2.462)**
TOTAL	-0.103 (3.428)***		0.129 (4.829)***		-0.029 (1.127)	

Note: Figures in parentheses are t-values.

*** = Indicates significance at the 1 percent level.
** = Indicates significance at the 5 percent level.
*   = Indicates significance at the 10 percent level.

Table A.5.4: **Trends in Instability in the Benefits from Trade and its Components: Country Results**

A. COCOA

	WELFARE		DBT		IBT	
	Trend	Quadratic trend	Trend	Quadratic trend	Trend	Quadratic trend
Cameroon	−0.554 (1.191)	0.038 (1.999)*	−0.038 (2.663)**	0.001 (2.219)**	0.006 (1.419)	
Côte d'Ivoire	0.167 (1.133)		0.002 (1.024)		0.007 (2.053)*	
Brazil	0.199 (1.504)		0.011 (1.792)*		0.013 (1.913)*	
Ghana	0.018 (1.602)		0.012 (1.805)*		0.007 (1.896)*	
Dominican Republic	0.016 (1.712)		0.016 (2.824)**		0.008 (1.438)	
Ecuador	0.215 (1.843)*		0.009 (2.103)**		0.013 (2.726)**	
Nigeria	0.014 (1.845)*		−0.002 (0.470)		0.007 (0.005)	
TOTAL	0.012 (2.903)**		0.005 (1.266)		0.020 (2.392)**	

B. COFFEE

	WELFARE		DBT		IBT	
	Trend	Quadratic trend	Trend	Quadratic trend	Trend	Quadratic trend
Mexico	0.099 (1.066)		0.009 (1.388)		0.006 (1.274)	
Côte d'Ivoire	-0.268 (2.094)**		-0.0009 (0.816)		0.012 (2.323)**	
Brazil	0.164 (1.165)		0.008 (2.245)**		0.120 (2.327)**	
Colombia	0.234 (1.608)		0.006 (1.679)		0.010 (1.979)*	
El Salvador	-0.146 (1.538)	0.006 (2.066)*	0.017 (2.440)**		0.012 (3.398)***	
Uganda	-1.872 (3.619)***	0.055 (3.101)***	0.014 (2.282)**		0.0140 (2.282)**	
Kenya	0.195 (1.678)		0.008 (1.616)		0.009 (2.581)**	
Indonesia	3.411 (3.810)***	0.098 (3.233)***	0.140 (2.094)*	-0.007 (2.292)**	-0.021 (0.704)	
Ethiopia	0.124 (2.041)*	-0.004 (1.794)*	0.006 (1.376)		0.009 (2.224)**	
TOTAL	-0.032 (1.677)		0.006 (1.866)*		0.042 (2.715)**	

C. TEA

	WELFARE		DBT		IBT	
	Trend	Quadratic trend	Trend	Quadratic trend	Trend	Quadratic trend
Indonesia	-1.976 (4.251)***	0.076 (3.380)***	0.001 (0.312)		-0.002 (0.306)	
Malawi	0.011 (0.760)		-0.008 (1.704)		0.018 (3.148)***	-0.0005 (2.301)**
Brazil	-0.294 (2.216)**		-0.033 (1.757)*		0.004 (1.110)	
Kenya	0.182 (1.535)		0.003 (0.752)		0.004 (1.026)	
Sri Lanka	-0.533 (1.742)*	0.038 (2.778)**	0.009 (2.211)**		0.005 (1.513)	
India	-0.074 (2.295)**	0.007 (4.619)***	0.001 (0.312)		0.005 (1.319)	
Bangladesh	-1.450 (4.162)***	0.051 (3.333)***	0.047 (1.682)	-0.002 (1.865)*	-0.006 (0.738)	
TOTAL	-0.009 (0.635)		-0.012 (1.076)		0.002 (1.689)	

D. SUGAR

	WELFARE		DBT		IBT	
	Trend	Quadratic trend	Trend	Quadratic trend	Trend	Quadratic trend
Mauritius	0.267 (1.996)*		-0.004 (0.537)		0.002 (0.434)	
Thailand	-0.695 (2.170)**	0.040 (3.043)***	-0.0001 (0.030)		-0.005 (0.351)	
Brazil	0.145 (1.341)		-0.008 (1.799)*		0.019 (0.646)	
Guyana	0.257 (2.894)***		0.011 (2.358)**		0.003 (0.518)	
Philippines	-0.645 (1.987)*	-0.025 (1.947)*	-0.004 (2.194)**		0.010 (1.943)*	
Dominican Republic	0.060 (0.466)		0.008 (1.024)		0.012 (1.653)	
TOTAL	0.031 (1.350)		-0.003 (0.378)		0.008 (0.845)	

Note: Figures in parentheses are t-values.

*** = Indicate significance at the 1 percent level.
** = Indicate significance at the 5 percent level.
*   = Indicate significance at the 10 percent level.

Table A.5.5: **Instability of Benefits from Trade and its Components: Country Results**

(Average of percentage absolute deviations around log linear trend)

Instability for Sugar:
(%)

	Welfare	DBT	IBT
Philippines	169.52	11.95	19.65
Thailand	303.78	17.17	65.55
Dominican Rep.	42.10	19.50	24.39
Mauritius	446.39	30.90	12.78
Brazil	170.33	21.73	26.09
Guyana	312.74	25.99	21.42
TOTAL	38.22	65.67	91.47

Instability for Cocoa:
(%)

	Welfare	DBT	IBT
Ecuador	335.57	13.99	19.46
Cameroon	648.67	13.26	12.39
Dominican Rep.	41.33	23.48	21.75
Brazil	341.76	26.22	27.27
Ghana	29.89	19.09	14.64
Côte d'Ivoire	249.72	6.57	15.87
TOTAL	14.01	14.24	26.21

Instability for Coffee:
(%)

	Welfare	DBT	IBT
Indonesia	569.33	113.41	30.41
Ethiopia	89.53	19.38	15.71
Uganda	447.71	65.58	20.12
El Salvador	46.94	21.47	15.69
Mexico	245.09	16.13	15.23
Côte d'Ivoire	537.96	5.75	15.69
Brazil	263.58	17.23	18.61
Colombia	332.94	9.43	17.97
Kenya	225.44	17.26	16.48
TOTAL	107.69	107.69	107.69

Instability for Tea:
(%)

	Welfare	DBT	IBT
Indonesia	526.94	17.12	22.34
India	80.84	10.13	9.00
Sri Lanka	423.55	14.22	7.28
Malawi	157.30	11.91	9.69
Brazil	469.67	22.39	12.93
Bangladesh	528.27	25.37	25.50
Kenya	222.26	12.11	11.53
TOTAL	54.62	65.67	91.47

BIBLIOGRAPHY

Adams, G. and S. Klein (1978). Stabilizing World Commodity Markets. Lexington, MA: Heath & Co.

Adams, G. and J. Behrman (1982). Commodity Exports and Economic Development. Lexington, MA: Lexington Books.

Akiyama, T. and R. Duncan (1982). "Analysis of the World Coffee Market". World Bank Staff Commodity Working Paper, No.7. Washington, D.C.

Akiyama, T. and R. Duncan (1982). "Analysis of the World Cocoa Market". World Bank Staff Commodity Working Paper, No.8. Washington, D.C.

Amin, S. (1976). Unequal Development. Sussex, England: Harvester Press.

Aubrey, H. (1955). "The Long Term Future of U.S. Imports and its Implications for Primary Producing Countries". American Economic Review, Vol.45, No.2, pp:270-295.

Atallah, M.K. (1958). The Long Term Movements of the Terms of Trade Between Agricultural and Industrial Products. Amsterdam, Netherlands: Economic Institute.

Bacha, E. (1978). "An Interpretation of Unequal Exchange from Prebisch-Singer to Emmanuel". Journal of Development Studies, Vol.5, No.4, pp.319-330.

Baer, W. (1962). "The Economics of Prebisch and ECLA". Economic Development and Cultural Change, Vol. 10, No. 2, part 1, January, pp. 169-182.

Bairoch, P. (1970). Diagnostic de l'évolution économique du Tiers Monde, 1900-1968. Paris: Gauthier-Villars.

Bairoch, P. (1975). The Economic Development of the Third World Since 1900. London: Methuen.

Baldwin, R.E. (1955). "Long-Term Trends in International Trade, Secular Movements in the Terms of Trade". American Economic Review, Papers and Proceedings, May, pp. 259-269.

Batra, R. and P. Pattanak, (1970). "Domestic Distortions and the Gains from Trade". The Economic Journal Vol.80, No.139, pp: 639-649.

Behrman, J. (1977). International Commodity Agreements. London: Overseas Development Council, monograph, No.9, October.

Belsley, D.A., et al. (1980). Regression Diagnostics. New York: John Wiley & Sons, Inc.

Bernstein, E.M. (1960). "International Effects of U.S. Economic Policy", in Joint Economic Committee, Study of Employment, Growth and Price Levels, January.

Bettelheim, C. (1970). Chine et URSS: Deux Modèles d'Industrialisation. Paris: Temps Modernes.

Bhagwati, J. (1958). "Immiserizing Growth: A Geometric Note". Review of Economic Studies, Vol.25, June, pp.201-205.

Bhagwati, J. (1960). "A Skeptical Note on the Adverse Secular Trend in the Terms of Trade of Underdeveloped Countries". Pakistan Economic Journal, December.

Bhagwati, J. (1965). "The Pure Theory of International Trade: A Survey", in The American Economic Association and The Royal Economic Society. Survey of Economic Theory, Vol. II, pp:156-239, New York.

Bhatia, B.M. (1969). "Terms of Trade and Economic Development: A Case Study of India, 1861-1939". Indian Economic Journal, Vol. 16, No. 45, April-June, pp. 414-433.

Box, G.E.P. and G. M. Jenkins (1976). Time Series Analysis: Forecasting and Control, revised edition. San Francisco: Holden-Day.

Box, G.E.P. and D.A. Pierce (1970). "Distribution of Residual Autocorrelations in Autoregressive Integrated Moving Average Time Series Models". Journal of the American Statistical Association, Vol. 65, pp.1509-1526.

Brecher, R.A. (1974). "Minimum Wage Rates and the Pure Theory of International Trade". Quarterly Journal of Economics, Vol.88, No. 1, February, pp.98-116.

Burgess, D.F. (1974). "A Cost Minimization Approach to Import Demand Equations". Review of Economics and Statistics, Vol.56, pp.225-234.

Cairncross, A.K. (1961). "International Trade and Economic Development". Economica, Vol. 28, No. 111, August, pp. 235-251.

Choeng-Hoy Chung (1979). "A Preliminary Model of the World Tea Economy". World Bank, Commodities and Export Projections Division. Washington, D.C.

Chow, G.L. (1960). "Tests of Equality Between Sets of Coefficients in Two Linear Regressions". Econometrica, Vol. 28, No.3, pp. 591-605.

Chu, K. and T.K. Morrison (1984). "The 1981-82 Recession and Non-Oil Primary Commodity Prices: An Econometric Analysis". IMF Staff Papers, Vol. 31, No. 1, pp. 93-140.

Chu, K. and T.K. Morrison (1986). World Non-Oil Primary Commodity Markets: A Medium-Term Framework of Analysis. IMF Staff Papers, Vol. 33, No. 1, pp. 139-184.

Clark, C. (1938). *The Conditions of Economic Progress*. New York: MacMillan.

Clark, C. (1942). *The Economics of 1960*. London: Macmillan.

Clement, M.O., R.L. Pfister and K.J. Rothwell (1968). *Theoretical Issues in International Economics*. Boston: Houghton & Mifflin.

Cooper, R. and R. Lawrence (1975). "The 1972-75 Commodity Boom". *Brookings Papers on Economic Activity*, Vol. 3, pp. 671-715.

Coppock, D.J. (1962). *International Economic Instability*. New York: McGraw-Hill.

Coppock, D.J. (1977). *International Trade Instability*. England: Saxon House, pp. 4-5.

Commonwealth Secretariat (1975). "Terms of Trade Policy for Primary Commodities". *Commonwealth Economic Papers*, No. 4; A Study Directed by J.P. Hayes, London.

Diakosavvas, D. (1983). "The Measurement of Commodity Market Instability with Particular Reference to Food Consumption Instability". *Manchester University Discussion Paper in Development Studies*, No. 8302.

D'Hérouville, H. (1975). "Termes de l'échange des pays développés et des pays en voie de développement". *Economie et statistique*, I.N.S.E.E., No. 67, May, pp. 23-26.

Edgeworth, P.T. (1894). "The Theory of International Values". *Economic Journal*.

Ellsworth, P.T. (1956). "The Terms of Trade between Primary Producing and Industrial Countries". *International American Economic Affairs*, Vol. 10, Summer, pp. 47-65.

Emmanuel, A. (1972). "Unequal Exchange: A Study of the Imperialism of Trade". New York: *Monthly Review Press* (translated from the French).

Enoch, C. and M. Panic (1981). "Commodity Prices in the 1970s". *Quarterly Bulletin, Bank of England*, Vol. 20, No. 1, pp. 42-53.

Erb, G. and S. Schiavo-Campo (1969). "Export Instability, Level of Economic Development and Economic Size of Less Developed Countries". *Oxford Bulletin of Economics and Statistics*, Vol. XXI, November, pp. 263-283.

FAO *Production and Trade Yearbook*, various issues.

Findlay, R. and H. Grubert (1959). "Factor Intensities, Technological Progress and the Terms of Trade". *Oxford Economic Papers*, February.

Findlay, R. (1981). "The Fundamental Determinants of the Terms of Trade". In Grassman, S. and E. Lundberg, (eds.) The World Economic Order: Past and Prospects. London and Basingstoke: Macmillan.

Flanders, M.J. (1964). "Prebisch on Protectionism: An Evaluation". Economic Journal, Vol. 74, No. 294, June, pp. 305-326.

GATT. (1980). International Trade 1979/80. Geneva.

Gelb, A.H. (1979). "On the Definition and Measurement of Instability and the Costs of Buffering Export Fluctuations". Review of Economic Studies, Vol.46, No.1, pp. 149-162.

Glezakos, C. (1970). "Export Instability and Economic Development: A Statistical Verification". (unpublished Ph.D. Thesis, University of Southern California).

Glezakos, C. (1983). "Instability and the Growth of Exports: A Misinterpretation of the Evidence from the Western Pacific Countries". Journal of Development Economics, Vol. 12, No.2, pp. 229-236.

Graham, F.D. (1932). "The Theory of International Values". Quarterly Journal of Economics, Vol. XLVI, No.3, pp. 581-616.

Granger, C. (1966). "The Typical Spectral Shape of an Economic Variable". Econometrica, Vol.34, No.1, January. pp. 150-161.

Grenander, U. and M. Rosenblatt. (1957). Statistical Analysis of Stationary Time Series. New York: John Wiley & Sons.

Haberler, G. (1947). The Theory of International Trade. London: Macmillan.

Haberler, G. (1954). "The Relevance of the Classical Theory Under Modern Conditions". American Economic Review, May, pp. 543-551.

Haberler, G. (1958). Évolution du commerce international. New York: UN.

Haberler, G. (1959). "International Trade and Economic Development". National Bank of Egypt, 15th Anniversary Commemoration Lectures, Cairo.

Haberler, G. (1961a). "Terms of Trade and Economic Development", in Ellis, H.S. and Wallich, H.C. (eds.), (1959). Economic Development for Latin America. New York: St. Martin Press, pp. 275-301.

Haberler, G. (1961b). A Survey of Internatonal Trade Theory. Special paper in International Economics, International Financial Section. Princeton, N.J.; Princeton University, No. 1, July.

Haberler, G. (1964). "An Assessment of the Current Relevance of the Theory of Comparative Advantage to Agricultural Production and Trade". International Journal of Agrarian Affairs, Vol. 4, No. 3, May, pp. 130-149

Hall, R. (1962). "Commodities Prices and the Terms of Trade". Lloyds Bank Review, No. 63, January, pp. 1-15.

Hallwood, P. (1979). Stabilization of International Commodity Markers. Greenwich, Connecticut: JAI Press.

Hallwood, P. (1982). "Instability in the Terms of Trade of Primary Producers". Discussion Paper, No. 82-06, University of Aberdeen.

Hamada, K. and K. Iwata (1984). "National Income, Terms of Trade and Economic Welfare". The Economic Journal, Vol. 94, No. 376, pp. 752-771.

Hanson, J. R. (1983). "Export Earnings Instability Before World War II: Price, Quantity, Supply, Demand?". Economic Development and Cultural Change, Vol. 31, No. 3, pp. 621-637.

Harkness, J.P. (1968). "A Spectral-Analytic Test of the Long-Swing Hypothesis in Canada". The Review of Economics and Statistics, Vol.50, November, pp. 429-436.

Hausman, J.A. (1981). "Exact Consumer's Surplus and Deadweight Loss". The American Economic Review, Vol. 71, No. 4, pp. 662-677.

Henner, H.F. (1976). "Termes de l'échange". Revue d'économie politique, March-April, pp. 261-264.

Hicks, J.R. (1953). "Inaugural Lecture". Oxford Economic Papers, Vol. 5, pp. 117-135.

Hyde, F.L. (1963). "A Critique of the Prebisch Thesis". Economia Internazionale, Vol. 16, No. 3, pp. 463-487.

Hwa, E.C. (1979). "Price Determination in Several International Primary Commodity Markets: A Structural Analysis". IMF Staff Papers, Vol.26, pp. 157-188, March.

International Monetary Fund (IMF), and International Bank for Reconstruction (IBRD) (1969). The Problem of Stabilization of Prices of Primary Products. A joint staff study, part I, Washington, D.C.

Jabara, C.L. (1980). Terms of Trade for Developing Countries: A Commodity and Regional Analysis. Economics and Statistics Service, Foreign Agricultural Economic Report, No. 161, USDA, Washington.

Jevons, W.S. (1865). The Coal Question, an Inquiry Concerning the Progress of the Nation and the Probable Exhaustion of the Coal Mines. 2nd edition, London: Macmillan, 1906.

Johnson, H.G. (1955). "Economic Expansion and International Trade". Manchester School of Economic and Social Studies, Vol.23, pp. 95-112.

Johnson, H.G. (1959). Economic Development and International Trade". Nationalokonomisk Tidsskrift, pp. 253-272.

Johnson, H.G. (1958). "The Gains from Freer Trade with Europe: An Estimate". Manchester School of Economic and Social Studies, Vol. 26, No. 3, pp. 247-255.

Johnson, H.G. (1967). Economic Policies Toward Less-Developed Countries. Washington D.C.: The Brookings Institution.

Johnston, J. (1972). Econometric Methods, 2nd edition. New York: McGraw.

Josling, T. (1984). "Agricultural Prices and Export Earnings: The Experience of Developing Countries". FAO Economic and Social Development Paper, No. 43, Rome.

Kahn, A.E. (1946). Great Britain in the World Economy. New York: Columbia University Press.

Kaldor, N. (1963). "Stabilizing the Terms of Trade of Underdeveloped Countries". Economic Bulletin for Latin America, Vol. VIII, No. 1, pp. 1-7.

Kaldor, N. (1983). "The Role of Commodity Prices in Economic Recovery". Lloyds Bank Review, July, pp. 21-34.

Kemp, M.C. (1962). The Gain from International Trade. Economic Journal, Vol. LXXII, December, pp. 803-819.

Kemp, M.C. (1968). "The Terms of Trade." International Encyclopedia of Social Sciences, pp. 105-108.

Kendrik, J.W. (1961). Productivity Trends in the United States. Princeton, N.J.: Princeton University Press.

Keynes, J.M. (1912). "Return of Estimated Value of Foreign Trade of United Kingdom at Prices of 1900". Official Papers, Economic Journal, Vol.22, No. 88, December, pp. 630-631.

Kindleberger, C.P. (1943). "Planning for Foreign Investments". American Economic Review, March.

Kindleberger, C.P. (1950). The Dollars Shortage. New York: Technology Press and Wiley.

Kindleberger, C.P. (1956). The Terms of Trade: A European Case Study. New York: Technology Press and Wiley.

Kindleberger, C.P. (1958). "The Terms of Trade and Economic Development". Review of Economics and Statistics Supplement, Vol. 40, February, pp. 72-85.

Kindleberger, C.P. (1964). "Terms of Trade for Primary Products" in Clawson, M. (ed.). Natural Resources and International Development. Baltimore: Johns Hopkins University Press.

Kindleberger, C.P. (1968). _International Economics_. Homewood, Illinois: Irwin, 4th edition.

Knudsen, O. and A. Parnes (1975). _Trade Instability and Economic Development_. Lexington, Mass: Heath-Lexington.

Koester, U. and P.M. Schimtz (1982). "The EC Sugar Market Policy and Developing Countries". _European Review of Agricultural Economics_, Vol. 9, May, pp. 183-204.

Kohli, Ulrich (1978). "A Gross National Product Function and the Derived Demand for Imports and Supply of Exports". _Canadian Journal of Economics_, Vol. 11, No. 2, pp. 167-182.

Kohli, Ulrich (1982). "Production Theory, Technological Change, and the Demand for Imports: Switzerland, 1948-76". _European Economic Review_, Vol. 18, No. 1/2, pp. 369-386.

Kohli, Ulrich (1983). "The Le Chatelier Principle and the Demand for Imports in the Short Run and the Medium Run: Australia, 1959/60 - 1978/79". _Economic Record_, Vol. 59, No. 165, pp. 149-165.

Kohli, Ulrich (1984). "Terms of Trade and Welfare: Estimates". _Kyklos_, Vol. 37, No. 4, pp. 577-597.

Krueger, A.O. and H. Sonneschein (1967). "The Terms of Trade, The Gains from Trade and Price Divergence". _International Economic Review_, Vol. 8, No. 1, February, pp. 121-127.

Labini, S. (1982). "On the Instability of Commodity Prices and the Problem of Gold". Paper presented to the World Conference on Gold, Rome, February.

Labys, W. and Y. Perrin (1976). "Multivariate Analysis of Price Aspects of Commodity Stabilization." _Review of World Economics_, Vol. 112, No. 3, pp. 557-564.

Labys, W. and P. Polak (1984). _Commodity Models for Forecasting and Policy Analysis_. New York: Nichols Publishing Company.

Lam, M.V. (1980). "Export Instability, Expansion and Market Concentration: A Methodological Interpretation". _Journal of Development Economics_, Vol. 7, No. 1, pp. 99-115.

Lancieri E. (1979). "Instability of Agricultural Exports: World Market, Developing and Developed Countries". _Banca Nazionale del Lavoro_, Vol.XXXII, No.130, pp. 287-310.

Law, A. (1975). _International Commodity Agreements_, Lexington, MA: Lexington Books.

Lawson, C. (1974). "The Decline in World Export Instability - A Reappraisal". _Oxford Bulletin of Economics and Statistics_, Vol. 36, No. 1, pp. 53-65.

League of Nations (1938). *Review of World Trade.*

Leith, J.C. (1970). "The Decline in World Export Instability: A Comment". *Bulletin of Oxford Institute of Economic and Social Studies,* Vol. 21, pp. 139-191.

Lerdau, E. (1959). "Stabilization and the Terms of Trade". *Kyklos,* Vol. 12, No. 3, pp. 362-374.

Lerdau, E. (1965). "Some Notes on the Terms of Trade and Economic Development". *Quarterly Journal of Economics,* Vol. 76, No. 3, pp. 464-470.

Lewis, W.A. (1949). *Economic Survey, 1919-39.* New York: UN.

Lewis, W.A. (1952). "World Production, Prices and Trade, 1870-1960". *Manchester School of Economic and Social Studies,* Vol. 20, No. 2, May, pp. 105-133.

Lewis, W.A. (1955). *The Theory of Economic Growth.* London: Allen & Unwin.

Lewis, W.A. (1969). *Aspects of Tropical Trade, 1883-1965.* Stockholm: Almquist & Wiksell.

Lewis, W.A. (1978). *Growth and Fluctuations, 1870-1913.* Boston: Allen & Unwin.

Lipsey, R.E. (1963). *Prices and Quantity Trend in the Foreign Trade of the United States.* Princeton, N.J.: Princeton University Press.

Love, J.L. (1980). "Paul Prebisch and the Origins of The Doctrine of Unequal Exchange". *Latin American Research Review,* Vol. XV, pp. 45-72.

MacBean, A.I. (1966). *Statistical Methods of Econometrics.* Amsterdam: North-Holland.

MacBean, A.I. and V.M. Balasubramanyam (1978). *Meeting the Third World Challenge.* 2nd edition, London. Macmillan for Trade Policy Research Centre.

Maizels, A. (1963). *Industrial Growth and World Trade.* Cambridge: Cambridge, University Press.

Malinvaud, E. (1966). *Statistical Methods of Econometrics.* Amsterdam: North-Holland.

Malthus, T.R. (1820). *Principes d'économie politique.* Paris: Calmann-Levy.

Marshall, A. (1903). *Memorandum on Fiscal Policy of International Trade,* quoted by W.W. Rostow (1950), "The Terms of Trade in Theory and Practice", in *The Economic History Review,* Vol. 4, No. 1, pp. 53-76.

Marshall, A. (1926). Official Papers, p. 367, quoted by W.W. Rostow (1950), op cit.

Martin, K. and F.G Thackeray (1948). "The Terms of Trade of Selected Countries, 1870-1938". Bulletin of the Oxford University Institute of Statistics. Vol. 10, No. 11, November, pp. 373-398.

Massel, B.E. (1970). "Export Instability and Economic Structure". American Economic Review, Vol. 60, No. 4, pp. 618-630.

Meier, G.M. (1952). "Long Period Determinants of Britain's Terms of Trade, 1880-1913". Review of Economic Studies, Vol. 20, No. 52, pp. 115-130.

Meier, G.M. (1968). The International Economics of Development. New York: Harper & Row.

Mikesell, R.F. (1954). "Economic Doctrines Reflected in United Nations Reports". American Economic Review, Vol. 44, No. 2, pp. 570-610.

Mill, J.S. (1848). Principles of Political Economy. 6th ed. (reprint ed. 1865). London: Longman.

Montgomery, S.S. (1960). "The Terms of Trade of Primary Products and Manufactured Goods in International Trade 1870-1952". Ph.D dissertation, Madison: University of Wisconsin.

Moret, M. (1957). L'échange international. Paris: Librairie Marcel Riviéres et Campagnies.

Morgan, T. (1959). "The Long-Run Terms of Trade Between Agriculture and Manufacturing". Economic Development and Cultural Change, Vol. 8, No. 1, pp. 1-23.

Morgan, T. (1963). "Trends in the Terms of Trade and their Repercussions on Primary Producers" in R.F. Harrod and D. Hague (eds.), International Trade Theory in a Developing World. New York: St. Martin Press.

Murray, D. (1978). "Export Earnings Instability: Price, Quantity, Supply, Demand?". Economic Development and Cultural Change, Vol. 27, No.1, pp. 61-73.

Myint, H. (1954-1955). "The Gains from International Trade and the Backward Countries". Review of Economic Studies, Vol. 22, No. 58, pp. 129-142.

Myrdal, G. (1956a). Development and Underdevelopment: a Note on the Mechanism of National and International Inequality. Cairo: National Bank of Egypt, 50th Anniversary Commemoration Lectures.

Myrdal, G. (1956b). An International Economy: Problems and Prospects. London: Routledge & Kegan Paul.

Myrdal, G. (1957a). Economic Theory and Underdeveloped Regions. London: Gerald Duckworth.

Myrdal, G. (1957b). Rich Lands and Poor Lands. New York: Harper & Row.

Naya, S. (1973). "Fluctuations in Export Earnings and Economic Patterns of Asian Countries". Economic Development and Cultural Change, Vol. 21, No. 3, pp. 629-641.

Nguyen, T. (1981). "Trends in the Terms of Trade of LDCs". Journal of Economics Studies, Vol. 8, No. 2, pp. 46-56.

Nurkse, R. (1953). Problems of Capital Formation in Underdeveloped Countries and Patterns of Development. London: Oxford University Press, (reprint ed.) 1967.

Nurkse, R. (1959). "Patterns of Trade and Development". G. Haberler and R.M. Stern (eds.), 1961, Equilibrium and Growth in World Economy. Cambridge, MA.: Harvard University Press, pp. 283-304.

Offut, S. and D. Blandford (1981). "An Evaluation of Alternative Indicators of Commodity Instability." Cornell University, Department of Agricultural Economics, Staff Paper, No.81-19, July.

Perkins, R. (1984). "Calculation of Variability in Grain Production, Prices and other Variables". Rome: FAO, mimeo.

Porter, R.C. (1970). "Some Implications of Post-War Primary Product Trends". Journal of Political Economy. Vol. 78 May/June, pp. 586-597.

Prebisch, R. (1950). "The Economic Development of Latin America and Its Principal Problems". Economic Bulletin for Latin America, Vol. 7, No. 1, pp. 1-22.

Prebisch, R. (1959). "Commercial Policy in the Underdeveloped Countries". American Economic Review, Vol. 44, No. 2, Papers and Proceedings, May, pp. 251-273.

Prebisch, R. (1964). Towards a New Trade Policy for Development. New York: UN.

Ray, G.F. (1977). "The Real Price of Primary Products". National Institute Economic Review, August, pp. 72-76.

Ricardo, D. (1817). Principes de l'économie politique et de l'impôt. Paris: Calmann-Levy, (reprint ed.) 1970.

Robertson, D.H. (1915). A Study of Industrial Fluctuations. London: London School of Economics, (reprint ed.) 1948.

Robinson, A. (1954). "The Changing Structure of the British Economy". Economic Journal, Vol. 64, No. 255, pp. 443-461.

Rostow, W.W. (1951). "The Historical Analysis of the Terms of Trade." The Economic History Review, Vol. 4, No. 1, pp. 53-76.

Samuelson, P.A. (1952). "Spatial Price Equilibrium and Linear Programming". American Economic Review, Vol. 42, No. 1, pp. 283-303.

Samuelson, P.A. (1962). The Gains from International Trade Once Again". Economic Journal, LXXII, December, pp. 820-829.

Sapsford, D. (1985). "The Statistical Debate on the Net Barter Terms of Trade Between Primary Commodities and Manufactures: A Comment and Some Additional Evidence". Economic Journal, Vol. 95, No. 379, pp. 781-788.

Sarkar, G. (1983). Commodities and the Third World. Calcuta, India: Oxford University Press.

Schloss, H.H. (1977). "Declining Terms of Trade: Myth or Reality". Economia Internazionale, Vol. XXX, No. 4, November 1977, pp. 466-469.

Schlote, W. (1938). British Overseas Trade from 1700 to the 1930s. Oxford: Blackwell, (reprint ed.) 1952.

Schultz, T.W. (1961). "Economic Prospects of Primary Products" in H.S. Ellis and H.C. Wallich (eds.). Economic Development for Latin America. New York: St. Martin Press.

Singer, H.W. (1950). "The Distribution of Gains between Investing and Borrowing Countries". American Economic Review, Vol. 15, No. 2, May, pp. 473-485.

Singer, H.W. (1982). "Terms of Trade Controversy and the Evolution of Soft Financing: Early Years in the U.N.: 1947-51". IDS Discussion Paper, No. DP181, November, Sussex.

Södersten, B. (1980). International Economics. London: Macmillan.

Soutar, G. (1977). "Export Instability and Concentration in the Less Developed Countries". Journal of Development Economics, Vol. 4, No. 3, pp. 279-297.

Spraos, J. (1980). "The Statistical Debate on the Net Barter Terms of Trade Between Primary Commodities and Manufactures". Economic Journal, Vol. 90, No. 357, March, pp. 107-108.

Spraos, J. (1983). Inequalizing Trade? A Study of Traditional North-South Specialization in the Context of Terms of Trade Concepts. Oxford University Press.

Spraos, J. (1985). "The Statistical Debate on the Net Barter Terms of Trade: A Response". Economic Journal, Vol.95, No. 379, p. 789.

Streeten, P. (1974). "World Trade in Agricultural Commodities and the Terms of Trade with Industrial Goods". Agricultural Policy in Developing Countries, N. Islam, (ed.). London: Macmillan pp. 207-223.

Sundrum, R. (1983). Development Economics. New York: John Wiley & Son.

Takayama, A. (1972). *International Trade*. New York: Holt Rinehart and Winston.

Tan, G. (1983). "Export Instability, Export Growth and GDP Growth". *Journal of Development Economics,* Vol. 12, No. 2, pp. 219-227.

Thirlwall, A.P. and J. Bergevin (1985). "Trends, Cycles and Asymmetries in the Terms of Trade of Primary Commodities from Developed and Less Developed Countries". *World Development,* Vol. 13, No. 7, pp. 505-817.

Torrens, R. (1815). *An Essay on the External Corn Trade*. (reprint ed.) 1829. London: Longman.

Torrens, R. (1821). *An Essay on the Production of Wealth*. (reprint ed.) 1965. New York: Kelley.

Triantis, S.G. (1952). "Cyclical Changes in the Balance of Trade". *American Economic Review*, Vol. 42, No. 1, pp. 69-86.

United Nations (1949). *Relative Prices of Exports and Imports of Underdeveloped Countries*. New York: under the direction of R. Prebisch.

United Nations (1950). *The Economic Development of Latin America and its Principal Problems,* Economic Commission for Latin America, April, New York: under the direction of R. Prebisch.

United Nations, *Yearbook of Trade Statistics*, various issues.

United Nations (UNCTAD/CNUCED) (1975). *Commerce des produits de base: Indexation*. Rapport du Secrétaire Général, TD/B/563, Geneva, July.

UNCTAD (1982). *Trade and Development Report*, Vol. II, UNCTAD/TDR/2, July, Geneva.

UNCTAD. *Handbook of International Trade and Development Statistics*. various issues.

van Ewijk, C. (1982). "A Spectral Analysis of the Kondratieff-Cycle". *Kyklos*, Vol. 35, pp. 468-499.

van Meerhaeghe, M.A.G. (1969). "Observations sur la signification des termes d'echange des pays sous-developpés". *Kyklos*, Vol. 22, No. 3, pp. 566-584.

Viner, J. (1946). "The Process of Foreign Trade in the Post-War World". *Transactions of the Manchester Statistical Society,* an address given at the annual meeting, June 19; reprinted by American Economic Association (ed.) (1950) in *Readings in the Theory of International Trade*. Homewood, Illinois: R.D. Irwin.

Viner, J. (1952). *International Trade and Economic Development,* Lectures delivered at the National University of Brasil. Oxford: Clarendon Press, 1957.

de Vries, J. (1979). "The World Sugar Economy". Commodities and Export Projections Division, World Bank, Washington D.C.

Willig, R.D. (1976). "Consumer's Surplus Without Apology." American Economic Review, Vol. 66, No. 4, pp. 589-597.

Wilson, T., et al. (1969). "The Income Terms of Trade of Developed and Developing Countries." Economic Journal, Vol. 79, No. 316, December, pp. 213-232.

World Bank (1978). World Development Report 1978, Washington, D.C.

World Bank. Commodity Trade and Price Trends, various issues.

Yotopoulos, P.A. and J.B. Nugent (1976). Economics of Development: Empirical Investigations. New York: Harper & Row.

Young, J. (1951). The International Economy. New York: Harper & Row.